ENGAGING COMMUNITIES AND SERVICE USERS

Engaging Communities and Service Users

Context, Themes and Methods

By Billie Oliver
& Bob Pitt

palgrave
macmillan

First published 2013 by
PALGRAVE MACMILLAN

Palgrave Macmillan in the UK is an imprint of Macmillan Publishers Limited,
registered in England, company number 785998, of Houndmills, Basingstoke,
Hampshire RG21 6XS.

Palgrave Macmillan in the US is a division of St Martin's Press LLC,
175 Fifth Avenue, New York, NY 10010.

Palgrave Macmillan is the global academic imprint of the above companies
and has companies and representatives throughout the world.

Palgrave® and Macmillan® are registered trademarks in the United States,
the United Kingdom, Europe and other countries

ISBN: 978–0–230–36307–6 paperback

This book is printed on paper suitable for recycling and made from fully
managed and sustained forest sources. Logging, pulping and manufacturing
processes are expected to conform to the environmental regulations of the
country of origin.

A catalogue record for this book is available from the British Library.

A catalog record for this book is available from the Library of Congress.

To all those women and men, children and young people whose voices have yet to be heard.

Contents

List of Figures and Tables

Figures

Tables

List of Activities, Case Studies and Boxes

Activities

Case Studies

Boxes

Acknowledgements

We are indebted to a number of colleagues and friends for their support, advice and generosity in contributing ideas and suggestions to guide our thinking as we developed this book. In particular we would like to thank Jane Dalrymple, Pat Taylor, Harry Shier and Robin Hambleton for their collegiality and insight and for sharing with us some of their own models and ideas. We are also grateful to Frank Harle (Restless Development) and Hen Wilkinson (Community Resolve) for work they are engaged in and for their generosity in helping to develop the interesting case studies we have drawn on. Finally, and in no small measure, we would like to thank our families, and in particular Penny and Iain, for their patience and encouragement.

The author and publisher would like to thank the following publishers and organisations for permission to reproduce copyright material:

Danny Burns, Robin Hambleton and Paul Hoggett for Figure 1.1 on page 17 from D. Burns, R. Hambleton and P. Hoggett: *The Politics of Decentralisation: Revitalising Local Democracy* (1994), Palgrave Macmillan Publishers LTD.

John Wiley and Sons for Figure 1.2 on page 19 from H. Shier: Pathways to participation: openings, opportunities and obligations in *Children & Society,* 15: 107–117.

PART I

Context

CHAPTER 1

Introducing Concepts and Meanings

CHAPTER OBJECTIVES

By the end of this chapter you should have an understanding of:

- some of the key terminology and theoretical models that can help us to understand and analyse approaches to participation and engagement;
- some of the developments in thinking that have influenced approaches to engaging with communities and service users;
- some of the critiques and analyses that highlight the contested themes covered later in this book;
- useful resources to improve knowledge and practice;
- guidance on how to make effective use of this book.

Introduction

The ideas and content in this book have emerged from our experience of working with students on a range of both undergraduate and postgraduate degree programmes across social care, education and health. Our teaching experience has been with students on programmes of study ranging from community and youth work, social work, community and public health, mental health and work with children, young people and families. Increasingly, today, students and practitioners from a range of health, welfare and social care professions are being required to involve the people and communities with whom they work in decisions that affect them. As a result, a patchwork of practices has emerged, often all grouped under the same, seemingly commonly understood, label. It has been our experience that students and practitioners often struggle to understand the complexity behind this seemingly straightforward terminology and as a consequence engage in often limited critical evaluation of their practice.

Our own experience as practitioners has been in community settings as community engagement and community education workers. As such we have direct experience of the complexities of policy and practice and of often firmly held differences in perspective and theoretical orientation between and within professional groupings. A key focus for us, in our teaching and in our writing, has always been to encourage engagement with a discourse that sets user involvement within a framework of *community engagement* and away from an individual case management model, currently so prevalent in a lot of practice with which we are familiar. Community engagement approaches to user involvement are essentially concerned with working to find ways to involve people *with others* to achieve positive change in their lives. However, when attempting to introduce this framework into our teaching we have found that we frequently have to 'back-track' and engage in a process of unpicking the complex and contested ideas upon which this approach is built. In our experience, students encountering constructs of community and participation for the first time, especially from a perspective of attempting to theorise their practice, do not find it easy to engage with some of the existing texts presenting political analyses of community and community empowerment. As a consequence their ability to analyse policy and practice is weakened.

How to use this book

Our aim with this book is to commence with a broad focus that reflects on some of the contested constructs of engagement and participation with individuals, groups and communities and to build a framework for understanding and analysing community practice and community engagement. For us, the key word in the title of this book is *engaging*. We offer an approach that explores complex and contested concepts to which the study of engagement with people and communities gives rise. In so doing, our aim is to extend readers' understanding of theories, skills and issues in practice and to help students and practitioners to articulate and evaluate their work. To do this we draw on contemporary reflective and practice-based activities and resources to engage the reader in ideas and policy debates that we introduce and to stimulate your capacity to critically explore the conceptual ideas. The chapters all attempt to illustrate the practical application of those ideas through case studies from a range of practice using both UK and international examples. At the end of each chapter we include resources that you might use. Throughout the text there are activities to help you to extend your theoretical and practical understanding. In each chapter you will be encouraged to consider how you might progress your learning further and to reflect on your progress and development. Each chapter aims to move beyond a superficial understanding and help you begin to engage with the complexity in more depth and to develop your own emergent analyses and critiques.

This book is aimed, primarily, at students and student practitioners in fields of study across social care, welfare and health and will be of direct relevance to those on practice-orientated programmes. However, we hope that it will also be useful as a resource for students on applied social sciences and social policy courses and practitioners working in human services who might be interested in deconstructing some of the principles behind the study of community and user engagement.

The book is structured into ten chapters within three parts: Context, Themes and Methods. Each of the chapters makes links between engaging communities and service users, and includes contemporary debates, case studies and practice examples. We have not written this book with the belief that you will start at Chapter 1 and read through the book in a sequential manner. We expect, and hope, that you will move between chapters and make conceptual links between some of the ideas and themes covered. As you will note when you read the later chapters in this book, there is a frequent overlap and connection between the themes and concepts covered. However, by breaking the themes and methods into separate chapters we aim to offer a starting point that will guide you to begin to engage with some quite complex ideas. The conceptual frameworks outlined in this first chapter will be further explored, analysed and applied in the chapters that follow. They are introduced, initially as a way to help you begin to think about some of the complexity behind seemingly simple ideas and policies.

This first chapter outlines and begins to critique some of the attempts to define the constructs of *community, service user, engagement* and *participation*. We also begin to consider the impact of the developing role of the service user over the past 30 years in influencing policy, services, practice and community. In Chapter 2 we will build on the contextualising concepts covered in this chapter to consider how some of these ideas have been embraced and interpreted by policy makers and politicians. An interesting question to ask yourself as you read the next chapter will be to consider the extent to which policy drives practice or practice drives policy.

Chapters 3 to 5 further build on the conceptual frameworks and theoretical models outlined in this chapter and on the policy trends explored in Chapter 2 to develop an analysis of theories and practice of association, citizenship and community capacity building. Chapter 6 will then progress to a consideration of some of the ethical and professional boundary dilemmas that can arise when working closely with communities and service users. Chapters 7 and 8 summarise some of the methods and approaches often associated with participatory practice with communities and service users, such as informal education, social pedagogy, advocacy and mentoring. Case studies and practical examples illustrate ways of empowering people to be involved in decision making and present methods to facilitate their voices being heard. Chapter 9 will also apply theoretical analyses to the practice of participatory evaluation and research. Finally, Chapter 10 concludes with an exploration of what can be concluded about the future direction of travel and outlines our framework for understanding and analysing community practice and engagement. It outlines developments in the political arena and invites the reader to reflect on some recent initiatives. The final chapter provides an overview of some of the practice contexts that have emerged, and are still emerging, as a result of the policy agendas outlined in the book.

ACTIVITY 1.1

Engaging with this book

Our aim in writing this book is to present an accessible starting point that enables engagement with some of the complex and contested concepts that the study of engagement with service users and communities gives rise to. We want you the reader to engage with some of these ideas and to participate in thinking about how they apply to your own experience and practice. This activity is designed to get you started!

Choose a chapter that, on skimming through the book, seems to be of particular interest to you. Skim read the chapter to make brief notes to identify the following:

- A key policy or political initiative that illustrates the chapter's focus.
- A theory or model presented that resonates with your experience.
- A case study or example that you could apply to your own practice.
- A useful resource or an item of further reading to look up and from which to make notes.

Attempting definitions

Our discussion, in this chapter, introduces some historical perspectives and traditions that have influenced practice and policy. Many of these themes will be built on and extended in the chapters that follow. Our intention in this first chapter is to enable you to begin developing a conceptual framework for analysing and critiquing some of the policy and practice you will be exposed to throughout the book and beyond, in your own practice. There have been numerous attempts to define *community* and mostly these have led to the development of typologies that commonly refer to communities of attachment, identity, interest and affiliation. In Chapter 2, we explore how policy often has a tendency to conflate these meanings leading not only to confusion about what is meant, but also to confusion over the aim of particular interventions. When we attempt to look for definitions of *community* and *service user* we encounter the elusive nature of them as conceptual constructs. They begin to appear imprecise, contradictory and controversial. Both terms tend to be imbued with evaluative or ideological associations.

ACTIVITY 1.2

Defining community
What communities do you belong to? What does the word *community* mean to you? Try to map out for yourself a spider diagram that explores the range of communities you feel that you belong to.
Can you cluster these in a way that begins to identify different types of community or different meanings that the word holds for you?
Summarise some of these definitions and concepts.
What patterns do you note?

In attempting this activity you have probably experienced some tensions surrounding your different experiences of *community*. These tensions may well relate to whether, for you, the nature of *community* is objective or subjective, or whether you experience it as inclusive or exclusive.

> **ACTIVITY 1.3**
>
> **Defining service user**
> Think about some of the communities that you identified in Activity 1.2.
> Would you say that within any of these communities you could be labelled as a
> service user? Why do you say this?
> What might be an alternative label for your role within each of these
> communities?

In much the same way that the concept of *community* is contested and endlessly debated, recent years have also witnessed an increasing attempt to critique the concept of service user. Dinham (2007, p.181) has suggested that there has been a tendency to use the words as 'umbrella terms' and as 'hurrah words'. As with the pre-occupation with definitions of community, these debates are usually driven by competing ideological positions and shifting values. As others have pointed out (e.g. McLauglin, 2009, Braye, 2000), the meanings that we attribute to the words we use to describe our practice do not always have universal understandings and the nature of the language we use is imbued with assumption and power that is notoriously difficult to unpick. Too often the words are used with an assumption that there is agreement over their meaning, whereas, when examined more closely, one begins to uncover a confusion that suggests more support for the rhetorical principles than for examining the reality of how to make it work in practice.

The difficulty of what to call the people we are trying to involve continues and the literature is full of debates on the pros and cons of different terminology. This debate often reflects the changing balance in how the responsibility between the *professional* and the *user* has shifted. In the 1970s and 1980s, for example, recipients of social services were commonly referred to as *clients*. However, with the emergence of the service user movement this term grew to be seen as 'patronising and stigmatising' (Cowden and Singh, 2007, p.18) and the term *user* became far more common. Coulter (2011, p.9) suggests that similar controversy surrounds the use of the term *patient* with arguments against the use of this label associating it with an 'inferior status'. Coulter (2011, p.10) has also argued that she finds the use of the term *service user* 'clumsy' and that it 'implies a relationship with an inanimate object instead of an active partnership'. It also, she argues, 'carries connotations of drug misuse and can therefore be easily misunderstood'. What this debate tells us is that there is no single, agreed definition of *service user*, just as there is no single definition of *professional* and as Barnes and Cotterell (2012a, p.xxiii) remind us the term *service user* needs to be examined and defined 'in each context that it is employed to describe'. They go on to argue that when thinking about the language that we use to describe user involvement 'it is important to be conscious of the purposes this serves and to recognise that language is one of the sites of struggle in the power relations between those who provide and those who use services' (Barnes and Cotterell, 2012a, p.xxiii).

In this book we have chosen not to stick to one common label throughout. Instead, we use different terms in different contexts and where appropriate adopt the convention of the organisation or profession to which we refer. Box 1.1 'Who is a service user?' illustrates some of the complexity and difficulty with choosing an appropriate terminology and reflects some of the varied contexts and perspectives that will be explored in the forthcoming chapters. Thinking back to your answers in Activity 1.3, which of these words do you consider refers best to your role in that setting? Which labels do you prefer?

BOX 1.1 WHO IS A SERVICE USER?

A range of words and labels are to be found in the literature and in different professional practice contexts. These include:

stakeholder,
resident,
patient,
student,
customer,
consumer,
young person,
client,
citizen,
expert-by-experience,
carer,
member of the public,
survivor,
advocate, and
lay person

You might find it helpful at this stage to 'fast forward' to Chapter 10 to pick up on where we revisit some of these ideas and contested terminology and reflect on the nuances of the arguments behind some of these labels.

Community

Cunningham and Cunningham (2008, p.107) offer a useful example of a typology of community. They have placed the different ways that we think about our experiences of community under three headings: aesthetic community, community of interest and geographical community.

Aesthetic communities

In developing their typology, Cunningham and Cunningham draw on the work of Zygmunt Bauman (2001) to argue that there are two forms of aesthetic community. The first type, which they refer to as 'idol-centred', is described as being 'related to taste, fashion ... and the here and now' and often 'emerge around particular fads, fashions, trends or celebrities'. They include within this category online communities such as Facebook, Twitter and community forums such as Mumsnet. Aesthetic communities such as these tend to be, it is argued, about 'personal belonging' or individual need rather than about 'the achievement of community goals in a wider sense' and they do not necessarily always lead to the sort of values that 'facilitate the development of a community spirit' (Cunningham and Cunningham, 2008, p.110). Hoggett (1997, p.7) refers to this type of community as 'elective groups' and 'intentional communities' and describes them as being a key feature of contemporary life.

The second type of aesthetic community described by Cunningham and Cunningham (2008, p.107), 'spontaneous communities', emerge 'in response to spontaneous, one-off ... issues' or 'supposed panic-arousing events'. Examples might include neighbours or residents who come together to campaign to save their local swimming pool or library or against a new housing development. In common with 'idol-centred' communities, these kinds of spontaneous communities tend to be viewed as transient and temporary. They form because of a particular focus but, even when they result in positive outcomes in terms of community provision, are not usually sustained. While they can provide a sense of belonging and identity, creating bonds and lessening feelings of isolation for individuals 'spontaneous communities' can also lead to unreasonable or unlawful behaviour such as illegal occupations or 'lawless witch hunts' against vulnerable people (Cunningham and Cunningham, 2008, p.110).

'Aesthetic communities' may have characteristics that engender a sense of belonging and a sense of a shared identity. They can also, in some cases, lead individuals to develop the 'confidence and skills that may lead them to engaging in more substantive community work' (Cunningham and Cunningham, 2008, p.108). However, some would argue (Bauman, 2001) that these sorts of communities have emerged in response to the decline in what are sometimes referred to as *traditional* communities, where close ties, bonds and associations have been weakened. We will return to and pick up on some of the themes within this understanding of the concept of community in Chapter 3. You might also be interested to read, at this point, the discussion in Chapter 10 of some more recent analyses of online communities.

Communities of interest

These communities tend to comprise of people who share common characteristics, interests or identities. They tend to be more permanent and often require personal commitment. The focus is usually on a wider social transformation such as gender equality or disability rights. People within these communities may have diverse backgrounds but they come together because they are 'united by a bond of common commitment' (Cunningham and Cunningham 2008, p.110). It has been argued (Williams, 1992, p.205) that communities of interest and identity have tended to replace traditional class-based politics as a way to initiate change in recent years. Communities of interest and identity have particular relevance to our consideration of the growth of the service user movement as discussed later in this chapter. We will also apply some analysis of these themes to our discussion of the concept of citizenship in Chapter 4.

Geographical community

Geographical communities, or *communities of place* as they are sometimes referred to, are most commonly associated with the traditional conceptualisation of community. These communities relate to a sense of belonging to a particular locality or area. Within such communities there are often common values and norms, a sense of permanence, shared responsibility, reciprocity, kinship and duty. People may continue to feel an affiliation to a geographical community long after they have moved away to another location. Geographical communities have often provided the focus for policies advocating community development practice and regeneration and, as we will see in Chapter 2, have been a popular focus for politicians who very often refer to the breakdown of such communities as being the root cause of a number of social 'problems'. There have been a number of studies interrogating the validity of this conceptualisation of community (for example, Hoggett, 1997; Taylor, 2011), nevertheless, as we will note in Chapter 5, this way of thinking about community has most often been associated with approaches to community development and this has led to difficulties for interventions that have not taken sufficient account of diversity and tensions within these geographic areas.

There have been other, similar attempts to create typologies that help to understand and explain the concept of community. Gilchrist (2009, p.21) for example offers an extended analysis of eight categories that include: communities of 'locality', 'interest', 'identity', 'purpose', 'practice', 'inquiry', 'support' and 'circumstance'. Dinham (2011, p.530) organises his exploration of community around notions of 'location', 'shared history and values', 'common activities' and 'solidarity'.

ACTIVITY 1.4

Overarching themes in 'community'

Thinking about these different attempts to categorise definitions of community into typologies, can you identify one or two over-arching themes that all these definitions and categories have in common?

Smith (2001) suggests that an over-arching theme to the concept of community is that it offers a conceptualisation of a sense of belonging, of having something in common and of, therefore, offering a sense of identity. Smith suggests that this sense of belonging to a community can be associated with a 'place, an interest or a communion with others'. Territorial or place community is most often associated with a locality, where the sense of something in common is understood geographically. Communities of interest or what Smith calls 'elective' communities share something in common other than place.

'They are linked together by factors such as religious belief, sexual orientation, occupation or ethnic origin' (Smith, 2001). Smith's third classification, 'communion', is described as a 'sense of attachment' or what is often referred to as a 'spirit of community'.

Dinham (2011, p.531), however, introduced a further conceptualisation in the notion of the 'unchosen community' wherein we might find ourselves caught up in a 'rich matrix of involuntary interconnections'. For example, Eriksson (2011) discusses the responses of a group of disabled people in order to discover their experiences of community. Eriksson asserts that the group only partially shared an identity as *disabled* and that what they actually share is an identity based on 'the experiences of the label of disability. The group denies that they share an identity in other contexts. They argue that their identity as disabled has been imposed on them by others' (p.410). This is a helpful framework for our analysis of engaging with communities and service users and leads us to pose questions such as: *Who is in a community and who is not ... and on what basis? Who speaks for the community?* and *How are its members represented?*

ACTIVITY 1.5

Unchosen communities

Reflect for a moment on your own situation. Can you identify any communities to which you feel you have been assigned and that were not of your choosing? How do you feel about this? Does it cause any conflicts or tensions of loyalty for you? What is the impact on your sense of identity or belonging?

Typologies such as these offer a simplified way to help us make sense of the complexity behind certain taken-for-granted terms. As Smith (2001) points out, there is, of course, a strong possibility that these different ways of approaching community will overlap, but in breaking them down into different definitions we can begin to understand how our policies and practice might be based on unshared assumptions or rhetorical over simplifications. For example, as we will explore in more depth in Chapter 2, many current policy responses to social issues tend to embrace a concept of community from what many people argue (Williams, 1958, Hoggett, 1997, Brent, 2009) is a romanticised view of a 'golden age' of community where, it is assumed, everyone knew and looked out for their neighbours, left their back doors open and shared common values that led to social cohesion and civil society. These analyses tend to take the view that our experience of *community* in the twenty-first century has been lost.

You might like, at this point, to 'fast forward' to Chapter 10 and read the section where we revisit the nature of community in the light of some more recent events and developments to reflect on whether you agree with this analysis that the experience of community has been lost. Yerbury (2012, p.188), for example, set out to research with young people their understanding of the vocabulary of community in the early twenty-first century. She found themes running through the young peoples' 'lived experience of community' that included a sense of belonging and a sense of being connected to others. A sense of community is formed, she argues, when people keep in touch 'either face-to-face or when mediated through some form of technology'. Only one young person in her sample had a 'geographical notion of community'. Place was not an important factor. 'A few referred to websites and social networking sites as a meeting place' but most indicated that they see themselves as 'mobile'. For most it was about a sense of belonging and a sense of 'recognition'. Yerbury concluded that community 'is no longer seen as an entity into which an individual can be absorbed', instead it should be seen as 'something that grows out from the individual and that is endlessly created and re-created' (p.196).

The service user movement

The emergence of a wide range of groups of service users who felt dissatisfied with the services and support they received can be traced back to the 1980s and linked to our earlier discussion of 'communities of interest'. The growth of self-help groups and projects based on the centrality of personal experience as a powerful tool for change established a different relationship between service users and professionals and began to meet needs previously ignored. The traditional view of professional autonomy has come to be seen as categorising service users as dependent and passive with the focus being on problems, failings or inadequacies rather than the service users' abilities, strengths, resources and capacities. Historically, there has been a tendency for professionals to place more emphasis on their own professional judgment than on service user's views. As a consequence, there were demands from those using services for a greater involvement in decision making and in determining how their needs should be met.

Service user-led groups provide a space where people can collectively articulate their experiences and explore responses and solutions to the problems they encounter. Such spaces allow people to 'experiment with their voices and plan and prepare to enter into dialogue with those who might exert considerable power over their lives' (Barnes and Cotterell, 2012b, p.1). Service user groups seek to make health, education and welfare provision more accountable to the people who use it and 'less dominated by professionals who decided what was best for the service user' (Cowden and Singh, 2007, p.9). The service user movement emphasises people's social, political and civil rights as citizens and their participation in planning and decision making as fundamental to active citizenship. It is also argued (Taylor, 2007, p.100) that listening to and understanding people's experience of the services they receive can create 'continuing mechanisms for dialogue and debate' that can help to continuously improve practice.

Reflecting this nuanced development in the relationship between service users and professionals, the terminology has shifted more recently towards embracing the concept of *expert-by-experience* in a challenge to the centrality of professional knowledge. The move towards greater service user inclusion has witnessed a shift in the client–worker relationship with a greater emphasis being placed on the rights and abilities of clients to define and understand their own situation. The recognition that worker and client possess different knowledge and skills has led to an increasing willingness by professionals to see clients as active and equal partners. This shift in conceptual thinking has led to other gradual changes in the language, reflecting the principles of *user-led services* or *user-centred services*. Taylor (2007, p.99) offers the term 'lay person' as yet a further alternative to *service user*.

However, it has been argued (Beresford, 1992) that the term *service user* changes the way we think about 'citizens', transforming them into unconnected individual consumers who are competing with each other to secure education, health and welfare needs. The consumerist model of service user involvement will be discussed more fully in Chapter 2, however, it has been argued (Milewa et al., 2002) that, despite the difficulties with the concept of service user as customer this approach did at least signal a shift from seeing people as 'passive recipients' of care towards a view of them as more 'active consumers'. It could also be argued that the emergence of the terminology of *service user* offers a more equalising conceptualisation when compared with patient, client or customer. Barnes and Cotterell (2012b, p.3), however, suggest that the increasing confidence and effectiveness of service users has led to 'questions being posed about their representativeness' with the term 'professional user' sometimes being used to 'undermine the credibility and legitimacy of those who speak on behalf of their peers' and some people even going so far as to suggest that such spokespersons are not 'real users'.

Later in this book we will examine the interface between some of the conceptualisations of community and of service user movements and some of the theoretical frameworks for considering their manifestation in practice. In Chapter 6 we will also consider some of the tensions that the challenges to power and accountability between *professional* and *user* have given rise to as we explore the shifting boundaries of practice. Now, however, we want to continue our exploration of frameworks for examining the meanings behind the language that is often used when talking about community and service user engagement.

Rhetoric or reality: Understanding engagement and participation

Braye (2000, p.9) has pointed out that one of the main difficulties with any attempt to unpick the concept and definition of terms such as 'participation and involvement' is that 'the language is complex and that the same term often means different things to different people'. Too often, she argues, an 'apparent consensus that participation is a good thing masks major differences of ideology' leading to 'ends and means' becoming confused. Often, when examined more closely, we can begin to uncover more support for the rhetorical principles than for examining how to make it work in practice.

ACTIVITY 1.6

Defining involvement

Think of a situation where you could be construed as having been a *service user*.
What was the service that you were using?

To what extent did you feel that you had any influence or control over the
service that you were receiving?

How did those who were providing the service treat you? Were you involved in
any decisions about the nature of the service you were receiving?

What sorts of things made you feel involved or consulted (or not)?

How could your involvement have been enhanced?

Cornwall (2008, p.269) has suggested that the language of participation and
involvement have become 'buzzwords and infinitely malleable' concepts that
can be used 'to evoke and to signify almost anything that involves people'. She
goes on to argue that attempts to involve people in so-called participatory
processes can also serve to deepen the exclusion of particular groups 'unless
explicit efforts are made to include them'. One of the mechanisms often used
for ensuring inclusion, she suggests, is the 'identification of predetermined
categories of stakeholders whose views are taken to represent others of their
kind' (p.269).

Taylor (2007, p.112) (see Table 1.1) outlines four different traditions and
approaches to involving service users that also serve to illustrate a range of
ways in which service users can be marginalised by professionals who purport
to be involving them. These include 'exploiting people and expecting them to
give their time and effort voluntarily without engaging with their need to be
resourced; incorporating them into the organisational culture of the organisation; taking no interest in how they can connect to the communities they come
from; and defining the agenda or using professional jargon which can block
all forms of partnership working'.

Defining participation

There have been numerous frameworks that attempt to explain and try to
make sense of the complexity surrounding both the terminology and the practice of participation. A variety of models and typologies have been developed
to explore the degrees of participation and involvement that we might identify
in different organisations or individual practices. The aim of these models is to
show the range of participatory practice that might exist – all within the same
label of *participation* or *user-involvement*. The range and extent to which
people can be involved or participate in decision-making processes that affect
their lives has been portrayed, traditionally, as a hierarchical process where the
level and nature of participation varies according to the degree of power that
an individual holds.

The most widely referred to model is that by Sherry Arnstein who, in 1969,
developed a typology depicting a ladder of participation outlining eight stages
in ascending order of power sharing, from 'manipulation' where participants

Table 1.1   Summary of Taylor's (2007) four traditions and approaches to involving service users

Approach to service user involvement	Details
Consumerist	In this approach people are 'asked for their views on specific services by those responsible for those services'. Their involvement can be time limited and the boundaries determined by the service provider. Such initiatives may take the form of surveys and focus groups and often participants are referred to as 'stakeholders'.
Representative	Taylor calls this approach 'quasidemocratic' (p.112). It involves the appointment of 'representatives' on public bodies to achieve some degree of public accountability. The role of these 'representatives' is to ensure that public interests and perspectives are considered. However, as Taylor points out, the key issue is to ask 'how far these appointed representatives are viewed as legitimate representatives' by the communities they purport to represent. Cowden and Singh (2007, p.15) highlight the danger within these first two approaches of user involvement becoming 'a fetish, something which can be held up as a representative of authenticity and truth, but which at the same time has no real influence over decision making'.
Interest group	This approach is through the activities of 'organised interest groups who have an independent status' (p.112). These groups develop their own agenda that they then attempt to promote through their various activities. Participants in these groups are likely to have developed a range of skills and expertise over time and may have developed from participation in small self-help groups into campaigning for social change in larger organisations. Participants in groups such as these very often reject the term *user* because of its implication and association with illegal drug use and also because they wish to be seen as 'people who give something back rather than people who just use' (Cowden and Singh, 2007, p.16)
Network	This approach, according to Taylor, seeks to access public involvement through informal networks and activities within communities and so tries to find out the way people understand and live their lives and to find ways to help them articulate their perspectives and influence the development of services.

are placed or encouraged to join groups and committees simply to give the appearance of consultation, through different levels of tokenism such as 'information giving' and 'consultation' that actually do little to challenge the balance of power, to levels of 'citizen control' where there are varying degrees of shared planning and decision making. This widely referred to model has, in recent years, been criticised for being over-simplistic and that simplicity was acknowledged and accepted by Arnstein herself. However, its significance as a framework for beginning to analyse participation should not go unrecognised and the fact that it has been widely adapted and further developed acknowledges its contribution to our understanding.

Both Barber (2007) and Boylan and Dalrymple (2009) offer an excellent overview of a range of alternative models of participation, in particular in relation to analyses of the involvement of young people. Barber's analysis charts developments in thinking about how to explain the different approaches to participatory practice and more importantly to how analyses have begun to focus on ways of translating the theory into achievable practice. As Barber points out, the contribution and strength in Arnstein's original model lies in its 'sense of gradations' and it provides a useful starting point for thinking about 'degrees of participation'. Its weakness relates mainly to its assumption of progression from one stage to another. Our own experience of developing and supporting people's participation also suggests that the process is 'more dynamic, unpredictable and situation specific' (Barber, 2007, p.25) than a simple graduated model would imply.

A refinement of Arnstein's model was offered by Burns et al. (1994) (see Figure 1.1). In developing their ladder they have tried to distinguish more clearly between the concepts of participation and control, conceptualise additional forms of empowerment, and emphasise that 'the rungs of the ladder should not be considered as equidistant' (p.161). It is their analysis that 'it is far easier to climb the lower rungs than to scale the higher one'. At the same time, many practitioners will also find it less challenging and more rewarding to support participation at some of the lower levels of consultation and advisory bodies than to work out how to enable citizen control. As Eversole (2012, p.37) has concluded, it is not that 'participation is impossible to achieve; but rather that it is impossible to achieve for others'.

Burns et al. (1994, p.164) argue that the lower four rungs ('citizen non-participation') are all fairly close together and can generally be summarised as 'unsatisfactory forms of pseudo-consultation' that treat 'participation as a charade or limit it to trivial matters'. Within the zone of their ladder concerned with 'citizen participation' they distinguish between informing and consulting, decentralised decision making, partnership and delegated control. It is at rung five of their ladder that they claim 'genuine citizen input begins'. However, it is not until the top two rungs that citizens have 'authority' or 'the ability to take action without prior confirmation from a higher level' (p.174).

ACTIVITY 1.7

Defining participation
Think back to your answers to Activity 1.6. Where would you place yourself in terms of Burns et al.'s (1996) gradations of participation? (see Figure 1.1). Why do you say this?

Dinham (2007) applied Burns et al.'s model to his research with members of a local community involved in a government initiative called New Deal for Communities. He found that there was a 'significant decline' in reported

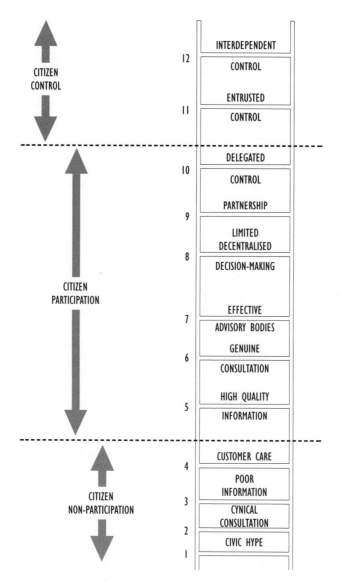

CITIZEN
CONTROL

12 INTERDEPENDENT
CONTROL

ENTRUSTED
11 CONTROL

DELEGATED
10 CONTROL

PARTNERSHIP
9

LIMITED
DECENTRALISED
8 DECISION-MAKING

CITIZEN
PARTICIPATION

EFFECTIVE
7 ADVISORY BODIES

GENUINE
6 CONSULTATION

HIGH QUALITY
5 INFORMATION

CUSTOMER CARE
4

POOR
INFORMATION
CITIZEN
NON-PARTICIPATION
3 CYNICAL
CONSULTATION
2 CIVIC HYPE

1

Figure 1.1   A ladder of citizen empowerment (Burns et al., 1994)

experiences of feeling involved and empowered between the start and six months into the project 'indicating a general perception that participation was significantly less empowering in experience than had been originally expected'. One explanation he gives for this difference is that people's confidence grew over the six months and consequently their expectations about their capacity to be involved also grew. The more confident they became, the greater their sense of cynicism and disillusionment with the sorts of participatory activity they were expected to become involved in. This analysis illustrates the dynamic nature of participation and capacity building and highlights some of the difficulties in evaluating participatory practice that we will explore in Chapter 9.

Ladder models, such as those discussed above, have been criticised for 'an underlying suggestion that the ladder must be climbed, with the upper rung as the ultimate goal' (Burke, 2010, p.46). The ladder analogy, it is argued, offers little to help us begin to understand how we can enable democratic participation to happen. As Barber (2007, p.26) points out, people may not be ready to climb the ladder and may need different forms of support to enable their participation. For some people, at the stage where they do not feel comfortable, confident or motivated to participate, consultation may be the preferred and more appropriate level of engagement. At other times, as we will explore in Chapter 7, different approaches such as advocacy or mentoring, might be the appropriate method of engaging people.

Treseder (1997) attempted to reflect this reality in a model that aimed to show how different types of involvement may be legitimate in different situations. The key significance about Treseder's model was that it attempted to differentiate between the nuances and realities of the terms involvement, consultation and participation and demonstrated how young people and children could be involved to varying degrees and possess differing degrees of power sharing. This model was significant for recognising that in certain settings involvement will never result in people completely controlling the decision that is made. Consultation, according to Treseder, can, however, lead to greater participation through involvement in further development activities. Cornwall (2008, p.273) develops a similar analysis arguing that models of participation could more usefully focus on the 'user of participatory approaches', suggesting that different purposes require 'different forms of engagement by different kinds of participants'. Taylor (2007, p.114) has conceived these different levels of involvement as an iceberg with people moving in and out of levels of participation and involvement. An individual, she suggests, has a limited capacity to be active in everything and while they might be active in one issue they may be a non-participator in others, happy for others to speak on their behalf. Participation in one activity, however, will build up skills and confidence and may lead to broader participation in other areas.

The Pathways to Participation model (Figure 1.2) developed by Shier (2001) introduced a further significant shift in emphasis and began to move the focus from the participant's capabilities towards how to conceptualise involvement and participation as a reality within organisational or policy cultures. Shier's model was originally conceived to focus on the willingness of organisations to involve children and young people. We have adapted it slightly to embrace the process of attaining democratic participation for all service users.

Shier's model outlines five levels of participation with each level seen as discrete but inter-connected. There are three stages of commitment at each level:

Openings: refers to an interest and readiness and desire to work to support people's democratic involvement;

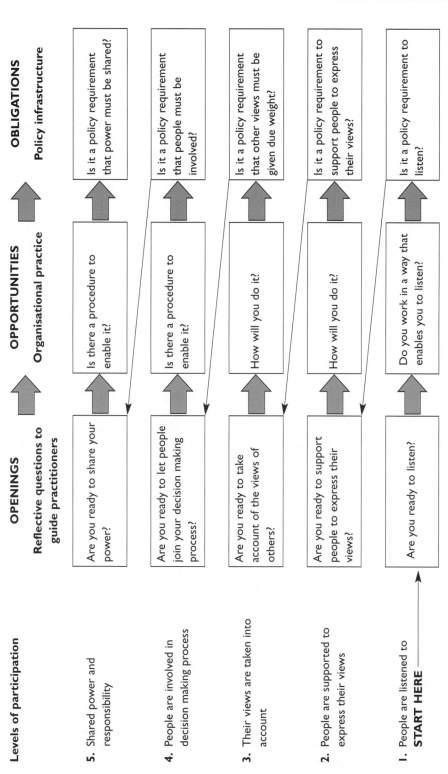

Figure 1.2 Pathways to participation model (adapted from Shier, 2001)

Opportunities: describes the procedures and activities within the practice of an organisation that are necessary to support participation;
Obligations: describes the infrastructure of policy that is built in within the organisation to enable democratic participation to become the norm.

The model has a structure similar to that of a flow chart that poses reflective questions to guide practitioners to reflect on 'where do we want to get to?' and 'what do we need to do in order to get there?' Shier's model has also been criticised for implying a hierarchical process (Sinclair, 2004). However, Shier (2006, p.18) responded to these criticisms by pointing out that 'in real life' while we do often use a ladder to climb to the top and move on, 'very often we just want to get to a rung some way up so as to work at the correct height for the job we are doing'. In many cases this may only be half-way up but 'without the ladder it would be impossible to climb to the appropriate height'.

Shier's model was important in shifting the emphasis towards a focus on what the organisation needs to do to create participative access and make espousal of the principles a reality. Barber (2007, p.34) conceptualises this process as creating an 'engagement zone' where practitioners attempt to match the needs of service users with the appropriate level of nurture and support and points out a critical 'shift from blaming ... people for failing to participate in civic life, to holding organisations to account for failing to develop method-ologies to enable participation' (p.36).

A further model for thinking about participation is through the conceptu-alisation of a bridge. This approach is described as 'significant' by Boylan and Dalrymple (2009, p.70) because it considers ways in which power can be negotiated and shared. The bridge model has been used by Taylor and Upward (1995) to demonstrate effective user involvement in community care and by John (1996) to demonstrate the politics of participation for young people. John (1996, p.16) argued that the 'participation bridge' model enables 'the construction of creative alliances'. In her view the 'rights discourse' should be more about 'transforming power' than about helping less powerful people into the world of 'the dominant majority' (p.15) and she goes on to suggest that there are three prerequisites to such empowerment: responsibility, unity and community action. These prerequisites, she argues, act as the pillars that support the bridge spanning the chasm between those with power and those without. Having built a firm and strong foundation of pillars, the service user or young person is in a position to act with the professional or adult, taking part in collaborative activities.

Taylor and Upward (1995) viewed participation as dynamic and ever changing. The bridge in this model, therefore, needs a firm foundation supported by pillars of legislation and developing knowledge through theory and practice. The flow across the bridge, they argued, needs to continue to be developed in both directions through on-going evaluation and the develop-ment of participatory ways of working. The strength of the bridge depends on the policy agenda, time and resources allowed to develop it. The bridge would therefore need good maintenance as well as firm foundations. This maintenance could be developed by 'individuals or collaboratively with all parties negotiating together in a process where the service users are not passive but active constructors and maintainers' (Boylan and Dalrymple, 2009, p.70).

ACTIVITY 1.8

'A potpourri of participation models'
Visit the website www.nonformality.org

Andreas Karsten has been engaged in a project for some years that has involved collecting information about, and tracing the origins of, different models, schemata and theories of participation.

On this website he has listed all the models he has found that have been developed between 1969 and 2012. There are, at the time of writing, 36 different models.

Look at some of the more recent models and reflect on how they have attempted to explain the nuanced debates about participation discussed above.

Reflexive engagement

ACTIVITY 1.9

Understanding engagement
Read back through the previous section. How many different words or phrases can you spot that could be used to define what you understand by *engagement*?

Some of the words you might associate with the concept of engagement probably mirror the debates outlined in this chapter. The practice of engaging others can include: consulting them on their opinion; listening and advocating for them or supporting them to develop confidence; recognising, valuing and drawing on their experience; having an active dialogue or debate; and inspiring and encouraging them to become active. There is, of course, no single widely agreed meaning for the term. The practice of engagement, as you will note as you work through this book, is influenced by a range of ideological, political and structural factors and it is our intention to encourage you to examine and reflect on each context in which the claims of engagement are employed.

Underpinning our own approach to engaging you, the reader, in the debates explored in this book is our commitment to reflexive dialogue and reflective practice. The importance of reflecting on our practice, as part of the learning process, has been emphasised for some time now. As Schön (1983) suggested, the capacity to reflect on action so as to engage in a process of continuous learning is one of the defining characteristics of professional practice. Schön argued that the model of 'technical rationality' described as filling learners up with knowledge so that they could discharge it as fully formed professionals when they entered the world of practice, has never been a useful or realistic description of how professionals operate, and that it is quite inappropriate in the ever changing context of practice that we encounter today. Developing the capacity to reflect *in* action (while doing something) and *on* action (after you have done it) has become an important feature of professional learning in many disciplines. Reflexivity is a process by which practitioners can better understand themselves in order to be able to build on their existing strengths and take appropriate future action. The word 'action' is key here, as the aim of reflection is to develop professional actions that are aligned with personal beliefs and values (Somerville and Keeling, 2004). As you work your way through the chapters in this book you will find reflective activities and suggestions for further reading and resources that are designed to engage you with the theoretical content and to apply it to the context of your own practice. The activities are designed to support your active engagement with what you are reading and to encourage you to develop your own analysis and theories-in-use (Argyris and Schön, 1974).

As you will note when you read the later chapters in this book, there is a frequent overlap and connection between the themes and concepts covered in this chapter. By breaking the themes and methods into separate chapters we aim to offer a starting point that will guide you to begin to engage with some quite complex ideas. The conceptual frameworks outlined in this first chapter will be further explored, analysed and applied in the chapters that follow. They are introduced here, initially as a way to help you begin to think about some of the complexity behind seemingly simple ideas and policies. Our aim is to establish a framework that will help you critically analyse the policy, themes and methods that we will cover in the following chapters.

Each chapter is structured in such a way as to introduce you to the key concepts relevant to the chapter focus. The chapters all attempt to illustrate the practical application of those ideas through illustrative case studies, reference to resources that you might use and a series of activities to help you to extend your theoretical and practical understanding. In each chapter you are encouraged to consider how you might progress your learning further and to reflect on your progress and development. Each chapter aims to move beyond a superficial understanding and help you begin to engage with the complexity in more depth and to develop your own emergent analyses and critiques.

Chapter summary

This chapter has briefly set out the conceptual terrain upon which we will build our critical analysis in the forthcoming chapters. It has introduced some models and typologies underpinning the concept of community and service user engagement. Different analyses of *community*, *service user* and *participation* have been explored in order to draw out some common themes that will be examined in later chapters.

As we explained in the opening paragraphs to this chapter, we have not envisioned this book as one that you will read in a linear fashion, starting on page one and reading each chapter in turn. We expect you to move back and forth between chapters, sections and reflective activities – and we encourage you to do so. The complex interplay between the analysis of conceptual ideas and the exploration of practice requires us to constantly revisit some of the frameworks and models introduced in this chapter. In practice, all the forms and meanings of participation and involvement outlined in this chapter may be found in a single project, to varying degrees and at different stages. As we have explained our intention has been to commence with a more general focus on constructs of involvement and participation and to build on these analyses to develop a framework for understanding community and service user engagement and the values that underpin it. Our purpose is to engage you in reflecting on these contested ideas and to offer an approach that can support your understanding of theories, skills and issues in practice and to help you to articulate and evaluate your practice.

Our aim throughout the chapters in this book is to introduce you to a variety of approaches and methods that might enable you to develop your understanding and critique of policy and practice that you may encounter. In the next chapter we will continue to establish the context within which we will explore the analyses that develop in the later chapters. In Chapter 2 we set out an overview of the ways in which some of the ideas introduced in Chapter 1 have been embraced and interpreted by policy makers and politicians in recent years. This overview will enable us to identify key themes and trends that will inform the focus for the chapters on methods in Part III. An interesting question to ask yourself as you read the next chapter, and those that follow, will be to consider the extent to which policy drives practice or practice drives policy.

USEFUL RESOURCES

Involve is an organisation set up to promote community engagement. It lists various tools and techniques to assist in public participation: **www.involve.org.uk**

Participation Works is a partnership of six national children and young people's agencies that enables organisations to effectively involve children and young people in the development, delivery and evaluation of services that affect their lives: **vwww.participationworks.org.uk**

Participation Compass website offers practical information, resources and news for those working to involve people: **http://participationcompass.org/**

Social Care Institute for Excellence website contains a wealth of practical, theoretical and research based resources covering work with service users of all ages: **www.scie.org.uk**

FURTHER READING

Barber, T. (2007) Young People and Civic Participation. *Youth & Policy*, 96, 19–39.
This article presents a very helpful summary of the developments in theoretical models that attempt to explain and define involvement and participation. The article reproduces a variety of diagrams and models in a very accessible format.

Beresford, P. and Carr, S. (eds) (2012) *Social Care, Service Users and User Involvement* (London: Jessica Kingsley).
This book provides a helpful collection of chapters that contextualise and examine the experience, contribution, impact and perspective of a diversity of communities and service users.

Cornwall, A. (2008) Unpacking Participation: Models, Meanings and Practices. *Community Development Journal*, 43, 3, 269–283.
This is another helpful article that examines the meanings and practices associated with participation, in theory and practice. It stresses the importance of paying attention to who is participating, in what and for whose benefit.

CHAPTER 2

The Policy Context

CHAPTER OBJECTIVES

By the end of this chapter you should have an understanding of:

- some of the UK policy initiatives that encourage engagement with communities and service users;
- why participation and involvement are considered important by policymakers and government;
- two models of participation – *consumerist* and *democratic* models – whereby service users and communities influence policy;
- policy changes and continuities in the UK from the 1990s presented under themes of *vision, empowerment, participation* and *partnership*;
- examples of practice emerging in response to policies; and
- policy development reflecting service user involvement including the personalisation agenda viewed from different political contexts.

Introduction

In this chapter we explore UK policy initiatives that encourage engagement with communities and service users and why participation and involvement are considered important. We begin with policies introduced by the New Labour government elected in 1997. The need for government to re-engage with communities was launched by Prime Minister Tony Blair's declared determination to 'recreate the bonds of civic society and community' (Blair, 1997). He spoke of the need to 'engage the interest and commitment of the whole of the community to tackle the desperate need for urban regeneration' (Blair, 1997). We outline government legislation and policy documents introduced by New Labour that sought to address Blair's vision and by the Coalition government elected in 2010.

Our policy overview is presented under four themes rather than chronologically as a means to highlight what we see as key changes and continuities. The themes offer a common thread through the policies as they each present a *vision* with the purpose of *empowerment* by means of *participation* and *partnership*. We are aware that the legislation and policy documents from the UK Parliament mostly relate to England; however we acknowledge differences in political context arising from devolved government within the UK.

The introduction of devolution by New Labour established the National Assembly in Wales and in Northern Ireland, and the Parliament in Scotland. Devolution gives those national governments powers to make or change laws in areas that include education, health, social services, local government and housing. Financial powers give the governments opportunities to exercise discretion over public spending. For example, unlike England, NHS prescription charges have been abolished in Wales since 2007 and there are currently no university tuition fees for Scottish students studying in Scotland. Different histories, cultures and voting behaviours mean these national governments are often formed by different majority political parties and coalition partners from the UK Parliament in London. This results in different principles and priorities influencing policy development and implementation in those countries. In Scotland, for example, 'the government has built the principle of community engagement into policy and guidance to public services' (SCDC, 2012). It is responding to its own commissioned report on the *Future Delivery of Public Services* (2011) that called for 'radical change in the design and delivery of public services' (p.xiii) The section on 'Personalisation' uses examples of how policy operates differently within the UK and in other countries.

Policy and practice

At the end of Chapter 1 we invited you to consider the extent to which policy drives practice or practice drives policy. In thinking about what and who drives policy we distinguish between 'legal, policy, professional and user mandates' (Kemshall and Littlechild, 2000). The Children Act 1989 (Great Britain, 1989) and NHS and Community Care Act 1990 (Great Britain, 1990) refer to informing, consulting and involving service users. These are examples of *legal* or *policy mandates* that make it a requirement or statutory duty, for example for an individual service user and their carer to be involved in an assessment and care management process. The *UN Convention on the Rights of the Child* (United Nations, 1989) stresses the importance of listening to the child. UK courts apply guidelines set out by Lord Fraser in a judgement in the House of Lords in 1985. The ruling recognises the right of young people under the age of 16 to make decisions about their health care if they have sufficient understanding and intelligence (NSPCC, 2012).

'Professional mandates' derive from professional codes of conduct, ethics or practice. For example social workers are expected to show respect for 'each individual's preferences, wishes and involvement in decision-making' (BASW, 2012, p.12). Health and care workers must 'promote and protect the best interests of service users' (HCPC, 2012, p.8). Youth workers have a commitment to 'respect and promote young people's rights to make their own decisions and choices' (NYA, 2004, p.6). It would be difficult for professional practitioners to work in these ways without ensuring service user involvement, participation and engagement to determine those preferences, interests and choices. There is also the pragmatic consideration noted in Chapter 1 that involving service users, families and carers creates better outcomes in interventions by professionals.

'User mandates' bring pressure from service users and communities to be heard by policymakers, arising from the development of the service user movement as discussed in Chapter 1, and can be demonstrated by two models of participation: consumerist and democratic models (Kemshall and Littlechild, 2000). The consumerist model emphasises ideas around choices of, access to and information about services with opportunities to complain or claim redress where the service on offer falls short. The democratic model focuses on attempts to gain greater collective involvement, influence and control by challenging the power of those who determine needs, priorities and entitlements. Policies promoting greater user involvement signal a shift from the consumer to the democratic model in that policy aims not just to seek greater and wider participation in the service relationship but to challenge the balance of power between those making decisions and those on the receiving end. Participation with the purpose of achieving greater influence and control by individual and collective action is explored within the wider context of citizenship in Chapter 4. The focus of this chapter is on 'legal' or 'policy mandates' as the main policy drivers.

New Labour to coalition: From neighbourhood renewal to building civil society

This section explores policy documents (reviews, reports, papers and guidelines) in order to outline the aims and purpose of government interventions since 1997. Analysis will consider the language of the policies and the ideas, principles and thinking behind them. By tracking a selection of policies related to communities it is possible to build up a narrative of change and continuity linked to a number of key themes – *vision, empowerment, participation* and *partnership*.

Vision

First, to what extent does the vision expressed in policy demonstrate change and continuity? New Labour (1997–2010) came to power with a vision of promoting social justice, ending child poverty and tackling inequalities. The Treasury carried out a review of spending that tied future departmental budgets to the overall purpose of reform and modernisation. The *Modernising Government* document (Cabinet Office, 1999) set out New Labour's determination to deliver high-quality services to meet the needs of citizens rather than for the convenience of professionals. It called for closer monitoring of service user views on public services and sought to encourage 'joined-up working' through local partnerships.

New Labour focused on addressing the causes of poverty and social exclusion across governmental departments. The Social Exclusion Unit was established to report on integrated approaches to dealing with problems such as housing, crime, unemployment, poor schooling and community breakdown. In 1998 it recommended a national strategy for neighbourhood renewal. The report by Policy Action Team 17 (DETR, 2000) on the *National Strategy for*

Neighbourhood Renewal referred to involving communities, investing in people and tackling the poorest neighbourhoods. The strategy called for long-term commitment and an integrated approach with clear leadership so that 'within 10–20 years no one should be seriously disadvantaged by where they live' (SEU, 2001, p.8).

As part of the strategy the New Deal for Communities programme was launched in 1998 to regenerate poor neighbourhoods introducing schemes such as Sure Start to support young children and families in deprived areas (see Case Study 2.1). The Local Government Act 2000 (Great Britain, 2000) placed a statutory duty on local authorities to produce a 'community strategy' to promote social, economic and environmental well-being for their area. Local Strategic Partnerships were established for areas of particular need or disadvantage consisting of representatives from the voluntary, community, public and private sectors. They had access to funds to support involvement in the partnerships to improve the quality of life of the locality.

Vision and purpose surrounding these policies were about reconnecting councils with local communities and moving towards service provision that was responsive to the demands of users and taxpayers. There was the attendant notion of invigorating local democracy by promoting participation in democratic processes and establishing greater community cohesion. New Labour believed neighbourhood renewal would lead to more jobs, better education, improved health, better housing and less crime.

ACTIVITY 2.1

Policy and community

Table 2.1 summarises a range of government policy from 2000 to 2010. Choose an example of a Coalition policy document such as *Building a Stronger Civil Society* (Cabinet Office, 2010) to compare with an example of a New Labour policy from the selection of policies in Table 2.1.

What similarities and differences do you notice in key words and phrases used in the documents, the aims and objectives, who the policy is aimed at, how the aims will be achieved and the intended outcomes? What unintended outcomes may arise?

Answering Activity 2.1 you may note similarities with reference to principles of empowerment from New Labour and the Coalition that cause you to question how they interpret this term. Differences may be seen in the roles envisaged for central and local government, frontline professionals and voluntary and community sector organisations. You may find it helpful to fast forward to Chapter 5 and to read the discussion about different interpretations of the concept of empowerment that we offer there. Reflecting on the models presented in Figure 5.1, what critique would you make of the interpretation of empowerment embodied in policy initiatives described in this chapter?

Initially the New Labour vision was neighbourhood renewal as a response to neighbourhood deprivation (DETR, 2000). Deprived neighbourhoods were perceived as 'fractured' areas that required building and strengthening through

Table 2.1 UK Government policies 2000–2010

Policy document	Aims	How the policy is implemented	Principles underpinning the policy	Intended outcomes
National Strategy for Neighbourhood Renewal: Joining it up Locally (DETR, 2000)	To tackle neighbourhood deprivation and problems of crime, low educational attainment and poor health.	By local joint working.	Empowerment with residents as partners; strong leadership and commitment from all partners; joined-up working; government as facilitator.	'Improving skills and changing cultures; and building ownership of the neighbourhood renewal vision throughout communities and service providers' (p.5).
Building Cohesive Communities (Home Office, 2001)	To build stronger, more cohesive communities.	By measures 'to promote dialogue and understanding'; by working in partnerships.	Based on 'robust evidence' and 'understanding of what works'; 'Government cannot create or impose community cohesion. It is something that communities must do themselves with Government's help as enabler and supporter' (p.34).	Unite people 'around a common sense of belonging'; for 'fractured communities' to become 'cohesive ones'.
Firm Foundations: The Government's Framework for Community Capacity Building (Home Office, 2004)	To support community capacity building; to engage more people in decision making and setting priorities for policies affecting their localities and neighbourhoods.	By a community development approach; through 'programmes and activities which enable people to take a more active part in their communities' (p.2).	Build on what exists; take a long view; embrace diversity and adapt solutions to local circumstances.	Community-led service providers 'plan and deliver activities and programmes'; increasing the confidence and capacity of individuals and groups to participate actively in their communities' (p.7).

continued overleaf

Table 2.1   *continued*

Policy document	Aims	How the policy is implemented	Principles underpinning the policy	Intended outcomes
An Action Plan for Community Empowerment: Building on Success (DCLG, 2007)	New relationship between Government and citizens 'making public involvement the rule, not the exception' (p.2).	By producing an Action Plan; embed community empowerment approaches in key programmes; and 'give citizens means of participating in decision-making at every level' (p.2).	'Moving away from "top down" working to ways of working that take the needs and wishes of communities into account' (p.6).	'Greater participation, collective action and engagement in democracy'; 'changes in attitudes towards community empowerment'; and 'improved performance of public services and quality of life' (p.5).
Communities in Control: Real People, Real Power (DCLG, 2008)	Strengthen local democracy; make institutions more accountable.	By harnessing the energy and innovation of frontline professionals, local government, citizens and communities	Shift power 'into the hands of communities and individual citizens'; belief that communities and individuals 'can take difficult decisions and solve complex problems for themselves' (p.1).	'More people becoming active in their communities as volunteers, advocates and elected representatives' (p.iii).
Building a Stronger Civil Society (Cabinet Office, 2010)	For the voluntary and community sector organisations 'to play an even more influential role in shaping a stronger sense of society and improving people's lives'; 'to create a Big Society' (p.3).	By establishing a 'community right to buy and to bid to run community assets' and 'to challenge their local authority'; by encouraging volunteering and philanthropy; training 5,000 Community Organisers to build and mobilise local networks; reducing bureaucracy and red tape; improving access to finance 'for social entrepreneurs'.	Empower communities; shift power from Whitehall to local communities; open up public services; promote social action.	Mobilising civil society with local people and businesses offering 'their skills and time to support small scale local charities, voluntary organisations and community groups' (p.10).

community cohesion (Home Office, 2001). A breakdown in tolerance and understanding within and between communities was seen as the root of sporadic 'serious disorder' in Bradford and other UK cities during April to July 2001. This breakdown was to be addressed by building a common sense of belonging. Civil renewal replaced neighbourhood renewal and the vision shifted to building capacity for people to become more active in their communities (Home Office, 2004).

New Labour during its third term in government sought to present its proposals and policy approaches to community as 'fresh and radical'. Policy referred to 'safe and friendly neighbourhoods' and 'decent society' (DCLG, 2006, p.1) yet the aim of more people becoming active 'as volunteers, advocates and elected representatives' remained (DCLG, 2008). To counter the idea that vision can lack substance New Labour persistently stressed the word 'real' with reference to the aims and implementation of policy and to those involved. For example, 'real control' and 'real people, real power' (DCLG, 2008, p.1). However, there was often a lack of detail in how exactly some ideas and approaches to policy would be implemented, monitored and evaluated.

The vision of Prime Minister David Cameron for the 'Big Society' (see Case Study 2.2) has continued ideas and themes seen in New Labour policy. New Labour developed a wider vision of creating a 'decent society' rather than simply renewing or regenerating neighbourhoods and localities. Cameron tapped into a sense of breakdown and fracture with reference to a 'Broken Britain' characterised by crime, social disorder and deprivation on sink estates populated by generations of families who have never worked for which a 'Big Society' can offer solutions. Cameron (2011) persists with his 'Big Society' agenda and a vision to 'build a bigger, stronger society' 24 years after a previous Conservative leader, Margaret Thatcher, declared in a magazine interview that 'there is no such thing as society' (Keay, 1987). It is an attempt to offer more substance to a vision backed by a government office with a budget, the Office for Civil Society; by legislation such as the community right to buy and bid to run community assets in the Localism Act 2011 (Great Britain, 2011) outlined in Box 2.1; by recruiting and training 5,000 *community organisers* to support local people to take action on issues that affect them (see 'Useful resources'); and by establishing the Big Society Bank. The bank was officially launched in July 2011 as Big Society Capital using unclaimed assets left dormant in bank accounts to offer investment to social enterprises, that is, organisations seeking social and environmental change (see 'Useful resources').

As an incoming Government it is unsurprising that the language of Coalition policy included words such as 'refreshed', 'renewed' and 'radical' (Cabinet Office, 2010) to present ideas and approaches that are intended to bring different benefits and more lasting solutions to the complex problems policy is seeking to address. Yet similarities remain embedded. The Coalition has continued New Labour's idea of both shifting and harnessing the power of communities, but with a different emphasis.

Empowerment

New Labour's view of empowerment was initially for local residents to be part of local decision making and to work on solutions to their own problems (DETR, 2000). 'Empowerment' saw residents of deprived neighbourhoods as partners with government and others in joint working. *The Community Development Challenge* (DCLG, 2006) referred generally to 'encouraging and empowering people' (p.1) and to the 'dispersal of power' (p.8). This signalled a shift in central government thinking that was acknowledging its inability to micromanage complex and diverse modern developments and coming to regard its function as lying in an 'enabling' role rather than as a service provider.

An Action Plan for Community Empowerment (DCLG, 2007) again emphasised the new, for example a 'new statutory "duty to involve"' (p.3) and a new relationship between Government and citizens hailed as 'a reinvention of the way we govern' (p.2). This was to be achieved by passing power from central government to local government and rebalancing power between parliament and government. Details on how this empowerment was to be achieved were through measures such as online consultations on planning issues and citizen juries to prioritise and shape policy.

The *Action Plan* saw community engagement by public bodies as reaching out to communities 'to create empowerment opportunities' (DCLG, 2007, p.12). This acknowledged the need for public bodies to change their approaches and attitudes by 'really listening, being prepared to be influenced, and giving real responsibility and support to local citizens' (p.11). 'Community empowerment' was defined as 'giving the confidence, skills and power to communities to shape and influence what public bodies do for them' (p.12). To ascertain as to whether this was achieved the *Action Plan* stated that 'real empowerment ... must make people feel differently about themselves and their power to influence' (p.12).

The Action Plan referred to the Local Government and Public Involvement in Health and Social Care Act 2007 (Great Britain, 2007) that introduced Local Involvement Networks. These networks of local people and groups were created to ensure communities monitored service provision, influenced decisions and had a stronger voice in the process of commissioning health and social care. Empowerment initiatives were more clearly linked to improving the quality of services.

Communities in Control (DCLG, 2008) saw power as something tangible that can be transferred, distributed or shifted 'both to front-line professionals and to users' (p.i) and 'from existing centres of power into the hands of communities and individual citizens' (p.1). The power being passed to communities and individual citizens is to be able to 'take difficult decisions and solve complex problems' (p.1). However, we would argue that passing on difficult decisions and problem solving, for example about cuts in services, is not a genuine transfer of power where the state retains the authority 'to set national priorities and minimum standards' (p.1).

Similarities can be observed where the Coalition government talks of transferring power to the voluntary and community sector 'to find better solutions to our social problems' (Cabinet Office, 2010, p.3). 'Empowering communities' is a core component of the 'Big Society' policy agenda by shifting more power to local councils and neighbourhoods. An example of new powers in the Localism Act 2011 is the community right to challenge the local authority if it believes services might be run better by other organisations, for example youth service provision. However the emphasis of empowerment under the Coalition government does not lie in delegating power to communities to make decisions and work out solutions to their problems but rather to open up contracts and services to wider competition from alternative providers.

Participation

Policy is not just the text and words in government documents and legislation it is also about action and deeds (Ball, 1994). The nature of the action called for in policies highlighted in Table 2.1 envisages some kind of *participation*. What do the policies tell us about changes in who is expected to participate and in what ways? The report on the *National Strategy for Neighbourhood Renewal* (DETR, 2000, p.5) referred to 'involving communities properly', for example, by including residents in local decision-making. *Building Cohesive Communities* (Home Office, 2001) sought 'to promote dialogue and understanding'. Dialogue between local people and communities would be encouraged by the development of projects through neighbourhood initiatives. This illustrates two government departments working at that time in different ways to establish participation, the former by promoting involvement in decision-making processes and the latter by developing projects as a means of establishing dialogue within and between communities to build cohesion.

Community capacity building (see Chapter 5), it was claimed, would lead to greater participation with 'the active involvement of citizens and communities with public bodies to improve the quality of life' (Home Office, 2004, p.2) and well-being of communities. A benefit of this approach was seen as 'sustainable involvement' (p.7) where individuals and groups would participate actively supported by their communities thereby increasing their confidence and capacity. *The Community Development Challenge* (DCLG, 2006) presented participation as 'community engagement' to 'boost democratic consent' and 'to engender pressure "from below" on underperforming services' (p.11).

An Action Plan for Community Empowerment (DCLG, 2007) reinforced the view of participation as 'community engagement' giving citizens opportunities to participate in decision-making 'at every level' (p.5). A key outcome was seen as 'greater participation, collective action and engagement in democracy' (p.5) with more emphasis on local involvement in planning and shaping policy. *Communities in Control* encouraged a wider view on participation when Prime Minister Gordon Brown referred to harnessing 'the energy and innovation of front-line professionals, local government, citizens and communities' (DCLG, 2008, p.i). Participation would see 'more people becoming active in their communities as volunteers, advocates and elected representatives' (p.iii). This purpose has continued under the Coalition government that states: 'The Big Society agenda is not a Government programme; it is a call to action' (Cabinet Office, 2010, p.12). The nature of the action is based on volunteering (see Case Study 2.2) and continuing New Labour's promotion of *active citizenship* (see Chapter 4).

Partnership

At the launch of the *National Strategy for Neighbourhood Renewal* residents were regarded as partners in joint-working (DETR, 2000). The idea of local strategic partnerships was established bringing together representatives from the public, private and community-voluntary sectors as well as existing partnerships to produce local neighbourhood renewal strategies. *The Government's Framework for Community Capacity Building* was less focused on the idea of partnership and more on building 'stronger collaboration and co-ordination at local, regional and national levels' (Home Office, 2004, p.4).

New Labour's slogan of 'Together We Can' was aimed at giving citizens and communities a bigger say in the services they received and in the quality of communities in which they lived (DCLG, 2006). The Coalition government's *Building a Stronger Civil Society* begins 'together with citizens and communities, the voluntary and community sector sits at the heart of the Government's ambitions to create a Big Society' (Cabinet Office, 2010, p.3). It concludes by reminding us that 'citizens, communities and civil society providers all need to play a part in reducing the deficit' (p.12). This could be seen as a case of resurrecting the New Labour slogan to suggest 'together we can' identify 'the smartest way of making savings and finding better ways of doing things' (p.4). There is a similarity with New Labour offering power to local communities to make difficult decisions about complex problems (DCLG, 2008).

Benefits of partnership come from combining knowledge and resources so more can be achieved together. Working together exposes practitioners and organisations to different methods, approaches, ideas and opportunities to reflect on assumptions or taken-for-granted attitudes. For the community-voluntary sector in particular it can be useful to combine applications to gain access to additional funding sources. Problems arise where partnerships of convenience are built in which some partners may be silent or silenced. The tokenistic nature of the partnership may be further affected where the voices of communities and service users are not adequately represented and heard. Partners who are service providers may not like what they hear and there may be conflicts of interest within and between communities, for example, in relation to expanding a traveller site or setting up a hostel for homeless people in the neighbourhood.

Continuity and change

New Labour's vision for social policy emerged from the report of the Commission on Social Justice (1994) commissioned while in Opposition. The vision was to create greater social justice and tackle social exclusion by developing the economic well-being of individuals and communities. The Coalition likewise has adopted the mantle of social justice to find solutions to poverty following the establishment of the Centre for Social Justice in 2004.

Exploring the policy documents and reports show that an interest in social justice and community seeded in politicians while in Opposition has begun to blossom at the heart of government. Under New Labour what was going on locally came first under the responsibility of local government ministers in the Department for Environment, Transport and the Regions. From 2001 these roles and functions gained an upgrade as they were moved into the Office of the Deputy Prime Minister. From there *community* finally arrived at the Cabinet table with its own department and budget following the appointment of the first Secretary of State for Communities and Local Government in 2006. Under the Coalition the Office for Civil Society is part of the Cabinet Office. It includes the Deputy Prime Minister and works across government departments to translate the Big Society agenda into practical policies. The Centre for Social Justice operates as an independent think-tank that has the attention of ministers looking for policy ideas and solutions.

Where once it was practitioners and academics using language such as *empowerment, social capital, community cohesion* and *capacity building*, it is now the politicians and policymakers who use these terms, defining them and setting out ways they will be enhanced or achieved. This includes a renewal of central government interest in community development. This chapter suggests that the text and words in documents and policies show politicians and policy makers are still catching up with, or aspiring to achieve, the aims and principles of community development set out over two decades ago:

> Community development is concerned with change and growth – with giving people more power over the changes that are taking place around them, the policies that affect them and the services they use. (Taylor, 1992, p.6)

and

> [Community development seeks to] enable individuals and communities to grow and change according to their own needs and priorities. (Standing Committee on Community Development, 1990, cited in Taylor, 1992, p.6)

At this point you may find it useful to read Chapter 5 where we explore the potential for community development as an approach for releasing capacity to enable individuals and communities to grow and change.

Policy into practice

In the previous sections we used the texts and words of policy documents related to themes of *vision, empowerment, participation* and *partnership* and tracked continuities and changes in policies and practice. We now turn from the text and words of the aims, purpose, principles and rhetoric of government and policy makers to the action and deeds of communities, service users and practitioners, the 'street level bureaucrats' (Lipsky, 1979) who follow, promote, interpret, rewrite, obstruct, undermine or ignore policy. We explore how policies such as those in Table 2.1 translate into action with communities and service users.

New Deal for Communities (NDC) was 'billed as New Labour's big idea for reviving some of the country's most deprived areas' (Ball-Petsimeris, 2004, p.177). Toynbee (2011) regarded the programme as 'the boldest initiative ever tried'. Case Study 2.1 is an example of an area transformed by NDC funding.

CASE STUDY 2.1

Community at Heart

In 2000 local residents and agencies made a successful bid for £50 million to regenerate an area of east Bristol in the UK. The vision was 'to create a strong responsible community that has the ability to understand, engage and overcome its problems, enabling residents to build a safe environment that fulfils local needs, inspires and provides opportunities for all' (Community at Heart, 2010). The resulting partnership established eight 'key outcome areas': employment and business; healthy places, happy people; community safety; lifelong learning; housing; community services; arts and sports; tackling racism.

ACTIVITY 2.2

Devising a community programme

Outline ideas for a programme or project to address one of the eight 'key outcome areas' listed in Case Study 2.1 for a community or neighbourhood with which you are familiar:

What will the programme involve? How will you establish it? What benefits will it bring to the community?

Compare your ideas with what happened in Community at Heart as outlined in the final report (Community at Heart, 2010). The example of community safety is described below.

Refer to Chapter 1 and reflect on your use and understanding of concepts such as *community, engagement,* and levels of *participation.* Reflection on your programme ideas might include applying Burns et al.'s (1994) 'ladder of citizen empowerment' (see Figure 1.1) to assess the envisaged level of citizen control, participation or non-participation.

In Case Study 2.1 Community at Heart projects under the key outcome of community safety included: working with the police authority to establish a team of Police Community Support Officers for the area; CCTV, security-controlled access to tower blocks and improved street lighting; a project to install new locks and security lights to make homes safer; funding projects to help the rehabilitation of drug users; and employing a domestic abuse caseworker.

The Coalition's big idea for revival and renewal is rooted in the Conservative Party Conference of October 2009 when party leader David Cameron referred to the problems of 'broken society' and 'big government' being solved by a 'stronger' and 'responsible society' that later transformed into his vision of 'Big Society'.

> ### CASE STUDY 2.2
>
> **Big Society**
>
> Cameron's view was that government under New Labour had got 'too big', 'promised too much' and 'spent too much'– 'I have some simple beliefs. That there is such a thing as society, it's just not the same thing as the state. That there is a "we" in politics, and not just a "me"' (Cameron, 2009).
>
> Cameron developed this belief in a speech as leader of the Opposition in November 2009 where the vision of Big Society was introduced to challenge the 'big government' of New Labour. Voluntary groups and charities would take on a key role in tackling poverty. The emphasis in this initiative shifted from the state to 'civil society, the third sector and social enterprise' (Scott, 2011, p.132). Arguably Big Society is a comparable vision to Tony Blair's *Third Way* but is 'more tangible, dynamic and institutionally embedded' in the Office for Civil Society within Cabinet (Barnard, 2010).
>
> In 2010 Prime Minister Cameron launched his Big Society idea to mend what he perceived as Britain's 'Broken Society' (Cameron, 2010; BBC News, 2010). There are a range of perspectives from academics, media commentators, politicians and practitioners on what these terms mean. For example, Tam (2011) sees the repeated mantra that 'Big Government has failed' as the 'Big Con' to get people to accept the idea that 'the less the government does for you, the better off you and society would be in sorting things out' (p.30).

Hancock et al. (2012) see the 'big state' being presented and described by Cameron and others as inefficient, costly, limiting individuality, stifling freedom, encouraging 'welfare dependency' and the 'primary cause of the broken and sick societies'. They continue by noting how 'the notion of a "broken Britain" refers to "broken" families, "broken" communities, deprivation, welfarism, crime and disorder' rather than any acknowledgement that Britain has been 'broken' 'by economic change, by large-scale deindustrialization, disinvestment or by the everyday workings of the market' (p.348). Activity 2.3 provides an opportunity for you to scrutinise the evidence of a 'Broken Britain'.

Big Society will be created, according to the Centre for Social Justice, by charities, local organisations and an army of social entrepreneurs from the voluntary sector in the vanguard of fixing the broken communities of 'Broken Britain'. Iain Duncan Smith (2009), then chairman of the Centre, presented the following 'facts' within an article on its website as evidence that Britain is broken:

- 'Britain's social housing estates ... are now ghettos for our poorest people.'
- 'Life expectancy on some estates ... is lower than the Gaza Strip.'
- '20% of pupils who gain no GCSEs come from just 203 schools.'
- 'Social mobility is rare: more than 80% of social housing residents in 2006 had been in the sector ten years earlier.'
- '1.35 million children have a parent addicted to drugs and alcohol.'
- 'Predatory loan-sharks thrive on our social housing estates charging interest rates up to 1000%.'

- 'Marriage, far more stable than cohabitation, has rapidly declined in recent decades.'
- '15% of babies in Britain are now born without a resident biological father.'
- 'We have the highest teenage pregnancy in Europe.'
- 'Without strong families violent and lawless street gangs ... offer a deadly alternative.'

ACTIVITY 2.3

Is Britain 'broken'?

Read through the list above and consider how strong is the evidence presented that Britain is broken? What other evidence could you present to support or contradict the view that Britain is broken? How might you use statistics from the UK's Office for National Statistics (www.ons.gov.uk/ons/index.html) to support your view?

The claim that 'life expectancy on some estates ... is lower than the Gaza Strip' is based on a comment by a Scottish Nationalist politician attacking Labour's record on health in the build up to a by-election in Glasgow in 2008. The politician, Angus Roberson MP, declared 'life expectancy in Glasgow East is lower than in the Gaza Strip' (Channel 4 News, 2008). Channel 4 News (2008) uses its FactCheck blog to offer assessment and comment on the 'life expectancy' example data while reminding us to be cautious when comparing data from different sources. The FactCheck blog 'goes behind the spin to dig out the truth and separate political fact from fiction' (FactCheck blog, n.d.).

In July 2010 Prime Minster Cameron announced the launch of four Big Society 'vanguard areas' in Eden Valley (Cumbria); Windsor and Maidenhead; Liverpool; and the London borough of Sutton. The areas were invited to put forward proposals for innovative local projects embracing Big Society principles.

CASE STUDY 2.3

Eden Valley

Eden Valley is a rural area of villages and market towns in North West England bordered by the Lake District to the west and the Pennines and Yorkshire Dales to the east. Three communities in the area identified their main priorities as affordable housing, neighbourhood planning, superfast broadband, renewable energy and transport. The Community Plan of each area gives an idea of the type of projects illustrative of the Big Society agenda.

> *Upper Eden*: has set up an online superfast broadband centre based on a farm; established a cycle path between two villages as an alternative to a busy main road; and plans to build a wind turbine under community ownership for renewable energy.
> *Heart of Eden*: is promoting cycling and walking to boost the local economy and tourism; reviewing bus timetables with a focus on transport needs of

> young people; identifying need for affordable housing for local people; and
> lobbying to control second home numbers.
> *Lyvennet:* local residents set up a co-operative to buy and re-open their local
> pub as a community pub selling local beer and produce as well as using it as a
> venue for community events. (Eden District Council, n.d.)

Liverpool withdrew from the vanguard programme in February 2011 amid media headlines heralding the death of Big Society (Kruger, 2011) and politicians questioning its future. The withdrawal was illustrative of tensions arising where a local authority is run by one political party and central government by another. Against a backdrop of cuts in budgets to local government the Labour-led Liverpool City Council felt it could not make its plans for a Big Society programme work. Those involved in the initiative argued they supported the principles but that Big Society was launched at the wrong time since its intended outcomes were becoming associated with cuts in services and loss of frontline professionals. The leader of the Council declared 'Liverpool has been doing the "big society" for many years. We call it "working with our communities"' (BBC News, 2011).

The Coalition presents Big Society as handing power from bureaucrats to communities and individuals to create better neighbourhoods and local services, overseen by a newly appointed Minister for Decentralisation. For the Coalition this redistribution of power to localities offers new responsibilities and opportunities for volunteering, innovation and social enterprise. Others interpret this power shift as central and local government passing the buck to local people to make cuts to services. People are 'encouraged to be the bearers of their own predicaments' (Sage, 2012, p.375) within the Coalition's promotion of 'a highly individualized model of responsibility'. Sage views the beginning of Cameron's leadership as an attempt to show that the Conservative party had changed its predominant association with neoliberalism: 'through the Big Society, the Conservatives' renewed interest in social justice was interlinked with their desire to reinvigorate civil society' (2012: p.371). However, he notes how the Big Society agenda has been challenged by the deficit reduction programme of austerity and public spending cuts with reference to '£20 billion worth of welfare cuts' and '£4.5 billion worth of spending cuts imposed on already stretched charitable organizations' (p.374). Neoliberalism has remained a persistent influence and is again exerting its influence within the Coalition in its prioritising of 'a smaller state, marketization and personal responsibility' (p.378). It is such factors as these that limit the impact of Big Society.

In Scott's view Big Society 'as a contagious idea has broken through' (2011, p.133). It is reinvented and relaunched in the face of on-going criticisms (Toynbee, 2011). Policy designed around changing behaviour, such as central government calls for active citizenship or volunteering to run local services, is likely to risk accusations of rhetoric and being regarded as 'highly manipulative' (Scott, 2011, p.136). However Big Society is backed up by concrete initiatives and access to funding or other resources. Scott is critical of how high levels of funding given by New Labour to the community and voluntary sector failed to trickle down to grassroots communities with a rise of 'ever greater structural inequality within the voluntary and community sectors' resulting in 'the marginalization of community development' (2011, p.134). He recognises that renewed focus on civil society offers potential for community development to work to relocate 'the power to initiate' to communities (2011, p.134).

The renewed focus on civil society and 'power to initiate' are evident where the Minister for Decentralisation has set out actions for Big Society to flourish in the Localism Act 2011 with the 'right to bid' and the 'right to challenge'.

BOX 2.1 LOCALISM ACT 2011

> We think that power should be exercised at the lowest possible practical level – close to the people who are affected by decisions, rather than distant from them. (DCLG, 2011a, p.4)

The Act gives greater powers and rights to communities and neighbourhoods, for example, residents can instigate a referendum on any local issue; there are new powers to save local facilities and services threatened with closure; and voluntary and community groups have the right to challenge local authorities over services.

- *Community right to bid*: local authorities are required to maintain a list of assets of community value nominated by the local community. These might include a community centre, library, swimming pool, pub or village shop. If a listed asset comes up for sale or change of ownership then community groups are given time to develop a bid and raise money to bid to buy the asset.
- *Community right to challenge*: voluntary and community groups, parish councils and local authority employees have the right to express an interest to take over the running of a local authority service. (DCLG, 2011a, p.11–12)

A shift in thinking about how the duties and powers of local authorities are defined and exercised is signalled in the Localism Act. The Coalition government sees that the reason why councils are unwilling to try something new is because generally their work is determined by what duties are required in legislation and what powers they may choose to exercise. This means they are wary about being challenged in the courts for doing something beyond their established duties or powers. The Government has sought to turn this around so 'instead of being able to act only where the law says they can, local authorities will be freed to do anything – provided they do not break other laws' (DCLG, 2011a, p.7). The Localism Act includes a 'general power' of competence that 'gives local authorities the legal capacity to do anything that an individual can do that is not specifically prohibited' (DCLG, 2011a, p.7).

Overall the intentions are presented as making it easier for local people to take over amenities they value and to ensure those groups or others with ideas to improve services get opportunities to put these into practice (see Case Study 2.3). The expectation is that this will give councils increased confidence to be creative and innovative in meeting local needs. At the root of the Localism Act is the notion that power is a tangible entity that is 'hoarded and concentrated' (DCLG, 2011a, p.1) in the hands of central government and needs to be shifted from the bureaucracy of Whitehall to local public servants, communities and individuals.

The focus of Coalition policy in relation to communities broadly demonstrates on-going application of a democratic model that purports to create greater citizen involvement and to shift control and decision-making powers from central government to neighbourhood level. Neighbourhood renewal under New Labour was part of a strategy to tackle poverty by driving down to neighbourhood and street level to identify pockets of deprivation and target solutions to try to ensure that policy had an impact. The Coalition government continues to focus on groups and individuals within neighbourhoods but with a different emphasis. As part of the Big Society it is the active involvement of groups and individuals that can find and implement solutions to 'Broken Britain' while helping to address the debt crisis. The Localism Act uses the language of a democratic model to suggest it is seeking greater collective involvement and challenging the power of those who traditionally determine needs and priorities. In practice the Act is unleashing a consumer model where competing interests within and between neighbourhoods seek to have their voice heard over proposals affecting them all. Ultimately the power of local and central government will be used to resolve conflict.

ACTIVITY 2.4

Local decision making

Use your local newspaper to find examples of plans or proposals that affect different neighbourhoods or groups, for example, plans for a new supermarket, sports stadium, bus lane, mental health facility or primary school. Follow the newspaper's online discussion forum to get an idea of different issues, arguments and solutions being presented about the plans.

Reflect on whose interests are being put forward and whose are not. Consider the roles of those involved in the decision making. What evidence do you see of democratic and consumerist models being applied to affect the outcomes of the plans?

Activity 2.4 offers examples such as building a new supermarket where conflicts are likely to be expressed between residents, local traders, the wider business and enterprise community, and local planning authority. Bus lanes and other traffic-related plans generally lead to conflicting views between motorists, cyclists, public transport users and pedestrians. In these examples there may be periods of consultation, presentations of alternatives, and possibly public enquiries, challenges to decisions taken and judicial reviews. Local authorities and government ministers retain the power to initiate these processes and to make final decisions on plans in the absence of consensus.

The consumerist model is more clearly apparent in policies impacting on individual service users. The idea of mobilising active citizens using choice, charters and compensation to drive up quality of public service provision came to the fore during the Conservative government led by Margaret Thatcher from 1979 to 1991 and continued under John Major (1991–97). The neoliberal agenda used market forces to create competition so that consumers could choose to take their custom elsewhere for electricity, gas or rail travel. Where you felt you were not getting a good service then citizen or consumer charters with promises of performance provided the template for making complaints and seeking redress. The development of the consumerist model can be traced through the movement towards the personalisation policy agenda.

Personalisation

Alongside New Labour's vision for renewing and empowering communities came their ambitions for improving and transforming health and social care services in the UK (DH, 2006, 2008). Personalisation was introduced as 'the cornerstone of public services' that would mean every person receiving support within adult social care would be 'empowered to shape their own lives and the services they receive in all care settings' (DH, 2008). This ambition was presented as a reform of public services where people would be able to live according to their wishes and where their needs would be met by high quality services. Personalisation offered individuals choice and control of their support and marked a strategic shift towards early intervention and prevention. This shift would also result in significant changes for the service providers. Personalisation envisaged tailoring services to each individual's needs rather than delivering a one-size-fits-all provision. The idea was put into action through direct payments and individual or personal budgets. It is 'more than a passing political fad' (Dickinson and Glasby, 2010, p.1) and it is a commitment that has been taken on by the Coalition government.

The Community Care (Direct Payments) Act 1996 (Great Britain, 1996) gave disabled people in the UK who were eligible for adult social care the option to receive direct payments to pay for services. This idea of consumer-directed care was developed through work begun by disabled people in the US and was taken up by disabled people's organisations in the UK in the 1980s. The promotion of the concept alongside on-going lobbying of politicians resulted in the 1996 Act. Direct payments were one tangible and practical aspect of a struggle to ensure greater choice, control and independent living for those with disability. The payments were seen as part of a wider social movement to establish the social model of disability. This model defines disability by the social and cultural barriers and attitudes towards people with disability that prevent them participating as equal citizens. Where previously disabled people were assessed and provided with available services by professionals the introduction of direct payments under a Conservative government gave service users the choice to use money for their own care.

Dickinson and Glasby outline how this discretionary payment was extended to other user groups such as older people and carers. They also note criticisms of direct payments as a 'qualified form of empowerment' since 'they do not alter the basic needs-based and means-tested basis of the English welfare system' (2010, p.4). They go on to indicate how the introduction of personal budgets is having a wider impact on transforming the social care system. In particular they point to the work of In Control (see Case Study 2.4) in devising a new system of social care called 'self-directed support' to give people power, choice and control over their lives.

CASE STUDY 2.4

In Control

In Control is a UK national charity. Their website (www.in-control.org.uk) states that it operates 'to provide people with the knowledge, power and tools to control their support'. The organisation works directly with people needing support and their families. In Control has produced a fact sheet setting out a seven steps model of self-directed support to guide both individual service users and professionals through the process of establishing support.

Step 1: My money – finding out how much
Step 2: Making my plan
Step 3: Getting my plan agreed
Step 4: Organising my money
Step 5: Organising my support
Step 6: Living life
Step 7: Seeing how it worked

(In Control, 2011, p.3)

As noted in the introduction to this chapter there are different political contexts and policy development under the devolved governments of the UK. While personalisation and self-directed support may be seen as advanced in England there are different perspectives and priorities within other parts of the UK. In Wales personalisation is referred to as *citizen-directed support* and places more emphasis on building strong communities to enable people to support each other rather than on giving support to purchase services within the market. This demonstrates that a democratic model can be used in addressing the personalisation agenda. The Wales Alliance for Citizen Directed Support consists of local authorities that commission services, organisations that deliver services and organisations that represent people using services. Its aims, principles and ways of working indicate thinking beyond the individual service user by linking with people, organisations and communities and working together. Citizen-directed support is presented as developing a social movement rather than as an attempt by one consumer to secure the best possible care for that individual within the market.

Wales Alliance for Citizen Directed Support

The principle of the Wales Alliance for Citizen Directed Support is built from three main core beliefs:

- *Change*: I can work to create a better life for me and those around me ... We can work together to create a major change in the way we support each other and meet our needs.
- *Choice and control*: I will have the greatest possible choice and control to direct my own life ... We will work together to have lives that we can all aspire to.
- *Community*: I have a rightful place in my community and an opportunity to contribute to it ... We will help to build communities in which we all can exercise our responsibilities and enjoy our rights as citizens.

These core beliefs are expressed in detail on their website (http://welshcitizen support.files.wordpress.com/2011/08/wacds-principles-1-2.pdf) under the heading 'What we believe and what we will do'.

Think about how you could apply these principles to work with an individual or family experiencing social isolation within their neighbourhood.

Scotland, like England, is taking on the self-directed support strategy. Against a context of cuts in social care budgets and ensuring that all people needing support are allocated a share of diminishing resources Glasgow City Council (2010) offers to provide service users with an individual budget. The personalisation process starts with the service user completing a self-evaluation questionnaire to begin to identify their needs. They then devise a support plan in consultation with their social worker and are allocated an estimated budget used to plan and support arrangements to meet those needs. Those arrangements might involve employing a personal assistant, using technology or equipment, or purchasing support from different providers.

Individual budgets offer a transparent means of allocating resources to service users and letting them know exactly how much they have to plan and control to support their needs. An evaluation was carried out of an Individual Budgets Pilot Programme introduced in 13 local authorities in England between 2005 and 2007 to determine if individual budgets are a better way of supporting disabled adults and older people (IBSEN, 2008). The findings suggested service users welcomed the opportunity for choice and control over their support but that there were differences between groups; for example, satisfaction was highest among mental health service users and lowest among older people. Mental health service users saw individual budgets 'as an opportunity to access more appropriate support' (IBSEN, 2008, p.18) than was available under conventional arrangements. Older people, however, did not want 'what many of them described as the "additional burden" of planning and managing their own support' (p.19).

Impact on practice

The personalisation agenda raises issues for discussion where individual service users take on the role and responsibilities of a budget-holder or care manager in return for supposed choice and influence. Lymbery (2012) suggests that organising and planning of individual budgets may favour the more articulate and educated as well as erode the collective basis underpinning much public service provision. Personalisation illustrates the tension between a democratic and consumerist model. On the one hand there are the principles, for example, of the disability movement and of social work evident where services are determined by users who are experts in their own lives. On the other hand personalisation represents the marketisation of care where consumers use the market place to buy the best care for themselves. As Lymbery points out:

> the very reason why social care first emerged in the public sector appears to have been forgotten – to ensure that all people could be provided with support, particularly those that are least able to function as self-actualising consumers within the market (2012, p.5).

Dunning (2011) acknowledges there is also an impact on social care professionals and their core functions of care management such as assessment, producing a care plan and purchasing services. Under personalisation these functions transfer to the service user to assess their own needs, draw up their care plan and directly purchase services they want with their money, if they can afford it. As a consequence local authorities are creating new roles to support service users causing concerns in some areas about a reduction in qualified social workers and a rise in non-professional staff. Social workers complain of increased paperwork by the adding of user self-assessments to their workload (Dunning, 2011). However, while Lymbery notes the trend for employing fewer social workers within local authorities due to cuts in funding there 'remains a need for professional involvement – particularly in situations of complexity or acute levels of risk … It will be vital to assert the importance of social work in both assessment and safeguarding' (2012, p.13). He points out there is no requirement for social work to be undertaken within the context of local government and notes how social workers in countries such as Australia and the US are employed in a range of settings. How does personalisation work in those countries?

In Australia and the US the term 'consumer-directed care' is used rather than personalisation. Evidence from programmes for younger disabled people in Australia suggests that what consumers want includes 'reliability of staff, continuity of care … competence … and knowledge and experience of users' needs and wishes' (Henwood, 1999, cited in ACSA 2008). Consumer-directed care in the US was designed as a programme to contain costs. The costs of what service users want and need is not fixed and will change over a lifetime. The question is whether the costs and resources within any personal budget will continue to match those wants and needs. Consequently the skills of the professional offering support may become subsumed into the role of information gatherer to find cheaper alternatives and thereby cutting the costs of care.

Ongoing evaluation of how policies such as personalisation work in practice is required to check if the potential and the ambition are realised (see Chapter 9). That evaluation could: consider the extent to which personalisation leads to a wide range of high-quality services where service users have both real choice and control; assess where and how service users receive good quality advice and information to help make choices; and explore how the role of professionals changes to work with service users, families and communities to support themselves, build their independence and improve lives.

Chapter summary

In this chapter we explored why and how government policy initiatives have sought to encourage the participation and involvement of community groups and service users. We introduced two models of participation to distinguish between communities and service users exerting their power as consumers through choice, complaint and compensation or through democratic means of direct control of decision making. By mapping some of the continuities and changes in policy in relation to communities and to individual services users we have been able to identify similarities and new directions over recent years. We have noted the shift from neighbourhood renewal to renewal of civil society and Big Society; and from direct payments through personalisation to self-directed and citizen-directed support.

Having outlined the current policy context we will now move on, in Chapter 3, to consider some of the theoretical frameworks for examining community and engagement. We look at theories of attachment, association and social capital and critique their application in practice and their contribution to the *well-being* of service users and communities.

USEFUL RESOURCES

Community Organisers programme website enables you to find out more about the organisers, ask questions and get in touch (see: **www.cocollaborative.org.uk**).

Department for Communities and Local Government develops UK policy on supporting local government, communities and neighbourhoods. By 2014 all UK government departments will be available on the website (**www.gov.uk/government**).

In Control is a UK national charity whose mission is 'to create a fairer society where everyone needing additional support has the right, responsibility and freedom to control that support' (**www.in-control.org.uk/**).

Social Care Institute for Excellence (SCIE) website has a 'rough guide' to Personalisation (**www.scie.org.uk/publications/guides/guide47/?dm_i= 4O5,128CJ,UF1JP,39PG5,1**).

Social Enterprise UK is a national body presenting news, offering advice, support and promoting the growth of the social enterprise movement (**www.socialenterprise. org.uk/**).

FURTHER READING

Diamond, J. (2004) Local Regeneration Initiatives and Capacity Building: Whose 'capacity' and 'building' for what? *Community Development Journal* 39, 2, 177–189.
This article offers an interesting discussion of different approaches to community capacity building in Glasgow and Manchester.

Lupton, R. and Power, A. (2005) Disadvantaged by Where you Live? New Labour and Neighbourhood Renewal, in Hills, J. and Stewart, K. (eds) *A More Equal Society? New Labour, Poverty, Inequality and Exclusion* (Bristol: Policy Press), pp. 119–143.
This chapter presents discussion of some of the results of New Labour's neighbourhood renewal strategy.

Taylor, M. (1995) *Unleashing the Potential: Bringing Residents to the Centre of Regeneration* (York: Joseph Rowntree Foundation).
This report usefully summarised lessons from 33 research studies covering 100 housing estates in the UK looking at community involvement and how residents could play a major role in estate regeneration.

PART II

Themes

CHAPTER 3

Encouraging Association

CHAPTER OBJECTIVES

By the end of this chapter you should have an understanding of:

- relational approaches to understanding community and association;
- theoretical concepts such as social capital and civil society;
- the contested territory of policy approaches to encouraging voluntary association; and
- useful resources to improve knowledge and practice.

Introduction

Chapter 1 introduced a range of ways of thinking about participation in community and one of the themes that emerged from those analyses was the concept of attachment, association, affiliation and a sense of belonging. This approach to considering community through, what we refer to as a relational lens, acknowledges the value to the individual and to the collective of being connected to others. It is a way of thinking about community that stresses the importance of relationships and connectivity to an individual's emotional health and well-being. Community, in this sense, provides resources that are seen as supporting resilience.

As we noted in Chapter 1, Yerbury (2012) found that young people's understanding of the vocabulary of community revealed a theme about a sense of belonging and a sense of being connected to others. This *sense of community* is formed when people keep in touch with each other in some way. To the young people in this study, place was not an important factor in their notion of community. Yerbury (2012) concluded that community 'is no longer seen as an entity into which an individual can be absorbed'; instead it should be seen as 'something that grows out from the individual' (p.196). This is an important concept underpinning the frameworks in this chapter and, in our view, is a significant aspect informing the practice of engaging with service users.

In 2008 research by the Joseph Rowntree Foundation (Grayling, 2008) found a strong sense of unease about some of the changes shaping modern society. Top of the list of what they called 'modern social evils' was a sense that there was a 'demise of traditional forms of community' and a rise of individualism. We noted, in Chapter 1, how, in the perceived absence or weakening, of what have come to be seen as 'traditional' geographic communities people are increasingly turning to 'aesthetic communities' (Cunningham and Cunningham, 2008) in an attempt to create a sense of belonging and attachment. We also noted, in Chapter 2, how government policy has tended in recent years to try to create opportunities and interventions that are intended to encourage the creation of community groups and civic association where people can network, share and support one another.

In this chapter we consider some of the theoretical frameworks for examining community and engagement from this relational perspective. In particular, we discuss theories of association and social capital and attempt to critique their application in practice. These frameworks have particular relevance for considering current policy initiatives that stress the importance of *well-being*. Well-being has been described by the New Economics Foundation (NEF) as not only about 'feeling good and functioning well' but also as 'experiencing positive relationships and having some control over one's life' (Aked et al., 2008, p.1). This definition emphasises an individual's ability to 'function in the world' and to 'have a sense of purpose'.

ACTIVITY 3.1

Belonging to a community

Try to think of a group, club, network or community association to which you belong.

What emotions does being a part of this group generate in you?

You might express this as 'I feel … .'

When we have done this activity with people in groups (for example Oliver et al., 2011) they have usually come up with phrases such as 'I feel I belong', 'I feel at home', 'it feels like family', 'I feel that I am not alone', 'it was friendly', 'it is a safe place', 'it's a relaxed caring, supportive environment', 'it's my second home', 'it helps me deal with a heavy load', 'it offers a break – somewhere to go'. Like the participants quoted here, Begum (2003) found that active involvement in groups 'increased people's sense of belonging' and led to higher degrees of pride, attachment, trust and safety.

However, 'well-being', and the policies associated with it is another of those contested concepts that can lead us down unquestioning paths if we are not open to deconstructing them. White and Pettit (2004, p.2), for example, point out how concepts of well-being and participation have become 'highly contested, internally diverse umbrella terms' that have tended in recent years to become 'hurrah words: they are good things, engendering a warm glow and drawing people to them'.

Association and well-being

A frequent criticism of the concept of community as place is that such communities are often defined by outsiders or by government departments. We noted in Chapter 1 how these communities might sometimes be classed as 'unchosen communities' and we argued that commonality of place does not necessarily mean that individuals will have much to do with each other. Arnott and Koubel (2012, p.163) have also pointed out that marginalised groups and individuals are more likely to be overlooked when community is defined or labelled by an outsider. For example, a project established to work with an immigrant community could overlook the different experiences of women in that grouping.

It has been argued that participation in shared activities can lead to the development of close and caring relationships that contribute to well-being and resilience. Thomas (2012, p.131) for example, refers to research by the New Economics Foundation (2004) that estimated that 40 per cent of an individual's well-being is dependent on their outlook and activities and concluded that community involvement is a very important contributing factor to well-being. A recent report by UNICEF (Nairn, 2011, p.71) concluded that children are 'more likely to thrive' where the social context makes it possible for them to have time with family and friends and to get out and about without having to spend money. Jones et al. (2011) demonstrated that even simple, low-cost community group activities can have a beneficial impact on the well-being of adults with poor mental health. They found that participation in activities such as lunch clubs, cookery or arts and craft classes was positively associated with indicators of well-being such as personal optimism, clarity of decision making, community belonging, social interaction and neighbourhood trust. At the same time participation in such activities was also associated with reduced depression.

Most communities have a wide range of groups, including residents' associations, youth clubs, sports groups, pensioners' groups, city farms, community gardens, mental health support groups and a range of campaigning groups. In the UK, Europe and North America there is a long history and tradition of voluntary association in community and self-help groups that can be traced back to the nineteenth century. Voluntary groups are often mutual aid organisations involving people joining together to fulfil social needs. They might be small local groups or part of a national movement. In Britain there are said to be well over a million voluntary and community groups of varying sizes offering people the chance to share in decision making around things that affect their lives and in this way they can be a route to engaging in the wider political arena.

According to Begum, who has described voluntary groups as 'incubators of civic attitudes' (2003, p.12) voluntary groups can facilitate social connections and co-operation and engender trust, friendship and mutual aid among their members. Very often they provide a sense of belonging and identity and for many this can act as a stepping stone to paid employment. Informal, local groups offer the opportunity for local people to meet and to share their experiences. This can result in people realising that they share the same problems or concerns. From this kind of informal contact people often move to setting up self-help groups and support groups that can grow into groups that take on a campaigning focus.

However, recent reports by the Centre for Welfare Reform (Fulton and Winfield, 2011a, 2011b) found that practitioners often 'fail' to signpost service users to valuable sources of support and community organisations because of their lack of awareness of what is on offer and too little trust in service users' own abilities. The studies on community engagement and peer support found that personal budget holders were often missing out on valuable information, advocacy and help in support planning from fellow service users and local groups outside the care system such as churches, leisure clubs and neighbourhood groups. This was because many practitioners were unaware of what was available locally and did not trust service users to manage the support planning process without professional advice. The studies concluded that peer support through associational activity offers something distinctive to service users by enabling them to build relationships with people who have had similar experiences, boosting self-esteem and improving motivation.

ACTIVITY 3.2

Identifying a range of local services

Use a local voluntary sector directory, either at your local library or online to identify at least one local group offering support and/or activities for service users.

What sort of activities or support do they offer?

How could you enable or encourage a service user to access this service independently?

What short and longer term benefits could you or your service user gain by participating in this service?

Dinham (2007, p.192) notes that there may be many 'personal and individual' benefits from participation in community activity such as 'greater self confidence, new skills and improved relationships'. Brodie et al. (2011) found that association in social networks of friends, family, colleagues and others can be 'an invaluable resource' that can be called upon to give access to other resources, knowledge, connections and decision makers. Research by Phinney et al. (2007) concluded that encouraging social relationships among older service users can lead to an increased sense of safety and to a reduced sense of isolation. Phinney et al. (2007) found that social activities were important to people because they provided a sense of connection and belonging in the world allowing people to feel part of the wider community and to feel useful. Haslam et al. (2009) concluded that membership of social groups can be better for a person's health and well-being than diet and exercise. They cited studies that show that when people feel part of a close knit group, they are less likely to suffer heart attacks, are more able to cope with stress and are better at retaining memory than people who become socially isolated. Having a personal network or 'secure base-camp that encourages exploration' (Gilligan, 2000, p.39) has also been identified as one of the factors thought to contribute to the development of resilience. According to Gilligan, a sense of secure base is cultivated by a 'sense of belonging within supportive social networks and by attachment type relationships to reliable and responsive people'. The role of the practitioner in developing this type of relationship, for example through advocacy and mentoring, will be further explored in Chapters 7 and 8.

Association and civil society

Dinham (2011, p.530) has argued that a territorial dimension to people's relationships is not sufficient to make it a community. He asserts that 'relational factors are also a crucial part of turning a population into a community'. He goes on to argue that connection and association with others lead to the development of 'shared values' that are 'understood, accepted and internalised' by the community and, over time, become an 'aspect of the narrative of the community which people believe and perpetuate'. Association, attachment and solidarity with others, he argues, can lead to the development of 'moral obligations' to others within the community (Dinham, 2011, p.537).

This 'communitarian' (Etzioni, 1995) approach to understanding community has been very popular with politicians who have advocated policies aimed at strengthening family and social responsibility, volunteering, active citizenship and voluntary forms of association. The communitarian understanding of community suggests that communities consist of members' participation in shared activities such as residents associations and community groups that draw people into a 'collective participatory dialectic' (Barber, 1984, p.36). A communitarian approach, such as this, is based on reciprocity and mutual responsibility (Taylor, 2011, p.51) and views common values as emerging out of co-operative endeavours. According to Sage (2012) the communitarian view of the intrinsic value of participation in a strong community life is based on a belief that as social beings we desire to be part of a community and find it satisfying or fulfilling to achieve this. The challenge, as we will note later in this chapter, is for governments to avoid falling back on an authoritarian emphasis on personal responsibility when trying to engage people and communities with these ideas.

There has been much discussion, in recent years, of what is often referred to as a 'moral collapse' (Smith, 2011) and political debate about how to engender civil society within communities, neighbourhoods and nations has become increasingly popular. Concerns centre on a perception that there has been a decline in the ability to tell right from wrong and to act in an appropriate manner. Cohen (1972) first coined the term 'moral panics' to describe the phenomenon of a mass media reaction to youth culture that led to a perception that the values and principles that society holds dear were in jeopardy. He described its characteristics as 'a condition, episode, person or group of persons [who] become defined as a threat to societal values and interests' (Cohen, 1972, p.9). More recent examples drawn on to illustrate this apparent collapse, however, have not been restricted to young 'hooligans and rioters' as has been the case in 'moral panics' of the past. The abuse of position by elected members of various governments, the behaviour by the UK press and by those running the world's financial institutions are all used as examples of a general decline in moral responsibility.

Fox and Sandler (2004, p.11) have argued that, in recent years, 'larger society has replaced the small community as the basis for social life' and that 'religion, which helped to maintain order within community', no longer has the same role in people's lives. The perceived break down of attachments to religious or humanitarian communities is seen as leading to wider social problems, civic unrest and crime. Increasingly, politicians are seeking solutions that aim to maintain social order in a society that is no longer communally based. Smith suggests that:

> With secularisation, the growth of competitive individualism, and the decline of key mass membership organisations like unions and political parties, many people have less access to social environments where moral questions and collective responsibility are directly addressed. (2011, p.8)

Edwards (2009) has suggested that the idea of civil society embodies an ethical vision of social life and a social order that prescribes social norms and values of mutuality. Participation in a civil society entails equal rights and obligations for all, reciprocity and co-operation rather than authority and dependency, dialogue and respect for the other and recognition that we are mutually dependent on each other. It is believed that the norms and values of a civil society are embodied in voluntary associations where skills of co-operation are developed. In political terms, a return to civil society calls for a return to a manageable scale of social life emphasising voluntary associations, churches and communities. These themes are noticeable in recent government policy initiatives referred to in Chapter 2.

To Jochum et al. (2005, p.10) the key characteristics of a civil society are association and connection, two criteria that are seen as 'key pre-conditions of effective participation'. Their argument is that social ties and shared values, trust and reciprocity bind people together to facilitate collective action, which in turn strengthens social connectedness. Voluntary and community organisations can, therefore, play an important part in enabling people to 'come together for their own purpose and take part in community activity' (Jochum et al., 2005). Chanan (2003) has differentiated between vertical and horizontal types of participation in associational activity. Vertical participation refers to citizenship participation in local governance, such as being on a council committee, whereas horizontal participation refers to community activity such as participation in a faith group or support group. In Jochum et al.'s (2005, p.11) view, among others, horizontal participation in community activities not only serves to strengthen social ties, but can also stimulate or reinforce vertical participation.

> The passage from horizontal to vertical participation is neither automatic nor compulsory, however, effective participation is more difficult to achieve without the social connectedness that horizontal participation encourages. (Jochum et al., 2005, p.11)

However, as Hodgson (2004, p.140) has pointed out, the term 'civil society' is, like the term *community*, 'increasingly and unquestioningly accepted as part of the political lexicon, as if we all know what we mean when we talk about it. In reality this is far from the truth'. As you will have noted in Chapter 2 a range of government initiatives have sought to 'regenerate' communities and increase the role of and participation in the voluntary sector and to what Hodgson (2004, p.144) refers to as 'civil society becoming idealised' in ways that are unsustainable and unethical. Hodgson is critical of what she calls 'manufactured civil society'. Manufactured civil society refers to 'groups that are formed and funded through some sort of state initiative'. Hodgson (2004, p.145) states that 'the term manufactured is used because these groups have not developed organically, but have been engineered, created or manufactured by the state'.

Hodgson argues that there is no evidence to suggest that the benefits of association discussed above can be 'artificially created or manufactured from the outside' and furthermore that co-operation and trust 'are easily destroyed by government intervention'. Her analysis leads her to conclude that civil society in the eyes of government refers most often to organised large-scale voluntary or community activity as opposed to the informal networks and associations that individuals form and this sort of 'manufactured civil society' actually undermines social capital rather than encourages it (p.157). Hodgson argues that there needs to be recognition that 'authentic civil society is a complex, diverse, organically developing entity' that cannot be manufactured to suit the needs of government (p.160).

Packham (2008) adopts a similar position, arguing that one of the key requirements for a communitarian society is voluntary involvement in community. Packham argues that under some current government initiatives encouraging engagement in voluntary groups, volunteering is becoming formalised and increasingly used as a means of social control. She draws on Etzioni to support her argument that current initiatives aimed at encouraging volunteering place too great a concentration on the pursuit of individual rights, skills and productivity and that increasingly people are being coerced to be more responsible citizens. It is Packham's analysis that this trend has the potential to become a destructive force rather that a constructive force within communities. Dinham (2007, p.192) came to a similar conclusion, finding that disappointment about their level of participatory power, among participants in a New Deal for Communities project, actually led to 'the diminution of levels of well-being and therefore negatively impacted on the physical, psychological, social and spiritual health of participants'. Furthermore, he concluded, this could lead to a 'vicious cycle' in which 'disappointed participation leads to diminished well-being', which results in turn in the reduced likelihood of voluntary participation in the future 'since unwell people are likely to engage less in activities of this kind' (p.192). We will pick up on some of these arguments and examine them in more detail, in relation to volunteering and active citizenship, in the next chapter.

ACTIVITY 3.3

Constructed community

Look back at some of the contested themes discussed in Chapter I in relation to the concepts of *participation* and *community*. In particular you may find it helpful to read Taylor's analysis of different approaches to involving service users in Table 1.1.

What are the similarities in themes between some of the approaches and arguments made by Hodgson, Packham and Dinham, as outlined above, and those models and typologies covered in Chapter 1? Can you identify any examples from your own practice that might illustrate these analyses?

In a similar vein to some critiques of so called 'ladder' or hierarchical models of participation that we discussed in Chapter 1, Brodie et al. (2011) have challenged the notion of participation as a progression, or as something that gradually becomes more intense and more committed. They found that people tend to be involved to different degrees over the course of their lives in terms of the time spent participating, and that the level of responsibility they hold can develop and grow but it is actually 'unpredictable; it is not necessarily linear. It can deepen or become more formalised but does not necessarily do so' (p.8). Their research has focused on the factors that can help support people's participation in associational activity. Key features that they identified include the importance of participation being voluntary. Participation, they argue, can be encouraged, supported and made more attractive, but it should inherently be about free choice. They also found that people's upbringing, family and social connections play an important role in shaping participation in associational activity. People's access to practical resources such as time, money and health; 'learnt resources' such as skills, knowledge and experience; and 'felt resources such as confidence and sense of efficacy' are all important to people's ability to participate. Lack of access to these resources, they concluded, reduces people's ambitions and expectations of their own participation in a civil society. In Chapter 5 we examine in some detail the concepts of power and empowerment in relation to people's capacity to engage and participate. That analysis is relevant to our discussion here and it may be that you would find it helpful to read that before continuing with this chapter.

Association and social capital

Putnam (2001, p.414) concluded that the way to re-engage citizens in civil society is through the building of social capital and 'encouraging individuals to do things together, and to multiply picnics'. Those who argue that fostering collective engagement is beneficial often refer to the benefits in terms of building social capital (Coulter, 2011). The key indicators of social capital include membership of formal and informal groups and associations, social activities including volunteering, trust, social participation and civic engagement (Begum, 2003). Hawkins and Maurer (2011, p.356) have defined social capital as 'the by-product of social interactions that are embedded in and accessed via formal and informal social relationships with individuals communities and institutions'. It has been claimed (De Silva et al., 2005) that there is a close relationship between the quality of one's social capital and health and well-being and Begum (2003, p.10) has suggested that the absence of social capital 'leads to isolation and the lack of goodwill, trust, shared values, norms and generalised reciprocity among the population'.

Putnam (2001) has claimed that having social capital allows citizens to resolve collective problems more easily and he uses the concept of social capital to describe the norms, networks and interactions – the sense of belonging – that facilitate collective action. According to Putnam, there are three categories of capital involved in modern societies: physical capital, which refers to physical objects; human capital, which refers to properties of individuals; and social capital, which refers to 'connections among individuals, social networks and the norms of reciprocity and trustworthiness that arise from them' (Putnam 2001, p.9). Voluntary and community organisations can play a key role in generating and mobilising social capital, both within and between communities and in involving people in decision-making processes and enabling their voices to be heard.

Putnam suggested that there are different functions of social capital. 'Bonding social capital' is characterised by strong and close community network ties that help us cope with the challenges we face as we go through life. For example, in the UK there are currently over one million unemployed young people and many of these young people face a number of barriers in addition to the shortage of jobs available. It may be that they do not have anything suitable to wear when approaching employers, they may lack transport to get to an interview or to a job. These barriers become less problematic for a young person with a wide network of contacts than for someone without. The young person with higher social capital may be able to borrow a jacket, get advice on an outfit and find a lift to the interview.

'Bridging social capital' can be characterised by what Putnam calls 'weak ties', referring to associations or acquaintances between people in different communities or groups. These are the more distant connections between unconnected people in dissimilar situations and different communities that can enable access to a far wider range of resources than are available in one's own community. Putnam referred to bonding social capital as 'the glue' that binds people together and implies strong in-group cohesion and solidarity. He referred to bridging social capital as 'the oil' that facilitates smooth relationships between groups. This is characterised by the outward looking networks with friends, associates and colleagues. Woolcock (2001, p.13–14) added a further dimension to this analysis, that of 'linking social capital'. Linking social capital describes connections with people in positions of power (Taylor, 2011, p.55) and is concerned with linking people to the knowledge and resources in formal institutions and agencies. 'Linking social capital is generated from ties across different groups, class and political lines where different groups access power and resources across social strata' (Begum, 2003). Hawkins and Maurer (2012, p.359) suggest that individuals and communities should 'ideally have network connections that generate social capital ... at all three levels'. However, as Jochum et al. (2005, p.11) have argued the 'main challenge' for voluntary and community organisations is to 'go beyond bonding social capital and promote bridging and linking social capital by engaging with a wider cross-section of the community'. They suggest that 'high stocks of bonding social capital, around narrow self interest, can considerably undermine the development of bridging and linking social capital' (p.11) that ultimately lead to the development of a civil society.

Putnam linked the presence of social capital with the capacity for civic engagement and he pointed out how, in the US, this resource is in decline due to a number of factors such as increased commuting distances to work, changes in the traditional pattern of family, the increased trend to move away from the community where one was born, leading to a multitude of social problems. Embracing Putnam's argument, Hall (1997, p.35) claimed that building social capital through encouraging civic association

> can alleviate many social problems and ease the implementation of various kinds of public policy, for instance by using neighbourhood watch groups to minimise crime. … nations as a whole lose a resource when the ties between individuals erode. (Hall, 1997, p.35)

In Chapter 7, you can read a case study about the 'Big Brothers Big Sisters Mentoring Program' in the United States. This project emerged in response to the changes in family life that were noted by Putnam. It seeks to match volunteers with children and young people in mentoring relationships with the aim of facilitating greater social capital, higher aspirations and enhanced confidence.

Brodie et al. (2011) have argued that an individual's networked relationships are a resource, which play an important role in determining how 'powerful' they are, that is to say how able they are at achieving their aims. Social networks through participation in associational activity can also lead to new friendships, which can encourage bridging and linking social capital to develop. Other participants in the activity can provide a bridge between different activities and groups through their many memberships. These bridges can play an important role, linking an individual to wider social networks and broadening their participation. A recent report (Ofsted, 2011) found that the most effective programmes for engaging young people included practitioners who had been trained in areas such as group work, project-planning, sourcing up-to-date resources and community networking. In the less effective provision, providers were 'spoon-feeding' ideas to young people rather than working with them to develop their own projects. Two key factors emerged in relation to engaging more vulnerable young people: skilled practitioners who built strong and trusting relationships with them, and the effectiveness of an organisation in removing barriers to participation. For those young people who might have exhibited behavioural problems or been excluded from school, taking real responsibility helped build their self-esteem and sense of purpose. Some of the young people had come to their own realisation that this approach was a means of building their capacity and confidence in seeking employment.

The following case study is an example of all of these ideas in practice. When reading it, try to identify examples of bonding, bridging and linking social capital and how the project works to develop these.

The Swindon Family LIFE Programme

The Family LIFE Programme aims to support families in crisis to rebuild their lives. Risk factors facing such families include mental health issues, physical disabilities, substance misuse, domestic violence, poverty, unemployment, lack of education, lack of skills and capabilities, overcrowding at home and contact with multiple public services.

State intervention for families with complex needs has traditionally focused on some or many of these risk factors, with families engaging with many different professionals in any given week over a long period of time, often with no sustainable change. The LIFE programme approach aims to move away from thinking about people's 'needs' to focusing on the assets within communities and individuals and develop these as positive capabilities. By shifting the focus from problems and needs to capabilities and opportunities, the Swindon LIFE programme aims to support families through a developmental process that is led by the families themselves. The approach has been found to bring about long term sustainable and positive change for families and communities facing complex and multiple challenges. The programme works on the principle that strong community and social networks have a significant role in preventing and tackling vulnerability and that services and solutions need to be focused on networks that include families, friends and peers rather than on individuals.

The key approaches in the Programme include:

- co-building capabilities for families and workers to release innovation and resource in the family and the community;
- building social networks; and
- peer to peer learning.

In this approach, families are able to pick their own multi-agency team that begins by helping with practical tasks such as gardening, decorating, cooking and budgeting. There is no key worker in the team, and practitioner team members are expected to develop their own skills while helping families to boost theirs and access a range of support. This approach gives the families and the workers an opportunity to really get to know each other, and a chance to talk about their lives in an informal setting, creating the basis for a purposeful relationship. Developing new social networks within the community has been a focus for the Programme, and the building of new associational relationships has made a significant difference to the families involved.

Outcomes have included:

- sufferers of mental health issues engaging in social activities and work opportunities on which they had previously given up;

- parents developing skills in how to support themselves and their children emotionally;
- children choosing to return to school after long periods of exclusion;
- adults seeking employment and/or training after long periods of unemployment;
- families being more active and engaged in community activities;
- families building positive relationships with neighbours; and
- a reduced dependency on statutory service intervention.

The Swindon Family LIFE Programme won the Children & Young People Now 2011 Integrated Working Award for their outstanding multi-agency team approach to improving people's lives.

You can read more about the LIFE programme on the website: www.alifewewant.com

The concept of social capital has been very influential on public policy since 1997. However, you will by now have recognised that not all arguments or theories are straightforward and any critical analysis will seek to problematise assumptions and taken-for-granted arguments. Social capital theorists generally recognise that social capital can also have a negative side such as when excessive bonding can lead to the formation of groups who are inward looking and excluding of newcomers, or when social capital materialises as attachment to gangs or within prison populations.

Furthermore, Coulter (2011, p.163) has pointed out that while 'on the face of it people appear to welcome the opportunity to get engaged, the proportion who actually do get involved when invited to do so often shrinks to a tiny, unrepresentative minority'. Community participation in civic engagement tends to be dominated by a small group of what tends to be referred to as 'usual suspects', that is to say, the same small group of people who get involved in a wide range of activities. While the contribution of these enthusiastic activists cannot be ignored, it is often the case that the wider community do not experience any benefit, and may even feel yet further excluded from participation through the actions of these few.

Connectivity or collectivity

A number of commentators criticise the notions of bonding social capital and associational activity for their emphasis on commonality at the expense of diversity (Eraut, 2002; Avis, 2005). The argument is that 'communities' or networks of 'like-minded people' can become protective cliques that not only exclude others but can also lead to the perpetuation of poor and unaccountable practice. There may be situations where the community does not contribute towards a civil society or exhibits power relationships that seriously inhibit entry and equal participation. It has been noted that some faith communities are so tightly bonded that they 'forget to engage outside themselves as actors in wider communities' (Dinham, 2011, p.537). Sheppard et al.

(2008, p.67) have written about the phenomenon they describe as 'service users as gatekeepers' whereby established users of services 'lack responsiveness' to new attendees who may be 'initially tentative about involvement' leading to the development of 'cliques that can be off putting to new members'.

> There is an existing culture, set of expectations of people, which mean that it is the newcomer rather than existing members who need to adapt if they are to become a member. (Sheppard et al., 2008, p.67)

ACTIVITY 3.4

New members

Think back to the group or club you had in mind in Activity 3.1. How did you and your fellow members respond to new people who wanted to join your group? Did you encourage new membership? How did you do this?

How did you feel when 'newer' members tried to take leadership roles or try to change the customary way of doing things?

In their research with the people who use the services at a children's centre, Sheppard et al. (2008) found 'a subtle exclusivity' that they describe as 'the flipside to conformity'. While those attending regularly found the centre 'friendly' new attendees often found it an 'alien environment' where they felt that they did not 'fit in'. The implication of this was that those who were not prepared, or unable to 'adapt were unlikely to feel welcome and stay' (p.67). Voluntary groups and associations may also sometimes display narrow areas of interest that can lead to threats to democratic governance because of the danger of the agenda being led by groups with the louder voices. In some smaller voluntary groups there may be a lack of transparency where communication channels are mostly invisible and not open to public scrutiny. Some associations often claim, illegitimately, to hold a monopoly of interest representation. If too great an emphasis is placed on consensual models that ignore the underlying contradictions in a community, opportunities for more outward looking learning will be constrained.

CASE STUDY 3.2

Community Resolve: 'Tower block troubles'

Community Resolve is based in an inner city area in the South West of England and was set up in 2003 with the aim of exploring ways of working with community tensions in the UK's diverse inner city communities. The organisation has developed a model of community conflict transformation, based on the premise that conflict is inevitable and that it is how we react to it that is what needs to be addressed. Their work includes workshops in schools for young people to explore issues they are dealing with inside and outside school, support for families of young people involved in street violence and gangs, and community interventions using street-based teams and large-scale group facilitation.

They aim to use local knowledge and experience to build stronger communities and view *transformation* as a *process* rather than a one-off *resolution* event. This approach is based on theory and practice from international post-violence reconstruction in a number of countries around the world.

An example of their work was 'Tower block troubles'. They were approached by local community workers following the outbreak of violent verbal and physical clashes between white and newly arrived Somali residents. The tower block had seen a transformation of its population in a couple of years, with 50 per cent new arrivals in an area that was historically white. Over a period of six months they trained local residents from both resident communities to work in pairs, going door to door to visit all the flats and talk to residents about the difficulties they faced.

They found that lack of a common language, adequate housing support and little social contact between 'original' and 'new' residents were fuelling the difficulties and had led to physical and verbal clashes. So too had a stark difference in values and beliefs. For example, Somali residents disliked dogs, considering them unclean. The initiative highlighted the issues and challenges in building good community relations and led to a number of positive developments. These included a welcome pack for new residents in English and other languages, and a fully representative on-going residents group which monitors difficulties as they emerge. Following this initiative the number of clashes between residents fell, and when an incident did occur eight months later, it was quickly and effectively managed by the representatives of the residents group who stopped the rumour mill before the incident escalated. Some residents volunteered for further training in mediation skills and went on to work closely with the local community development workers over subsequent years.

Analysing their approach across a variety of contexts they have identified two themes to their work:

- establishing/re-establishing relationships, and
- addressing structural inequalities.

Key techniques that they use whatever the setting and which lead to successful community interventions are:

- Plan to have no plan: a worker should have no final solution in mind, this should emerge through working with the community.
- Share voices: keep people involved and try not to interpret along the way. Develop a shared and locally owned language.
- Use local expertise and knowledge: actively recruit from local communities and value local experience. The practitioner should act as facilitator, not expert.
- Facilitate relationships and knit the community

Knitting the community

What Community Resolve's wide range of experience working within communities has also highlighted is that it is important to ensure all perspectives and approaches are reflected in the final design of an intervention. This implies both time – building consensus is never quick – and flexibility. In the tower block example, a range of very different groups had to work together: residents from white and Somali populations, council workers, support agencies, the police and local young people. Each had something to contribute or a role to play, but keeping them on board required careful relationship building – almost 'knitting' the community back together. In their own words 'each relationship required a different style to suit their particular needs – some tight, some loose, some plain, some intricate – and it was important to find an approach that was sustainable and did not lead to the whole work unravelling at the first dropped stitch' (Wilkinson, 2012).

ACTIVITY 3.5

Reflecting on the case study

In what ways does this case illustrate some of the theory covered in this book/chapter?

What model or models of 'community' do you think are being used here?

What methods are being used to encourage association and to facilitate the building blocks of community cohesion?

What similarities can you observe between what Wilkinson refers to as 'knitting the community' and what you have read about bridging and linking models of social capital?

Gilchrist (2009, p.145) has observed how notions of 'network' and 'community' can have their downside, with relationships not always being universally beneficial either for the individual or society as a whole. She points out that where people tend to associate with 'people who are like themselves' this can lead to exclusivity and to the maintenance of only those connections that are 'comfortable or convenient'. Networking, she suggests, is 'easier and more enjoyable' where there are 'common interests and mutual affinity' but these characteristics can 'militate against inclusion and participation'.

In an attempt to address this difficulty, Engeström (1999, p.12) put forward the notion of 'expansive communities' as a way of building more effective bridges and links. Engeström's activity theory views contradictions and internal tensions as the engines of change. His premise is that when new members enter a community tensions are inevitable as tasks are redefined, reassigned and redistributed and that if progress is to be made towards creating new forms of knowledge and practice, these sorts of differences must be encouraged, articulated and debated openly. Engeström argued that 'contradictions' can generate 'disturbances' that can often promote innovative and transformative ways of doing things.

Gilchrist (2009, p.129) suggests a similar dynamic and adaptive process in her analysis of the 'well-connected community'. She argues that 'complexity theory' offers a model of a 'community poised at the edge of chaos' that is able to survive in turbulent times because it 'evolves forms of collective organisation that fit the environmental conditions'. In her analysis, the 'well-connected community' will demonstrate 'insight and intelligence, responding to local or external perturbations and accommodating internal diversity. It will be capable of learning from experience and developing strategies for dealing with unusual situations and eventualities' (p.174). In this context, the sorts of sites that can offer the most effective opportunity for connectivity tend to be multipurpose community hubs that provide spaces for a range of groups to meet, fostering interaction between them and supporting social networks. Practitioners and service users who participate in these community hubs often serve as brokers, linking individuals to other groups and projects. Research by Brodie et al. (2011) found that two key characteristics seem to be important to the success of such hubs. First, it is important that they are run by the people who use them and second that they do not become monopolised by a particular group of people as this can be off-putting for others and prevent links emerging between different groups and communities.

ACTIVITY 3.6

Community hubs
Revisit your list of community groups that you identified in Activity 3.2. How many of them might be described as *community hubs* that provide spaces for a range of groups to meet, fostering interaction between them and supporting social networks?

CASE STUDY 3.3

Restless Development (Tanzania)
In Chapter 5 you can read, in more depth, a case study highlighting the work of Restless Development a youth led international development agency and their work in the Southern Highlands region of Tanzania and in the urban areas of Dar Es Salaam and Iringa.

Their urban youth development programme (*Afya Bomba*), draws on the experience volunteers gained as peer educators in the rural villages and supports them to develop a range of skills and capacities to help them access employment opportunities. They do this through the setting up of youth hubs that are designed as community resource centres and libraries where events, training and careers fairs are held. A recent report (AMCA, 2011) concluded that participation in income generation activities by the young people involved in these youth hubs had led to an increase in young people's individual and household income and that involvement in associative activities had led to increased employability and entrepreneurship.

Restless Development has found that initial youth groups set up by the young people around a particular focus develop over time into wider community-based organisations where young people are involved as active participants in decision making.

Read more about the work of Restless Development at:
www.restlessdevelopment.org

Brodie et al. (2011, p.43) found that being 'well networked' tends to be something that 'grows exponentially; once someone becomes connected to one network, it becomes easier to tap into the wider networks' and this can lead to an individual's wider participation in associational and civic activity. Their research concluded that the networks of an individual's friends, family, colleagues and other participants can be an invaluable resource 'that can determine whether they have the opportunity to participate and whether they are able to achieve their purposes' (p.43). An individual's wider social network can be called upon to give them access to resources, knowledge, connections and decision makers and they concluded that 'being well connected can afford an individual better access to decision-makers and make it more likely that they will gain support for their ideas' (p.43).

Chapter summary

This chapter has explored a relational approach to considering engagement and community. Conceptual themes such as social capital, communitarianism and civil society have been discussed as perspectives on the theme of association and relational activity with others. The chapter has highlighted the importance of a social network perspective – connectivity rather than collectivity – as offering solutions to some of the dilemmas inherent in the concept of association and civil society.

The focus of this chapter has been on what might be called 'social participation' (Brodie et al., 2011) involving collective activities that individuals might be involved in. This kind of social engagement is often referred to as associational life or horizontal community participation. The next chapter will build on some of the arguments presented here and look in more depth at what has been called vertical, civic or 'public participation' (Brodie et al., 2011), the engagement of individuals with the various structures and institutions of the state and democracy and the concern of governments to re-activate citizenship.

▓▓▓ USEFUL RESOURCES ▓▓▓

Civil Society UK is an online source that has links to recent news items, reports and discussion blogs on issues of relevance to charities and other community organisations
www.civilsociety.co.uk

Community Resources magazine is operated by volunteers. Its aim is to save community organisations money and advertise resources they can call on. They signpost free and affordable resources. You can sign up for their e-magazine.
www.communityresources.org.uk

Inspiring Communities Guide was produced by the UK Department for Communities and Local Government in 2011. Its aim is to help people get involved in community activities and contains tips and advice designed to help encourage people of all ages and backgrounds to 'get further involved in local life and bring lasting improvements to their communities'. The guide *Inspiring Communities, Changing Behaviour* is available

online: **www.communities.gov.uk/publications/communities/**
inspiringcommunitiesbehaviour

NCVO website has a page about Social Capital with links to many useful and
interesting publications and reports about social capital and civil society
http://www.ncvo-vol.org.uk/socialcapital

OpenDemocracy is a political discussion website that publishes news analysis, debates
about governance issues. Their aim is to ensure that marginalised views and voices are
heard and they aim to facilitate argument and understanding across geographical
boundaries. They include on their website a section debating the concept of Civil Society
http://www.opendemocracy.net/topics/civil-society

Social Care Institute for Excellence (SCIE) website includes films illustrating the
benefits of participation and the issues involved. They also set out the benefits that result
from working with service users and carers, with users and carers describing how this
leads to improved practice. **http://www.scie.org.uk/socialcaretv**

STARS Foundation is an international organisation that supports work with children.
Through its Impact Awards, STARS, it supports local organisations that achieve excellence
in the provision of services to disadvantaged children and that demonstrate effective
management systems. **http://www.starsfoundation.org.uk/en/impact-awards/**

FURTHER READING

Beresford, P., Fleming, J., Glynn, M., Bewley, C., Croft, S., Branfield, F. and Postle, K. (2011)
  Supporting People: Towards a Person-Centred Approach (Bristol: Policy Press).
This book is based on the findings of a Joseph Rowntree funded UK study of Person
Centred Support. It argues care and support services must change radically if they are to
meet the rights and needs of the rapidly growing number of people who require them.
It explores with service users, practitioners, carers and managers what person-centred
support means to them, what barriers stand in its way and how these can be overcome. It
offers practical guidance and highlights the importance of a participatory approach.

Field, J. (2008) *Social Capital*, 2nd edn (Abingdon: Routledge).
If you are interested in the theory and concept of social capital you can read a more
extended interrogation of its origins, development and influence on public policy in this
book.

Jochum, V., Pratten, B. and Wilding, K. (2005) *Civil Renewal and Active Citizenship* (London:
  NCVO).
This booklet provides a helpful overview of how voluntary and community organisations
relate to wider associational life and democracy. The publication is aimed at practitioners
rather than academics and so aims to highlight some of the contested perspectives relating
to civil society in an accessible way.

Activating Citizenship

CHAPTER OBJECTIVES

By the end of this chapter you should have an understanding of:

- the concept of citizenship within current UK, European and global perspectives;
- the historical development of ideas on citizenship with a particular focus on the UK;
- citizenship in relation to rights, duties, identity and participation at both national and international levels;
- citizenship as both status and practice;
- the distinction between the 'good' and 'active' citizen;
- ideas and practice for activating citizenship.

Introduction

In this chapter we outline a range of definitions and concepts relating to citizenship from academic texts and policy documents. We describe the historical development of ideas on citizenship with a focus on the UK and how our legal, political and social rights as citizens evolved (Marshall, 1950). That evolution illustrates a liberal tradition that emphasises the importance of individual rights, and civic republican and communitarian perspectives stressing duty and responsibility to the wider community or state. This is a useful way of introducing and explaining the different sorts of rights that enable citizens to associate freely, exercise political power and access welfare provision. We discuss citizenship in relation to concepts of rights, duties, identity and participation at both national and international levels. We present citizenship as both status and practice, as something you have and something you do (Prior et al., 1995). The status of the citizen is considered acknowledging differences within the UK and outside with reference to European and global citizenship. We explore *active citizenship* as practice guided by changing political agendas under New Labour and the Coalition government's *Big Society*. We use case study examples and activities to offer opportunity for reflection, discussion and practical ways of activating citizenship with communities.

Defining citizenship

Citizenship is a term that is associated with rights, duties, identity and participation. Distinguishing between legal, philosophical and socio-political definitions of citizenship (Faulks, 2000) is useful in producing different questions to address in this chapter. Legal definitions focus on the content and extent of citizenship that raise questions about what rights are given to citizens and who has access to those rights. For example a nation-state like the UK might ascribe the right of abode or to own property to those it calls citizens. The extent of citizenship can be seen beyond national boundaries in the 'global citizen' (Delanty, 2000) or as a citizen of the European Union with the right to live and work in member states. An example of a legal definition of citizenship is:

> The link between an individual and a particular state or political community under which the individual receives certain rights, privileges and protections in return for allegiances and duties. (Willshaw 1992, cited in West, 1997, p.71)

Philosophical definitions explore the role of, and relation between, the state and the individual leading to questions such as the extent to which the state should meet the needs of its citizens. Socio-political definitions consider the power relationships within society and question why some individuals or groups may be regarded as 'second class citizens'.

The label of citizen binds a nation or union of nations. We also see it as linking community and service user where the individual has a status and recognition within their community. The status of citizen gives the individual rights and access to services with the expectation of carrying out certain duties and responsibilities such as paying taxes, voting or doing jury service. Contemporary debate considers the nature of citizenship and how the state, policymakers, practitioners and others can both identify and encourage the *good* or *active citizen*. Questions within debates about citizenship consider 'who gets what, how they get it and why they are seen as being entitled to it' (Dwyer, 2010, p.7).

There are few simple answers to many of the questions posed so far. While modern citizenship is regarded by some as 'inherently egalitarian' (Faulks, 2000) and where every citizen shares 'equality of status' (Marshall, 1950) there remain issues of difference based on age, ethnicity, culture, faith, gender, race, class and sexuality. Age is a useful way to begin exploring difference, exclusion and marginalisation experienced by some citizens.

ACTIVITY 4.1

'At what age can I ...?'

TheSite.com is an online guide to support and information services for 16–25 year olds in the UK. Use the site to find out at what age in the UK you can:

- Get a part-time job.
- Be sent to a young offenders institute for up to two years.
- Leave school.

- Join the armed forces.
- Learn to drive a motorcycle or car.
- Vote or stand for election.
- Get married without parental consent?
  (Available at: http://www.thesite.org/homelawandmoney/law/yourrights/whatagecani)

Where is the age different in other countries? What factors may account for the difference?

Reflect on how other issues such as ethnicity, sexuality and faith can impact on an individual's equality of status as a citizen. What examples can you think of that illustrate how children, women, prisoners, travellers or homeless people may be treated differently as citizens?

In reflecting on Activity 4.1 you might consider the denial of the right to vote for young people under 18, for homeless people with no permanent address or for prisoners serving their sentence. To understand better the relationships within society that lead to some being labelled or feeling themselves to be 'second-class citizens' we need to explore how ideas of citizenship have developed over time.

Historical development of citizenship

The concepts of citizenship and the citizen are generally traced back to the Greek city-states and the roots of democracy around 450 BC. As a citizen of the city-state you participated in and were members of the political community. As an adult male you gained the right to vote once you had completed military training. In return your duty and obligation was to take up arms to defend your city-state in 'the world of the male citizen-warrior' (Dwyer, 2010, p.18). There were no property ownership requirements to become a citizen but those excluded were women, children, slaves and foreign workers. This illustrates how citizenship has developed as status and identity acquired by some while others were excluded, and as practice and participation by setting out actions to be performed such as voting or fighting.

The American and French Revolutions presented individuals as citizens with political rights and freedoms. They challenged the idea of people being regarded as subjects ruled by monarchs applying arbitrary power. The philosophical and political principles expressed in the United States *Declaration of Independence* and in Thomas Paine's *Declaration of the Rights of Man and of the Citizen* underpinned the changes in those countries. However citizenship remained a status for men that continued to exclude women, children and slaves.

Modern notions of citizenship refer to the work of Thomas Marshall whose essay on *Citizenship and Social Class* was published in 1950. In this he mapped the evolution in the UK from subject to citizen through the acquisition of certain rights over time. This development began with legal or civil rights such as freedom of speech, of association, of religious affiliation and access to justice that were gained during the seventeenth and eighteenth centuries. Political rights such as the right to vote, to stand for election and to join a political party were added through the nineteenth century. In the twentieth century the establishment of the welfare state offered social rights with access to education, health and welfare services and benefits.

However, those rights do not come without reciprocal duties that include responsibilities to work, attend compulsory education, and pay taxes and National Insurance contributions. Marshall drew attention to both the civic republican perspective that places greater weight on an individual's duty, responsibility and obligation to the state and wider community as developed in the Greek city states, and the liberal tradition emphasising individual rights and freedoms seen in the change from subjects to citizens following, for example, the American and French Revolutions. Marshall's view of the historical development of citizenship in the UK is of constant ebb between these two traditions where one may sometimes gain ascendancy over the other.

Writers such as Jochum et al. (2005) identify a third tradition, that of communitarianism, which has developed both in the UK and US (see Chapter 3). This tradition is rooted in practice with the emphasis on civil engagement between individuals and communities, and between communities of locality, belonging or interest. However, Dwyer regards communitarianism as located within the civic republicanism tradition that emphasises shared values and loyalty to community helping shape individual identity and thinking (2010, p.25). In promoting the communitarian movement Etzioni (1995) sought to balance rights and responsibilities in his call 'for people to live up to their responsibilities and not merely focus on their entitlements' (p.ix). He referred to the 1980s as a decade 'in which "I" was writ large, in which the celebration of the self became a virtue' and called for 'an age of reconstruction, in which we put a new emphasis on "we", on values we share, on the spirit of community' (p.25). He argued for balance in 'a judicious mix of self-interest, self-expression, and commitment to the commons – of rights *and* responsibilities, of I and we' (p.26). His ideas and expressions have been taken up across party political divisions and are evident in recent declarations such as the speech by Cameron (2009) referred to in Chapter 2.

BOX 4.1 TRADITIONS OR TYPES OF CITIZENSHIP

Civic republicanism: origins in the Greek city states with the emphasis on duty, responsibility and obligation to the state and wider community where 'the rights of citizens are dependent on the fulfilment of their responsibilities' (Jochum et al., 2005, p.8). A civic republican approach promotes citizen engagement and participation in political affairs.

Liberal tradition: origins in the rise of capitalism and nation states consisting of citizens rather than subjects where the emphasis is on individual rights and freedoms. Within this tradition there are two strands: 'libertarian liberalism and egalitarian liberalism' (Dwyer, 2010). The former stresses the importance of individuals having freedom to pursue their own self-interests with minimal state intervention to ensure personal liberty and a free market. The latter sees a role for the state in recognising some social rights and organising the distribution of resources more fairly so all can pursue their idea of a 'good life'.

Communitarianism: emphasis is on a sense of belonging, shared group identity, values and loyalty to a community (Jochum et al., 2005, Dwyer, 2010). The aim is to encourage participation where individuals recognise their social obligations for the common good as well as exercise their individual rights. The communitarian model promotes citizen participation in governance at the community level in order to develop participatory democracy.

Within the liberal tradition citizenship as status comes to the fore with the emphasis on rights that are acquired, ascribed, retained or removed. The role of the state is to be neutral or at least minimal to ensure personal liberty and a free market. However it has a significant role in recognising and determining social rights including welfare entitlements and protecting individual rights. Citizenship as practice is more evident in the civic republican and communitarian traditions where citizens are expected to be active in exercising their duties and responsibilities within their communities. The problem is in determining the boundaries of those communities. To which communities does the individual belong? To which are they ascribed against their will or choose not to join?

Marshall's essay on citizenship has been a useful starting point in our thinking about the UK citizen. However we acknowledge that his theory has attracted a range of criticisms that include his 'limited universality' and 'Anglocentric' approach (Dwyer, 2010, p.46). In addition we note how many civil, political and social rights have been granted in the UK and elsewhere, not through evolutionary growth and a beneficent state, but through conflict. For example we could look at the role of the Chartists, Suffragettes and 'Tolpuddle Martyrs' in securing the right to vote for men and women or to belong to a trade union. Marshall's theory appears outdated and less relevant in other countries where conflict is often seen as a feature of individuals overturning their status as subjects to become citizens (see Case Study 4.1).

Lister (2003) views citizenship more widely as being rooted in Western philosophy and located in northern hemisphere Western style democracies. In such democracies citizenship can be viewed as an evolutionary process whereby the individual acquires status through gaining greater numbers of rights and responsibilities that give them a sense of inclusion as a member with an identity. However this process may be contested by considering recent examples within Eastern Europe and South Africa in the 1990s, or in the 'Arab Spring' from 2010. Here we can find examples of the nature of citizenship being defined as a result of regime change, conflict and revolution.

CASE STUDY 4.1

'Arab Spring'

The terms 'Arab Spring', 'Arab Uprising' and 'Arab Awakening' are used to describe a period that began as an expression of civil resistance in Tunisia in December 2010. This was followed by a series of demonstrations and protests across North Africa and the Middle East in countries such as Algeria, Morocco and Bahrain, with civil war in Libya and Syria and regime change in Egypt. Common features have been mass demonstrations and protests in main squares alongside the use of social media and the Internet to communicate, spread information and to present evidence of regime abuse in the face of state censorship.

The protests included demands for rights and freedoms from absolute monarchs or dictators in Saudi Arabia and Libya, and against human rights violations in Egypt and Syria. There are examples within these countries of how the nature of citizenship is being constructed differently to the model and perspectives developed and applied by Marshall to the UK. Part of the 'Arab Spring' is about gaining rights and freedoms by direct action, force of arms and extracting concessions from the ruling elites. However, it remains the case that some of those protesting may not acquire equal rights and freedoms from the state. Protests by stateless and nomadic Bedouin in Kuwait have not established the nature of their citizenship. In Saudi Arabia women remain unable to exercise political rights although the king has announced women will be able to vote and stand in municipal elections from 2015.

Research and consider current events in countries directly affected by the 'Arab Awakening'. What are people demanding in relation to their rights as citizens? To what extent are those demands being met by the state?

Despite criticisms Marshall's theory remains relevant to contemporary debates about citizenship for two reasons according to Dwyer (2010). First, his emphasis on linking social rights to citizenship 'helped to force welfare firmly onto the citizenship agenda' (p.48). Second, welfare rights are 'a potential benchmark against which full citizenship status can be measured' (p.49). In other words we can see who is included and excluded in access to welfare services and provision, and track changes over time. This is taken up in the next section, which outlines citizenship as a status that delivers different rights, freedoms and entitlements to citizens in the UK and Europe.

Citizenship as status

Citizenship is not just a list of rights, duties, responsibilities or obligations that we have been granted or acquired over the years. It is also about who ascribes citizenship and when. We have already considered what rights or entitlements come to us at a certain age and begun to think about how some individuals or groups may have greater or lesser access to rights than others. Let us now explore who can have citizenship and who cannot. How do we get it? Who can give it and who can take it away? What is expected in return? While answering these questions it is worth noting that 'the status of citizens in Britain is founded on no more than an act of faith in the reasonableness of their elected representatives' (Prior et al., 1995, p.8).

In the UK you become a citizen by birth or descent, or by registration or naturalisation. The meaning of citizenship is linked to legal definitions such as the right of abode to live in a country and to return if you leave. UK nationality acts ascribe or offer different levels of citizenship. To become a citizen through registration or naturalisation you need to show 'good character', pass a citizenship test or meet other criteria as set out, for example, in the Immigration, Asylum and Nationality Act 2006 (Great Britain, 2006) or Borders, Citizenship and Immigration Act 2009 (Great Britain, 2009).

ACTIVITY 4.2

UK Citizen test

To apply to become a British Citizen or for permanent residence, individuals must demonstrate knowledge of the English language and of life in the UK. One way is to take the *Life in the UK* test revised in March 2013. Access the *Official Practice Citizenship Test* on *Life in the United Kingdom* at www.officiallifeintheuk.co.uk/test/.

Complete the test. What is your reaction to your score? What do you notice about the types of questions asked? What questions would you include instead and why?

In a previous test example (available at: www.ukcitizenshiptest.co.uk/) one question asked, 'Ulster Scots is a dialect which is spoken in Northern Ireland. True or False?' This might seem an odd question to ask, and may be one to which you do not know the answer despite growing up in the UK. However, it shows that those wishing to become citizens need to be aware that the UK consists of four countries with their own languages or dialects, histories and culture where citizenship can bring different privileges. For example those born in Northern Ireland have the right to take up dual nationality and to have a passport for both the UK and Republic of Ireland.

ACTIVITY 4.3

'Refugee', 'asylum seeker' and 'migrant worker'

UK immigration and asylum legislation makes distinctions in status between 'refugee', 'asylum-seeker' and 'migrant worker'. Consider the difference in meaning between these terms. Which suggest a higher status because of certain rights that are gained such as access to health and welfare services? What about different rights for the families of a refugee, asylum-seeker or migrant worker?

What differences can you find in the use of these or similar terms in other countries such as Canada, New Zealand or South Africa? You should find the following websites useful: www.ukba.homeoffice.gov.uk/asylum/; www.refugeecouncil.org.uk/; www.migrantsrights.org.uk/

In the UK 'asylum seeker' refers to someone who has applied for protection as a 'refugee'. An 'asylum seeker' may be able to access some health services but will not have the right to welfare benefits or to live and work in the country. If granted refugee status then you gain broadly the same rights and entitlements to services as other UK residents and citizens. You may also apply for a National Insurance number to enable you to work and pay taxes.

Under the UK's Immigration, Asylum and Nationality Act 2006 (Great Britain, 2006) the Home Secretary has the power to remove your status as a British citizen if this is 'deemed conducive to the public good'. This applies only if you have dual nationality or acquired citizenship through registration or naturalisation by fraud or concealing material facts. The Home Secretary cannot remove your status as a citizen if it is acquired by birth or descent. However under New Labour the Home Secretary Jacqui Smith introduced proposals for migrants to 'earn' UK citizenship. The subsequent Borders, Citizenship and Immigration Act 2009 (Great Britain, 2009) introduced a process of three stages. At first the migrant is classed as a temporary resident, then given a new status of 'probationary citizen' without the entitlement to claim any government benefits. The process whereby they gain full UK citizenship can be speeded up or slowed down by their behaviour. The expectation is that probationary citizens will show they are actively seeking to integrate with their local communities. Evidence of integration includes learning and making progress in English and showing they are 'active citizens' by getting involved in activities such as voluntary work or local groups. This policy of 'earned citizenship' was due to come into effect in July 2011 but the Coalition government decided not to implement it as it was considered by the new Home Secretary to be 'too complicated, bureaucratic and, in the end, ineffective' (May, 2010). This is illustrative of the power of the Home Secretary and the state through legislation to introduce or remove hurdles to the process whereby migrants prove they deserve the status of UK citizen.

Earlier in this chapter we acknowledged the idea of citizenship extending beyond national boundaries with reference to the European Union and the concept of the 'global citizen' (Delanty, 2000). Citizens of the European Union (EU) have the right to live and work in member states and to have access to different welfare systems. Article 17 of the 1997 Amsterdam Treaty of the European Communities states that 'every person holding the nationality of a Member State shall be a citizen of the Union. Citizenship of the Union shall complement and not replace national citizenship' (EU, 1997).

Rights have been extended to over 500 million people since the expansion of member states with new EU citizens from Central and Eastern Europe (Czech Republic, Slovakia, Hungary, Poland, Slovenia, Estonia, Lithuania and Latvia in 2004; Bulgaria and Romania in 2007). According to Article 18 of the Amsterdam Treaty 'every citizen of the Union shall have the right to move and reside freely within the territory of the Member States' (EU, 1997). The extension of such rights and freedoms has led to increased migration to some countries of Western Europe that impact on the host nation and local communities. For the host nation there will be positive economic and cultural benefits as well as concerns about the effect of large-scale immigration on local labour markets and social cohesion.

CASE STUDY 4.2

European citizenship

EU citizenship may be viewed as undermining the ability of nation states to ascribe status as citizens or to control migration. Opportunities are offered to people living outside the EU to acquire the status of EU citizen. For example non-EU citizens are invited to invest in property in Bulgaria, which is a member of the EU. The 'Government approved Immigration Investment Program' allows individuals and their family to gain permanent residency in Bulgaria with 'no residency requirement' (key2europe, n.d.). This means that at no point do they need to live in Bulgaria to qualify. Permanent residency status may be obtained within six months and after five years the individual can gain EU citizenship and a passport. See www.key2europe.com/en/Acquire-EU-citizenship-and-permanent-residency)

Neither UK nor EU citizenship offer one level of citizenship with assigned rights, freedoms and entitlements for all within their borders. UK citizenship is given or acquired through processes that offer different rights filtered by a range of conditions, for example, by birth or naturalisation; as an asylum seeker, refugee or migrant worker; or to those with dual nationality. EU citizenship is 'a highly stratified status' (Dwyer, 2010, p.180) with the ideal of the citizen as paid worker. Entitlements and social rights are accorded to paid workers and their family from EU member states over both those regarded as economically inactive such as older retired people and those from non-EU countries who may have lived and worked for many years in the member state. Further differentiation of status is likely to arise from concerns within host nations about which paid workers are needed to boost the economy and whether intermittent or seasonal workers should continue to have the same rights as other paid workers.

Large-scale migrations, technological developments, global communication, and the development of transnational and worldwide organisations, multinational corporations, and banking and financial institutions undermine or at least challenge ideas of national citizenship. The perceived erosion of national citizenship has led writers to focus more on global age theories and to look at 'citizenship beyond the state' (Delanty, 2000, p.53). The view that human rights were becoming increasingly regarded as more important than social or economic rights led to ideas of 'global' and 'cosmopolitan citizenship' (Dwyer, 2010, p.200). The idea of 'cosmopolitan citizenship' or 'citizen of the world' suggests that in addition to our rights we have responsibilities to the wider world beyond national borders, for example, to the environment. Lister (2003) uses the term 'ecological citizenship' in reference to duties 'which stretch beyond the geographical and temporal boundaries of the individual citizen's community' (p.24). The challenge for proponents of these ideas is to provide more substance to the concepts. The citizen of a nation state is unlikely to give up a status that offers services and benefits enshrined in a mix of legal, political and social rights for more abstract protections and aspirations presented in a declaration of human rights.

It is not yet clear that we have moved towards a post-national or global citizenship with the inevitability suggested in Tambini's observation that 'national citizenship emerged and national citizenship will pass' (2001, p.198). Overall a picture develops revealing the complexity behind the idea of citizenship and of differentiated and limited rights based on one's status as, for example, an EU citizen, a non-EU migrant worker and their family, an economically active worker, or a child or retired person. Citizenship is shown to consist of many layers at local, regional, national or transnational levels. The on-going world economic crisis has revealed tensions emerging between nations and blocs of nations. Those tensions arise from decisions to tackle national debts through austerity or growth and an increasing visibility of, and support for, nationalist parties that challenge liberal and civic republican views of who should be regarded as citizens. While governments ultimately wield the power of ascribing, amending or removing our status as citizens, it is individuals and communities who demonstrate citizenship in action or practice.

Citizenship as practice

The practice of citizenship is of interest as it allows us to see the citizen in action. As Dwyer (2010) observes 'contemporary citizenship is characterised by changing modes of participation and belonging, where citizen engagement is played out in a range of spaces from local to global' (p.177). Citizen engagement and action is not limited to establishing status by demanding, defending and maintaining rights, freedoms and entitlements. It is also about active participation of citizens within and on behalf of their communities.

In the early 1980s in the UK Conservative government thinking, driven by concerns about both the economy and the creation of a dependency culture, challenged Marshall's citizenship based on entitlements to welfare. There was a feeling that there should be more emphasis on the duty and responsibility to be economically independent and usefully employed. By the late 1980s this economic imperative was softened by a new call from ministers for socially aware and responsible 'active' citizens willing to contribute to their community (Heater, 2004). However the level of engagement of these active citizens was less about direct involvement with political systems and more about establishing, for example, neighbourhood watch schemes aimed at self-policing by communities.

BOX 4.2 ACTIVE CITIZENSHIP

In 1989, the UK Home Secretary Douglas Hurd argued that 'the idea of Active Citizenship is a necessary complement to that of the enterprise culture' and that public service 'is a responsibility of all' (Heaton, 1991, cited in Lockyer, 2003, p.3). Active citizenship in the New Right era of the 1980s in the UK was seen as 'invented as the charity giving and community-serving caring face of capitalism' (Ledwith, 1997, p.41). Hurd's view also signalled an exhortation for citizens as consumers to drive up the quality of public services and make them more efficient and accountable by exerting choice and using complaint procedures. Practical activities introduced such as Neighbourhood Watch and the concept of active citizen continued under New Labour (1997–2010). However their policies took on a wider socio-political remit such as developing 'community spirit' (Etzioni, 1995) rather than focusing on individual citizens as consumers able to mediate the excesses of an enterprise culture.

> A strength of the active citizenship agenda is that it implies that citizens have a political relationship with the state and not simply a consumerist one. That is, they have a collective interest in the wider aims and objectives of policies and their underlying social values (such as equity and social justice) over and above their self-interest as users of services. (Jochum et al., 2005, p.10)

The balance between rights and responsibilities was further altered under the New Labour government elected in 1997 that developed ideas of civic republicanism and communitarianism. New Labour regarded active citizenship as a means of re-engaging citizens with decision-making processes within their local communities. It aimed to do this by developing opportunities in civic participation, volunteering, citizenship education and lifelong learning.

At the Home Office David Blunkett promoted 'civil renewal' and the 'active citizen' (Blunkett, 2003a, 2003b). Blunkett saw the active citizen as someone able to participate constructively in decisions shaping their lives. He referred to building community cohesion and devolving power to the community by engaging people in democratic processes to identify and meet local needs. Participation and engagement of individuals would be achieved through political processes such as voting or standing for election, by involvement with decision-making bodies, and as volunteers and campaigners. The two papers, published in 2003, show a shift from civic to civil renewal. In the first, Blunkett regards civil renewal as a civic republican process where active citizenship involved the 'cultivation of civic virtues' and required education for citizenship (2003a, p.3). In the second, he refers to the need to 'participate in the self-government of our communities' (2003b, p.2) for civil renewal.

Citizenship education and lifelong learning through formal and informal education were seen as ways of building capacity and developing skills, knowledge and confidence in citizens through schools and wider education and training initiatives developed in the Civil Renewal Unit's Active Learning for Active Citizenship strategy (see Case Study 4.3). New Labour designated 2005 the Year of the Volunteer to help promote and achieve a target of raising the level of volunteering and community participation by five per cent by 2006. Civic participation covered engagement with state institutions and the status of 'Civic Pioneers' was presented to local authorities committed 'to involve and engage local people in decision making processes on policy and implementation in public services' (Gaffney, 2005, p.7).

Active Learning for Active Citizenship programme (ALAC)

In 2006 the Civil Renewal Unit was established under New Labour to lead the Department for Communities and Local Government's *Together We Can* programme. One initiative was Active Learning for Active Citizenship that aimed to address the call 'to improve the capacity of individuals and communities to relate to the world around them as active, critical, engaged citizens' (Woodward, 2004, p.1). ALAC was set up as 'education for active citizenship' based within the voluntary and community sectors (Mayo and Rooke, 2006).

A pilot project ran from 2004 to 2006 'to initiate new work on active learning for active citizenship' (Woodward, 2004, p.6). These programmes were delivered through seven regional 'hubs' by building on existing networks, partnerships and educational provision. The South Yorkshire hub based in Sheffield saw the Workers' Educational Association (WEA) working with an adult residential college to run learning events including teach-ins, seminars and workshops on asylum, voting, combating racism and living in the UK. They ran a six-month programme on migration and Europe for participants from local organisations that included a study visit to Sweden.

In the West Midlands a community based hub in Wolverhampton, linking the Asian Women and Diabetes Group and a local college, concentrated on providing citizenship courses aimed at black and ethnic communities. The courses looked at issues of difference and diversity and explored how participants could work together to influence decisions that affected them (Mayo and Rooke, 2006). For Packham (2008, p.7) this 'social justice approach to citizenship' presents active citizenship as not just learning about how to participate but about political literacy, empowerment, working for change of structures and power relations to address social inclusion.

'Competing and contradictory strands within Government policy' (Jochum et al., 2005, p.37) were evident in the New Labour discourse on active citizenship. On the one hand government was promoting civic participation with a focus on individuals and how they relate to the state. Citizens were being encouraged to vote, participate in local decision making and get involved as users in overseeing public services. On the other hand it was also encouraging civil participation and ways citizens could relate to each other seeing them as members of communities rather than as individual consumers. Government was also seeking 'to strengthen community ties and to foster values such as mutuality, solidarity and altruism' (Jochum et al., 2005, p.37).

A mixture of political and social dimensions to active citizenship are evident in the *Communities in Control* report (DCLG, 2008) referring to New Labour as being 'committed to greater democracy, devolution and control for communities' and wanting 'more people becoming active in their communities as volunteers, advocates and elected representatives' (p.iii). The political dimension may be seen in calls for citizen participation in political processes and governance. The social dimension brings in the collective aspect related to being part of a community, a sense of belonging and engaging in collective action as volunteers or advocates.

The development of the active citizen under New Labour (1997–2010) indicates a shift from a citizenship status presented with ascribed universal welfare rights to one where access to social rights became a 'conditional entitlement' dependent on the citizen accepting responsibilities (Dwyer, 2010) or demonstrating acceptable behaviours as *probationary citizens*. However government does not have total control over the range and diversity of activities or behaviours by which the citizen expresses their active citizenship. The citizen retains agency or self-determination to exercise choice.

Marshall referred to the 'general obligations to live the life of a good citizen, giving such service as one can to promote the welfare of the community' (1950, p.45). John F Kennedy in his presidential inauguration speech in January 1961 said 'And so, my fellow Americans, ask not what your country can do for you; ask what you can do for your country' (*The Guardian*, 2007).

Such visions offer insights into what is expected of a *good* citizen. The Crick Report (Crick, 1998) wrote about education for citizenship and the teaching of democracy in the belief that knowledge, understanding, skills and aptitudes on these topics could be acquired through the school curriculum. Active citizenship has been part of citizenship studies within the UK's National Curriculum since 2002.

CASE STUDY 4.4

'Good' and 'active' citizen

Crick (2002) distinguishes between the 'good' and 'active citizen' within education for citizenship. 'Good citizenship' is where the pupil is involved in planning and participating in a community event. 'Active citizenship' is where the pupil considers political issues connected to the source of the community event. Crick illustrates the difference with an example of a class of school pupils planning and arranging a party for older people in a near-by residential home. He regards this as 'a very nice thing to do, perhaps "good citizenship" but not … by itself "active citizenship"'.

To demonstrate 'active citizenship' the pupils might look at the policies and relations between providers of care for older people such as social services, government departments and the voluntary sector to explore why they are in residential care in the first place. This activity would inform the pupils enabling them to offer ideas on improving public policy. They could then conclude with the party to celebrate the prior process.

The teaching of citizenship within countries of the UK helps demonstrate different priorities and strategies beyond distinguishing the good and active citizen. In Wales, for example, there is a focus on global citizenship linked with sustainable development in recognition that with finite resources there is a need 'to live sustainably and to be globally aware of the impact of our own lifestyles' (WAG, 2006, p.i). In Scotland there is recognition that young people are citizens now rather than 'in waiting'. The teaching of citizenship seeks to develop the learner's ability 'to take up their place in society as responsible, successful, effective and confident citizens' with understanding of fairness and justice (Education Scotland, 2012).

What do we know about those who are active in civil society? Research conducted by the *Pathways through Participation* project looked at participation and the role of civil society organisations (Brodie et al., 2011). It concluded that 'social, public and individual' participation was 'widespread', 'changing and dynamic' but primarily 'personal'

> People participate because they want to, and sometimes because they need to. They get involved in activities that have personal meaning and value, that connect with the people, interests and issues that they hold dear. (Brodie et al., 2011, p.69)

An example of tapping this personal motivation to participate in community activity is illustrated in the UK by the introduction of a Citizens' Day (see Activity 4.4). The publication of the *Citizens' Day Framework* booklet by the Citizenship Foundation (2007) launched the idea. The aim of a Citizens' Day is to build 'cohesive, active and engaged communities' (p.1). While mainly about local authorities, businesses, charities, voluntary and community organisations and others organising activities on a single day, it also suggests ideas for other events such as a Local Democracy Week or Black History Month. The framework adds to debate about our national identity and what it means to be 'British'.

ACTIVITY 4.4

Citizens' Day

Access the Citizens' Day Framework booklet at: http://www.citizenship foundation.org.uk/main/resource.php?s367

Read page 7 to think about the purpose of having a Citizens' Day in your neighbourhood and what events you might organise. Link those events into a programme for promoting active citizenship in a wider area.

Other countries acknowledge and celebrate citizenship and as with the UK some are relatively recent initiatives by government. In the United States 17 September is Constitution or Citizenship Day to mark the ratification of the US Constitution in 1787. Congress has designated the date as a holiday since 2004. Pride in citizenship is shown publically through ceremonial events and activities in schools, churches and other places. Australian Citizenship Day was introduced in 2001 and also falls on 17 September. It is used as an opportunity to reflect on pride as Australian citizens through, for example, hosting a citizenship affirmation ceremony, exploring citizenship in the classroom or volunteering to organise a barbeque in the neighbourhood. These examples suggest the *global* or *cosmopolitan citizen* has not yet superseded the concept of the citizen of a nation state.

Current ideas found in the Coalition government's Big Society response to the notion of 'Broken Britain', as discussed in Chapter 2, question who is meant to benefit from active citizenship: the individual, the community or the state. As noted in that chapter there is a view in government that 'Broken Britain' 'can be fixed by an army of social entrepreneurs, grass-root charities and focus on voluntary organisation' (Duncan Smith, 2009). As part of this 'fix' the UK Cabinet Office and Department for Education have piloted a new National Citizen Service (NCS) programme aimed at 16 year olds. It involves schools, local authorities, businesses and neighbourhood groups bringing together young people from different backgrounds to become community volunteers. During the eight-week programme the young people work on community projects and spend time away from home, for example, taking part in teamwork and leadership skills training on a residential week. The policy is illustrative of the neoliberal agenda pursued by the Coalition government seeking to contract services out to private companies at the same time as cuts are being made in public spending on youth services. Serco won the contract to run the NCS programme in six regions (Mair, 2012). Serco is a private company with global revenue of more than £4 billion, which shows the difficulty faced by charities and voluntary organisations with limited resources to bid for contracts (Boffey, 2012). Critics have noted the lack of reference to 'skilled workers in building positive relationships with and between young people' in NCS programme documents (de St. Croix, 2011, p.50). Activity 4.5 aims to show the impact of practitioner skills and knowledge on effective outcomes when working with communities.

ACTIVITY 4.5

Practitioners and active citizenship
Packham (2008) sees different approaches for practitioners, such as community and youth workers, to work with communities to generate active citizenship:

1. As providers of adult education for training and voluntary programmes for volunteers.
2. As practitioners working to support government programmes and initiatives.
3. As practitioners working with communities to facilitate association, civic and civil engagement.

Identify a local community and map out ideas on how you might work with that community in each of the ways suggested by Packham. What differences do you notice in the ideas you present and the likely outcomes? You may find it helpful at this stage to read Chapter 8 to develop your understanding of youth and community work approaches such as *informal education*.

Your responses to Activity 4.5 will show differences in how you plan to work with different groups and may cause you to question your role and relations with service users, communities and other practitioners. In 1, the education or training provided might need to be accredited and participants registered and assessed. In 2, some will see you as an agent of government implementing its aims and objectives. In 3, you will find you are working with more freedom and creativity using a range of communication and facilitation skills to promote organic growth in association and engagement.

The active citizenship agenda in the UK has been generated and promoted by successive Conservative, New Labour and Coalition governments deciding how and why citizens should be involved as well as determining what they should do and when. For example, the Localism Act 2011 (see Chapter 2) allows citizens to bid to take on services or buildings such as libraries, village pubs and shops. This is a top-down approach that is at odds with achieving the empowerment of communities suggested in policy visions and aims. Further, by focusing on 'active' citizens there is a danger that those regarded as 'inactive' are seen as failed citizens who, by not exercising responsibilities set by government, are undeserving of their ascribed rights. In this framework, Government defines or judges who are active where it suggests what this can involve, for example, volunteering or charity giving. However opportunities to volunteer will reduce where voluntary and community organisations struggle with the impact of public spending cuts. Governments are less likely to promote active citizen involvement in actions to defend social rights and cuts in public services.

Case studies and activities in this chapter highlight ways for communities and service users to work with practitioners and others to identify and take opportunities to create their own citizenship agendas. Tam (2010) has noted 'only a small minority believed that it was important for all citizens to attain some tangible influence over public decisions to help promote the common good' (p.8). Explaining to communities and service users why it is important to be involved in decision making to promote the common good is not enough. As Tam observes there is a role for civic activists 'to bridge the gap between remote state bodies' and those who 'have yet to be convinced that they would ever be taken seriously by government institutions' (p.8). Part of the solution may lie in developing community understanding of the 'complex governance arrangements and highly professionalised decision making processes' of modern public services (p.10). However, an alternative to assimilation into hierarchical processes lies in the initiative by ALAC (Case Study 4.3) that sought to strengthen organisations at community level 'to provide the civic space for people to come together to cultivate a shared understanding of the problems they faced' (Tam, 2010, p.9). That is how and where communities and service users will develop their own agendas for citizenship.

Chapter summary

We began the chapter by presenting definitions of citizenship and different understandings of its meaning. We offered an historical overview of how citizenship has developed as an idea from a liberal, civic republican and communitarian tradition. The status of citizenship was shown to rest with the state that uses legislation and processes to differentiate between who is or is not regarded as a full citizen, how and when rights are ascribed or removed, who can apply for citizenship and how what they do can hasten or slow the process. At an international level citizenship as status was further linked to issues of identity that may be seen in those with dual nationality or as citizens of the European Union (EU). International concepts of global or cosmopolitan citizenship were discussed in relation to the impact of globalisation and the movements of people across national borders. We acknowledged how citizenship may develop differently outside Western style democracies using illustrative examples such as the 'Arab Awakening' to remind us that citizenship rights 'are not fixed. They remain the object of political struggles to defend, reinterpret and extend them' (Lister 2003, p.198).

Turning to the duties, obligations and responsibilities that come with the rights associated with status we illustrated citizenship as practice. We explored the emergence of the *active citizen* in the UK and traced this concept through UK policy developments with New Labour's promotion of civic and civil renewal. The presented case studies and activities show ways of working to activate citizenship and how we might recognise the 'good' or 'active' citizen contributing to their local communities. We used examples of opportunities such as Citizens' Day and National Citizen Service programme, introduced under the Coalition government's Big Society brand, for citizens to contribute to their communities.

Discussions about activating citizenship tend to focus on ways of involving the individual in their wider community. In Chapter 5 we will broaden the focus and consider the capacity and resources that exist with communities. Our discussion in the next chapter focuses on an exploration of approaches that aim to support the empowerment of people and communities to release their capacity for self determination and to set their own agendas.

USEFUL RESOURCES

Citizenship Foundation is an independent education and participation charity that focuses on developing young people's citizenship skills: **www.citizenshipfoundation. org.uk**

Citizen Organising Foundation (COF) is a registered charity whose mission is to create a network of competent, informed and organised citizens who are able to influence decisions that impact on their communities: **www.cof.org.uk**

Europa website for the European Union. See link headed *Your Life in the EU*: **http://europa.eu/eu-life/index_en.htm**

Home Office is responsible for securing UK borders and overseeing the migration system: **www.gov.uk/government/topics/borders-and-immigration**

Sheffield Hallam University website presents case studies on active learning and active citizenship: **http://extra.shu.ac.uk/alac/**

Take Part offers online resources for active learning and active citizenship: **www.takepart.org**

FURTHER READING

Crick, B. (2000) *Essays on Citizenship* (London: Continuum).
This series of essays explores how citizenship can bridge the vocational aims of education and education for its own sake.

Tam, H. (1998) *Communitarianism: A New Agenda for Politics and Citizenship* (Basingstoke: Macmillan).
A useful introduction to communitarian ideas and their implications for citizenship and policy illustrated using international examples.

CHAPTER 5

Releasing Capacity

CHAPTER OBJECTIVES

By the end of this chapter you should have an understanding of:

- a range of meanings and approaches associated with community capacity building;
- some guiding principles for working with people and communities to release their capacity for self-determination;
- some of the opportunities, challenges and tensions in the community development approach;
- useful resources to improve knowledge and practice.

Introduction

As you will have read in Chapter 2, over the past ten years many countries around the world have, increasingly, been introducing schemes whereby people who have been assessed as eligible for social care support have had the option to hold personal budgets to purchase the support and activities they choose. According to Coulter (2011) the aim is to empower people to have more choice and control over their care. Carr (2010, p.13) has argued that service users who hold personal budgets are increasingly using them to 'increase their participation and activity in their communities', thereby reducing their social isolation and building links that help promote independent living. What she refers to as the 'co-production model of care and support' recognises that people who use services have 'assets and expertise' that should be valued and released. The Workforce Development Strategy for adult social care (Skills for Care, 2011, p.19) urged practitioners working in adult social care in England to recognise this potential of service users, carers, volunteers and user-led organisations to contribute to communities. The report stressed the importance of what it called 'community capacity building' as being one of the skills practitioners need to develop in order to improve people's lives and support 'local communities, neighbourhoods and citizens get involved in taking responsibility for local services'.

The term *community capacity building* has often been used interchangeably with the term *community development*, especially by policy makers and this has led to argument and disagreement about the underlying principles of both terms. Craig (2007, p.354), for example, has referred to community capacity building as a 'new umbrella term' and one that he concludes is 'none other than our old friend community development'. You will, by now, be unsurprised to learn that these approaches are commonly described as contested terms, often used without agreement or understanding of the complexity and values that their practice can highlight. As Hoggett et al. (2009, p.31) remind us 'community development has long been considered an elusive and contested concept, its purpose difficult to define even by those directly involved in its practice'. Eriksson (2011, p.410) asserts that 'the tradition of community development is not easy to describe' and cites Mayo's (1975) claim to having identified 'no less than ninety-four definitions'.

Community capacity building has been defined by the Scottish government as 'development work that strengthens the ability of community organisations and groups to build their structures, systems, people and skills so that they are better able to define and achieve their objectives ... it includes aspects of training, organisational and personal development and resource building ... reflecting the principles of empowerment and equality'. They go on to suggest that community capacity building takes many different forms but is 'linked by the common aim of strengthening the collective ability of the community' and that the 'starting point for community capacity building is within communities themselves' (Education Scotland, n.d.)

Community Development Exchange (CDX), an independent UK-based organisation promoting the potential of community development to transform communities, argued that community development 'specialises in encouraging and empowering people to gain control over the conditions in which they live and provides a very powerful way of turning alienation into engagement'. CDX defined community development as a way of working with communities that is based on 'social justice, equality and mutual respect'. Community development, they argued,

> involves changing the relationships between ordinary people and people in positions of power, so that everyone can take part in the issues that affect their lives. It starts from the principle that within any community there is a wealth of knowledge and experience which, if used in creative ways, can be channelled into collective action to achieve the communities' desired goals. (CDX, n.d.)

What we can observe in both these approaches is a commitment to the importance of the concept of *empowerment* and what is often referred to as a *bottom-up* approach of developing sustainable capacity within communities, neighbourhoods and individuals. In Chapter 1, we outlined a number of models and conceptual frameworks for thinking about community and about participation. In this chapter we will build on those frameworks to help us critique initiatives that claim to be about empowerment or which claim to be about developing community capacity for change and development. This chapter explores some of the theory and the practice behind the concept and practice of community development, building on some of the ideas introduced in Chapter 1 and Chapter 2 about power and privilege in the policy process and will acknowledge the complexity that can emerge when we discuss the nature of this approach. In this chapter we explore some theoretical frameworks that can be used to help clarify the dilemmas that emerge in community development projects, building on the discussion begun in Chapter 1 about the contested nature of community participation and involvement.

The chapter begins with a brief historical overview of community development practice in both the UK and globally, tracking some of the tensions and dilemmas arising from ideological shifts in thinking, such as the tensions arising from a move away from traditions of paternalism and colonialism towards more empowering models of practice. Key themes explored in this chapter are the notions of *community capacity building, community empowerment, community identity* and *community representation*. We also revisit some of the themes discussed in Chapter 3 regarding attempts to 'manufacture community' and whether a *sense of community* can be imposed or constructed by initiatives such as neighbourhood regeneration and community cohesion schemes.

From philanthropy to solidarity

Community Development Exchange (CDX), see Useful Resources, aimed to promote an understanding of community development by practitioners, funders and policy makers. CDX argued that community development practitioners should work 'alongside people in communities to help build relationships with key people and organisations and to identify common concerns' and that by 'enabling people to act together, community development practitioners help to foster social inclusion and equality'.

However, as Hoggett et al. (2009, p.31) have suggested, community development has all too often been seen as 'a form of state intervention' that is often linked with, or has been 're-branded' as 'community engagement, community cohesion or more loosely still to a variety of roles associated with combating social exclusion'. Partly, the roots of this complexity in use of the term lie in the historical traditions and values of community development practice and ideology, or as Gilchrist (2009, p.23) has expressed it the 'evolution as a form of professional intervention'. Gilchrist (2009, p.24) suggests that in the UK, community development 'derives its inspiration and rationale' from three historical traditions: 'philanthropy and voluntary service; mutual aid; and informal self-help and solidarity'.

Philanthropy

Rimmer (2005), like other commentators, has drawn attention to the important role played by philanthropic 'do-gooders' and 'missionaries' in the late nineteenth century and linked this with the origins of community development work. Whether we are talking about work to alleviate poverty and eradicate disease in the slums of London, or in the recently colonised countries of Africa, the missionaries and 'middle-class lady almoners' of the day were exercising a social conscience and attempting a social action upon which the discourse surrounding community development and community empowerment has been built. There is no doubt, however, that some examples of so-called community development work, both historically and currently, can be seen to be based on a desire to intervene with an expressed desire to 'help' or to 'change' people in order to make them more 'like us' (the white middle classes). These interventions take what has become known as a 'deficit' approach, seeking to address 'what are seen as deficits in poor communities preventing residents from achieving their potential' (Gilchrist, 2009, p.25).

Another goal, historically, has been to increase the rate of industrial and economic development across the globe. The nineteenth century was characterised by a high level of philanthropic activity as concerns grew about the growth of cities and the fear of the spread of disease and poverty. This was a 'time of tremendous unrest' (Pankhurst, 1914, p.19) when a number of people with a social conscience were successful in raising awareness of equalities issues and in forcing social change. Many of them were poor women and men whose names and voices have not been recorded but whose efforts and actions have left a lasting legacy. Many of them, also, however, were typically liberal-minded, middle-class women who became involved in voluntary, charitable work, very often as Poor Law Guardians. Boards of Poor Law Guardians were responsible for administering the 'poor rate' – the financial assistance for children, the elderly, the sick, unemployed working men, single mothers and anyone else suffering from poverty. As Taylor (2007, p.103), however, notes the 'charitable activities of the rich were not wholly altruistic, and were often underpinned by self-interest and moral superiority'.

ACTIVITY 5.1

Modern day philanthropists

The *Sunday Times Giving List* (McCall, 2012) indicates that the culture of philanthropy continues to grow in the UK with what is referred to as a 'more broadly based culture of philanthropy among the wealthiest people' in the country than ever recorded before.

Visit www.philanthropyuk.org and look there for details of current philanthropists or rich people who donate their residual wealth to charity. Who are some of these modern day philanthropists?

Reflect on some of the themes that you read about in Chapter 4. Can you relate the activities of some philanthropists to notions of 'good' or 'active' citizenship as described in Case Study 4.4?

What sort of work do these philanthropists contribute to? Do any of them contribute to or support community development projects?

Mutual aid

Mutual aid organisations are those that operate on the basis of the reciprocal exchange of resources and services for mutual benefit. Mutual societies tend to have neutral political, religious, racial and union affiliations and have many similarities with co-operatives and tend to be organised around the principle that an association should be owned and controlled by the people it serves. In the late nineteenth century, some Victorian social philanthropists, such as Eleanor Rathbone and Emmeline and Sylvia Pankhurst, while commencing their activity from a starting point of being voluntary visitors to the poor, went on to develop an approach of working *with* families to support them to improve their own life circumstances as well as campaigning for better housing and social conditions. The Cadbury, Fry and Rowntree families established lasting social philanthropic traditions that campaigned to improve the housing, health and social conditions of the poor.

Like many social justice practitioners today, Emmeline Pankhurst in the late nineteenth century, recognised that the poverty and unemployment experienced by so many people was not, as was considered by many at that time, due to some fault of the people themselves. She attempted, through her work as Poor Law Guardian to challenge the structural and underlying causes of unemployment and financial insecurity that many were experiencing. 'With sorrowful wrath and persuasive plea' (Pankhurst, 1931, p.133–134) she set about transforming conditions in the workhouse and within five years had 'changed the face of the earth' (Mackenzie, 1975, p.10) for the women, 'establishing a school, a gymnasium and swimming bath'. Her daily contact with the hardship experienced by those in poverty made her 'acutely aware of the wider social changes that were needed to bring about a fairer and more equal society' (Purvis, 2002, p.45). Her daughter Sylvia Pankhurst continued this work during the early part of the twentieth century in the East End of London. World War I created even greater hardship for working-class families and Sylvia Pankhurst worked with these communities helping them to develop cost-price community restaurants and to set up mother and baby clinics (Davis, 1999).

The social upheavals of the 1930s caused by an economic depression, mass unemployment followed by the impact on housing and food supply caused by World War II led to the publication of the Beveridge Report (Beveridge, 1942) and a political commitment to the establishment of the UK National Health Service and other welfare services. There was a widespread expectation that the new welfare state would lead to many social problems being solved (Taylor 2007, p.104) and it was not until the 1960s that it became clear this was not to be the case. In the early part of the twentieth century, the growth of the Labour movement and the trades unions led to the development of many co-operative societies and mutual aid groups to support working-class people who often felt patronised and judged by the actions of the charitable rich. The co-operative movement was driven by a desire to reject the implied judgmental principles that underpinned many welfare initiatives that sought to distinguish between the 'deserving' and 'undeserving' poor. One example of such a movement that still exists today is the Workers' Educational Association (WEA). The WEA, a charitable organisation, was founded in 1903, to support the educational needs of working men and women who could not afford to access further or higher education. Today, their mission continues to be to provide educational opportunities for adults facing social and economic disadvantage. Their courses are created and delivered in response to local need, often in partnership with local community groups and organisations.

> **ACTIVITY 5.2**
>
> **Co-operative organisations**
> Revisit the list of community or voluntary organisations that you identified in
> Activity 3.2. How many of them claim to be run on co-operative or mutual aid
> principles?
> What other modern-day co-operative organisations can you think of?
> You might think about including shops, housing associations, banks and credit
> unions, for example, in your search.

Self-help and community action

During the 1960s and 1970s there was an increased focus on the importance
of the voluntary sector. 'New kinds of voluntary and community action grew
alongside the traditional charitable voluntary groups' (Taylor, 2007, p.105).
These groups were founded on traditions of self-help and mutual aid and were
supported by state investment in community development projects. In the UK
in the 1960s and 1970s the growth of community development projects
witnessed a shift in philosophy towards neighbourhood work based on
community activism whereby service users and communities were encouraged
to change their situation through collective action. A new breed of community
development worker was introduced into neighbourhoods tasked with 'gaining resources and initiating community groups' (Rimmer, 2005, p.7) and new
social movements grounded in community action began to emerge where
groups were encouraged to 'take matters into their own hands' (Eriksson,
2011, p.413).

Craig (2007, p.339) has argued that 'many governments and international
organisations "re-discovered" community development' in the 1980s and
1990s and he offers examples of 'Third World Development projects' that
began, during this period, to view community participation as important for
promoting self-help and sustainability. In contrast, in Britain, the 1980s and
1990s saw a move towards a policy of individual care in the community.
Nevertheless, the sense of oppression and poverty that also accompanied this
period served to activate the growth of collective movements with communities and service users becoming active in campaigning for equal rights and
resources. For example, the growth of the City Farms movement really took
off during this period. City Farms – community managed farms and gardens
run often in deprived areas – exist all over the UK and Europe. They are
usually established in response to a lack of access to green space combined
with a desire to encourage strong community relationships and an awareness
of farming and gardening. These are groups set up by local people, run by
local people and primarily for the benefit of local people. As Barnes and
Sullivan (2002) noted, these new movements went further than aiming to
improve services and support; they wanted to achieve a transformation in
social attitudes and understanding. Other user-led groups and organisations
have developed their own theories, for example, those of independent living

and the social model of disability and have evidenced the value of user-controlled organisations to personal development and empowerment (Beresford and Branfield, 2012).

ACTIVITY 5.3

User-led organisations

Revisit, again, your research into local community organisations in Activity 3.2.
Are any of these user-led organisations who campaign for changes in attitudes and services?
What sorts of activity do they offer?
What support do they offer to other users who might want to join?

Eriksson (2011, p.413) has developed an analysis that places the historical view of community development practice within a framework of conservative/consensus and radical/conflict. She argues that the 1960s and 1970s were a period within which a movement emerged that rejected consensual/conservative models of trying to 'integrate a person (or group) into a community of which he (sic) is no longer a member. A more radical dimension' emerged that valued 'self-organisation among the marginalised' and stressed principles of social justice and human rights and a focus on 'social conflict instead of co-operation and consensus'. Eriksson's analysis reveals that recent years, in the twenty-first century, have witnessed a return 'to a more conservative dimension based on cooperation' and that community development 'has promoted the interests of those in power' through initiatives that aim to transfer responsibility from the public sector to the voluntary sector.

Participation and empowerment

As we noted in the introduction to this chapter, community development is defined as being about building active and sustainable communities 'based on social justice and mutual respect'; about changing power structures that prevent people participating 'in the issues that affect their lives'; and about enabling individuals and communities to grow and change according to their own needs and priorities and at their own pace. Community development practitioners adhere to an approach of working alongside people in communities to help build relationships and to identify common concerns. Hargreaves and Twine (2006, p.153) argue that the significance of this approach is its capacity to 'address the process of transformation' in communities and that core to this success is the importance of 'benefitting the least empowered'.

Community development practitioners ascribe to a strong value base underpinned by principles of empowerment, social justice and sustainability. However, community development, as an approach, has increasingly come under pressure to deliver results and has often been hijacked by politicians as a framework for consulting with 'the community' to short timescales and for delivering programmes and projects to contract. Craig (2007, p.337) has argued that, historically, usage of the term 'community development' has most often been associated with 'geographical' definitions of community: 'a discrete housing development, a neighbourhood, a rural village or a refugee camp' and that this has led to difficulties for some interventions that have not taken sufficient account of diversity and tensions within these geographic areas. A further difficulty has been with the increasingly used, but rarely commonly understood concept of empowerment.

In recent years, a number of writers (Lather, 1991; Fielding, 1996, 2004; Colley, 2003; Thompson, 2007) have subjected the concept of *empowerment* to interrogation, exposing its increasingly contested nature. Fielding (1996, p.399) suggests that the problem is one of semantics. The 'burgeoning use' of the notion of empowerment, he argues, has gone hand in hand with its 'increasingly elusive meaning', leading many to approach the concept with 'cynicism' and 'suspicion'. Fielding believed that such a response was inappropriate and that 'however fatuous or pretentious its utterance, empowerment is neither trivial nor trite in its ambitions or consequences'. The danger, as Fielding saw it, with the use of the word *empowerment* is that we are likely to be 'confused or duped or both' as the meanings surrounding the concept become 'increasingly ubiquitous and decreasingly helpful' (p.400).

Fielding (1996, p.401) and Colley (2003, p.140) both offer analyses of the different interpretations and uses of the term that help to unpick some of this confusion. The 'classical model' (Fielding, 1996) represents power as something that is handed on from the powerful to those whom they decide are 'appropriate' recipients. Power, in this sense, is seen as 'a commodity' (Colley, 2003) or as 'a property' (Fielding, 1996), which is transferred from one person to another (see Table 5.1).

Fielding (1996) suggests that this approach to 'empowerment' is frequently vulnerable to 'political hijack' and that one of the difficulties within this conceptualisation is 'the extent to which those doing the empowering retain control, often in covert rather than open ways' – what he calls 'empowerment as manipulation' (p.401).

Table 5.1 Models of empowerment

Model	Power belief	Approach
Classical (Fielding, 1996)	Power is a commodity that can be handed on from the powerful to the less powerful.	Top-down Tokenistic
Collective (Colley, 2003)	Power in numbers. Collective activity can generate capacity to challenge oppression	Transparent values but can serve to reproduce existing hegemonies.
Process (Lather, 1991)	Power is a personal relationship and is about having a sense of power to rather than power over	Empowerment is about realising one's own potential. Bottom-up

To make the question of values and purposes extrinsic to the notion of empowerment is to run a much greater risk of empowerment being used as a buzz word while enabling those who do the 'empowering' to covertly get on with the real business of ensuring the world remains much the same as it is. (Fielding, 1996, p.405)

The argument here is that if empowerment leaves traditional structures and processes untouched, it can only ever be regarded as empowerment in a minimalist sense. This is a rhetorical, or tokenistic, approach to empowerment, often shrouded in hyperbole. In a later paper Fielding (2004) went on to argue that the central problem of trying to empower others lies in our tendency to 'mistake or betray' their realities 'in favour of our own'. A crucial difficulty is the 'extent to which the social location or identity of the (practitioner) shapes the way they see and understand the world' (Fielding, 2004, p.299). One of the outcomes is that inevitably there are 'some voices we wish to hear and others we do not' and in dismissing those that make us feel uncomfortable we may often miss things of importance 'and of a deeper seriousness than our first impressions allow' (Fielding, 2004, p.303). This discussion about the contested nature of the concept of empowerment may remind you of the exploration in Chapter 1 of attempts to create models that explain different levels of participation, such as those by Arnstein (1969) or Burns et al. (1994). This could be a useful point to revisit that chapter and to check your developing understanding of some of the themes covered there.

Interventions by policy makers or practitioners, which are sometimes referred to as 'community development', can also be critiqued from this perspective. As we noted in Chapter 3, such approaches to engaging with communities and user groups often consist of introducing 'outside experts and methods' and trying to 'foster groups with the goal of bringing about local co-operation' encouraging association and fostering civil society (Eriksson, 2011, p.411). Eversole (2012, p.30) argues that engagement, such as this, is often framed in a discourse that implies 'we-as-professionals believe that they-as-communities have something important to contribute to the process of social change'. Eversole argues that this approach can become the 'direct inverse of people-driven change' subtly perpetuating the top-down expert-led model that it claims to correct.

Development initiatives typically seat people's participation firmly within 'projects' and 'programmes' managed and funded by professionals in organisations ... experts and their institutions are still cast as the initiators, the developers, the agents of change. (Eversole, 2012, p.30)

CASE STUDY 5.1

Community councils

Turner (2009, p.23) has observed that much existing community development practice documented in the literature 'appears to focus on outcomes and requirements frequently established by those with power outside the community and social context'.

Eriksson (2011, p.412) illustrates this with an example of a community

> initiative in the US. Local community councils were established where representatives from both the local authority and local community organisations worked together to address local issues.
>
> 'Community surveys' were used as a method of identifying 'social problems' with a view to agreeing appropriate remedial actions with the community. Unfortunately, however, because the local authorities initiated these 'inventories' this way of working 'meant that they resulted in exposed groups being blamed or made victims and even ending up in dependency situations'.

The discourse that considers community as something that is threatened and which must be restored or reconstructed is often associated with initiatives involving external intervention such as this.

Empowerment as emancipation

What Fielding (1996, p.403) saw as an 'emancipatory account' of empowerment has similarities with Colley's (2003, p.140) 'collective model'. This approach seeks to make its value base explicit and argues that it is values and purposes which provide the impetus and capacity to bring about change. The in-built inequalities between disadvantaged and advantaged people are acknowledged and 'attempts are made to facilitate collective activities which can challenge oppression and exploitation' (Colley, 2003). Within this view there is an 'obligation to challenge, critique and question' in ways which 'push the powerful back onto their ethical and political haunches' (Fielding, 1996, p.406). This version of empowerment is a perspective that has tried to be transparent about its commitment to certain values and is therefore open to explicit challenge or agreement. However, as both Fielding (1996) and Colley (2003) point out, this perspective has increasingly been contested, problematised and worried about.

Colley refers to this discourse as the 'empowerment as impossible fiction' account and summarises it as suggesting that the 'covert and unrecognised' ways in which individuals 'internalise and reproduce existing relations of power' actually serve to perpetuate 'domination by hegemonic groups' (Colley, 2003, p.148). In this tradition, power is seen as 'circulating', never localised and as exercised rather than possessed. Individuals are seen as 'vehicles of power, not its point of application' (Foucault, 1980, p.89). Eversole (2012) has revisited this perspective in a critique of the 'elusive goal' of community participation. Participation, she argues, often focuses on bringing people and communities in and inviting them to participate and the problem with this approach is that 'development is inevitably therefore flowing from us to them'. Eversole (2012, p.31) states 'participation becomes the problem we cannot live without: embedded in our best practice, yet inextricable from it; a central ideal, yet unachievable. It is a veritable mirage.'

Fielding (1996, p.410) would have dismissed such critiques as 'unsatisfactory' and 'unadventurous', suggesting that these endless attempts to deconstruct notions of power and privilege serve only to 'weaken its engagement with the reality it is trying so hard to transform' (p.411) and leading to the 'passion and ambition' of the emancipatory approach becoming 'debilitated' and 'immobilised' with 'those in the emancipatory vanguard' coming under attack 'for a seeming reluctance to acknowledge that they too are necessarily susceptible to distortions, limitations and partiality' (Fielding, 1996, p.408). Eversole (2012, p.30) adopts a similar position, arguing that such critiques 'tend to assume that participatory processes never intended to be participatory in the first place'. For Eversole, the problem of participation is not that participation is impossible to achieve, the problem is 'that it is impossible to achieve for others' (p.37). In saying this, Eversole is framing participation as a process that the individual needs to engage in at their own pace and on their own terms. It is not something that can be forced onto others. This discourse has many similarities with the conceptualisation of empowerment that is embraced by community development practitioners to which we now turn.

Empowerment and critical pedagogy

Lather (1991, p.3) has referred to the 'process of empowerment' as being about analysing the ideas about the causes of powerlessness, recognising systemic oppressive forces and acting individually and collectively to bring about change. This view of empowerment embodies a process not identified in the analyses by Fielding and Colley. It views an essential aspect of empowerment as being something one undertakes for oneself. It is not something done 'to' or 'for' someone. 'The heart of the idea of empowerment involves people coming into a sense of their own power, a new relationship with their own contexts' (Fox, 1988, p.2, cited in Lather, 1991, p.4). Thompson (2007, p.14) refers to this approach to power as referring to 'power to as opposed to power over'. To have power, he argues is 'to have the potential' and as such 'empowerment amounts to realising one's potential'.

This approach to considering the process of empowerment is strongly influenced by the ideas of Paulo Freire (1972) who advocated a *bottom-up*, person-centred and reflective approach to empowering individuals and communities to challenge the status quo. Freire's work has provided an important and influential body of theory underpinning community development practice. This perspective seeks to support people to challenge traditional notions of professional 'expertise' and to encourage collaborative approaches that value the experience and 'expertise' of the participants and service users. Freire's argument for a 'critical pedagogy' was underpinned by a belief that the feelings generated by a process of critical consciousness would motivate community-based action. In other words, 'the emotion generated by seeing life more critically motivates people to act together for change' (Ledwith and Springett, 2010, p.172). Freire called this process 'conscientisation' and suggested that it is an approach that can help people become aware of the influences that have previously (and currently) ruled their lives and especially shaped their consciousness. 'Critical pedagogy' attempts to understand how power works through the production, distribution and consumption of knowledge within particular contexts. Craig (2007, p.353) has observed that for practitioners, or what he refers to as 'the powerful partners', this process means recognising that communities 'have skills, ideas and capacities: that are often latent or unacknowledged ... and listening to their demands and responding appropriately'. We will return to consider the influence of Paulo Freire on liberatory and transformative practice in Chapter 8 where we explore the potential of informal education and social pedagogy to working with people in communities in this 'bottom up' way.

ACTIVITY 5.4

Service user or powerful partner
Revisit the discussion and Activity 1.3 in Chapter 1 about the different labels used to refer to *service users*. Try to map the developments in thinking about service users and their role against the different ways of thinking about *empowerment* and *participation* as summarised in Table 5.1.

For example, which perspective in Table 5.1 would you associate with the use of the terms client, patient, service user, expert-by-experience, young person or ordinary citizen to describe those with whom we work?

You might have noted how Cowden and Singh (2007) suggest that the use of the term 'client' is seen as 'patronising and stigmatising' and how Coulter (2011, p.10) suggests that the use of the term 'patient' is seen as associating people with an 'inferior status'. Coulter also argued that she finds the use of the term service user 'clumsy' and that it 'implies a relationship with an inanimate object instead of an active partnership'. Such terminology could be compared to the classical model of empowerment as defined by Fielding (1996) and seen as a top-down or tokenistic approach. In Chapter 1 we noted how the move towards greater service user inclusion has involved a shift in relationships with a greater emphasis being placed on the rights and abilities of service users to define and understand their own situation. The recognition that we possess different knowledge and skills has led to an increasing willingness by professionals to see the people with whom they work as active and equal partners. This shift in conceptual thinking, and the associated changes in the language to, for example, 'expert-by-experience' might reflect the principles of a bottom-up approach. This could be viewed as embracing the process model of empowerment as conceptualised by Lather (1991) in which the individual grows to realise their own potential and capacity.

Releasing capacity

Community membership, as we have noted in Chapter 3, can lead to the development of strong affiliations, bonds and solidarity that can prevent the community looking outwards. As Dinham (2011, p.537) has noted, solidarity adds 'fraternal feelings characterised by special concerns and moral obligations which do not exist in relationships with people outside the community'. Community development has the potential to facilitate the linking and bridge building that can help to overcome these concerns. Community development can support ways of articulating difference and of celebrating being in communities, and not just from 'a' community.

In 2004, an international community development conference (Budapest Declaration, 2004) defined community development as

> a way of strengthening civil society by prioritising the actions of communities and their perspectives in the development of social economic and environmental policy. It seeks the empowerment of communities ... It strengthens the capacity of people as active citizens through their community groups, organisations and networks ... It plays a crucial role in supporting active democratic life by promoting the autonomous voice of disadvantaged and vulnerable communities.

Community development, as we have seen, involves changing the relationships between ordinary people and people in positions of power, so that everyone can take part in the issues that affect their lives. It starts from the principle that within any community there is a wealth of knowledge and experience that, if used in creative ways, can be channelled into activity that supports the community to achieve its desired goals. Community development programmes seek to equip people with the knowledge and skills and support that allow them to participate at the level of their choice. This is frequently referred to, these days, as developing the *capacity* of the community.

Craig (2007, p.349) has argued that the term 'community capacity building' has, in common with words like 'community' and 'community development' been hijacked by policy makers and funders around the world and used as a 'spray on additive to a very wide range of activities' that are effectively 'top down interventions where local communities are required to engage in programmes with pre-determined goals'. Craig refers to a study with Aboriginal Koori people in Australia (Tedmanson, 2003) that noted ways in which 'capacity building jargon' has tended to replicate 'top-down' approaches and where so called, 'capacity builders' are seen as working to develop those seen as 'capacity deficient'. The study goes on to argue that the Koori people had '40 to 60,000 years of survival and capacity' and that the problem is not that they do not yet have capacity, rather it 'is that their capacity has been eroded and diminished [by colonialists]'. The Koori people involved in the study argue for an approach characterised by 'restoring rather than building capacity' and one that 'avoids the paternalistic construction of a deficit'. This is the definition of community development that we are embracing in this chapter and is the lens through which we have sought to critique the themes and models covered in this book.

The conundrum with this perspective, however, as Eversole (2012, p.32) has suggested is that it can feel like a 'contradiction ... trying to create bottom-up development within a top-down frame'. Cornwall (2008, p.275) has observed that much depends on how people are supported and nurtured to take up and make use of what is on offer, emphasising that 'the contrast and the relationship between spaces that are created through invitation to participate and those that people create for themselves becomes especially important'. Cornwall is referring here to the problematic nature of what she calls 'invited spaces' and the need for community development workers to be careful not to raise unrealistic expectations. In Chapter 3 we illustrated this danger with reference to research with participants in a New Deal for Communities project (Dinham, 2007) whose disappointment over their level of influence led to a diminution of their well-being and their subsequent reluctance to ever participate again.

Botes and van Rensburg (2000, p.53) advise that in order to overcome this challenge community development workers need to become 'good facilitators and catalysts of development' assisting and stimulating energies and activity that is already emerging. They stress the importance of exploring with the community both the successes and the failures, since failures can often be informative and can lead to further insights that can assist development. They argue that process-related 'soft' issues are as important as product related 'hard' issues and the aim should be to release the energy in a community without exploiting or exhausting them. In a similar vein, Eversole (2012) argues that community development practitioners need to frame their interactions within communities as creating a 'participatory space' and that this requires practitioners to pay particular attention to facilitating a meeting point between the knowledge and expertise of both the community and of the 'professionals' and that the first challenge is to reframe how we conceptualise 'knowledge'. In this analysis, Eversole (2012, p.33) differentiates between 'expert knowledge' and 'situated knowledge', with 'expert' knowledge being brought by the 'professional' and the 'situated' knowledge being brought by the community. The community and its members 'know and respect the particular constraints and possibilities ... instinctively', in a way that outsiders seldom can. Situated knowledge is seen as important because it is the contextual knowledge that is vital for enabling development activity to succeed.

In framing professional knowledge as 'expert' and local knowledge as 'situated', however, there is a danger that we could be accused of trying to bring people and communities into our way of doing things and that it is the 'experts' who hold the only real knowledge. Eversole (2012, p.37) recognises this difficulty but argues that 'bottom up development will still need the support of formal institutional allies to help overcome the barriers that communities cannot shift for themselves'. The challenge, she suggests, for community development practitioners is to enable a 'participatory space' whereby this process does not become a 'one way journey'. Community development practitioners, in this analysis, become 'translation agents who are comfortable in the circles of both the powerful and the powerless and who are able to facilitate the journeys of both' (Eversole, 2012, p.37). We find this analysis helpful and in Chapter 10 we pick up on and take forward some of our own thinking about these ideas. You might find it helpful to fast forward and read that chapter now before reflecting on the next activity.

Revisiting Swindon Family LIFE Programme and Tower block troubles

Reread the case studies in Chapter 3 (Family LIFE Programme and Tower block troubles) and your answers to the questions following those case studies. What are some of the strategies that those initiatives are using to help support the creation of a participatory space?

In what ways, would you say, are the practitioners in those two case studies working from within a community development approach to practice?

You might have noted that one of the themes from those case studies is an approach that moves away from thinking about people's 'needs' to focusing on the assets within the communities and individuals and developing these as positive capabilities. You might also have noted an approach aiming to support a developmental process using local knowledge and experience. You might have reflected on the way in which this approach views transformation as a process that seeks to address structural inequalities rather than being a one-off intervention.

Hargreaves and Twine (2006, p.153) have argued that the key to putting community development into practice lies in reflecting on a number of guiding principles:

- The principle of human dignity – recognising that people have the ability to make their own decisions and take responsibility for their own actions.
- The principle of participation – making use of local knowledge and ensuring people have a stake in project development.
- The principle of empowerment – involving all members of a community in decision making.
- The principle of ownership – an intervention or initiation of a project by an external change agent should lead to transfer of ownership to the community itself.
- The principle of learning – all those engaged should learn from the process.
- The principle of adaptiveness – where mistakes are seen as learning opportunities.
- The principle of relevance – new initiatives or innovative approaches may require adaptation to and appropriate promotion in the local context to maximise their relevance.

Hargreaves and Twine (2006) recognise, however, that achieving these principles is not always easy and that not all of them will necessarily be attained at the same time.

Reflecting on community development principles in practice

What are some of the challenges and tensions you may have encountered in your own practice when attempting to work within these community development principles? How did you resolve them?

Botes and van Rensburg (2000) identified what they called 'nine plagues' or obstacles and impediments to participatory development, which, in their analysis illustrate how complex, difficult and challenging the process can be. The factors that they found commonly constrain the promotion of participatory development and, as a consequence, often lead to the application of non-participatory approaches, include both external and internal obstacles. External obstacles include 'the paternalistic role of outside development experts' who 'just arrive' and 'who already know the answers'. This can lead to dependency and can 'hinder participatory development by undervaluing the input and experiences of the non-professionals' (p.43). Community participation is also often constrained by 'the prescriptive role of the state' who frequently have their own political agendas. Another problem is what they refer to as 'the over-reporting of success' at the expense of examining the failures for what can be learned from them. 'We need more studies of what went wrong', they argue 'and some suggestions as to how the same mistakes can be avoided'. This will be a theme that we will develop in Chapter 9 when we consider some of the tensions inherent in trying to evaluate participatory practice and community development.

BOX 5.1 NINE PLAGUES

1. The paternalistic role of development professionals
2. The inhibiting and prescriptive role of the state
3. The over-reporting of success
4. Selective participation
5. Hard issue bias
6. Conflicting interest groups within communities
7. Gate keeping by local elites
8. Excessive pressures for immediate results
9. The lack of public interest in becoming involved.
   (Botes and van Rensburg, 2000, p.41–58)

'Internal obstacles' identified by Botes and van Rensburg (2000) (see Box 5.1) include the tendency for 'the most visible and vocal, wealthier, more articulate and educated groups' to be the ones invited to be partners and for the involvement of 'local leaders' producing an over-representation of 'self-appointed people' that do not accurately reflect the views and perspectives of the broader community. This can also lead to 'gate keeping by local elites' or the marginalisation of one or more interest groups within the community. A further 'impediment' is the tendency for funders to favour 'hard issue' outcomes over 'soft issues such as community involvement ... capacity building and empowerment and excessive pressure for immediate results'.

In overcoming these 'plagues', Botes and van Rensburg (2000) offer 'twelve commandments' or guidelines for promoting community participation. These include the importance of respecting the community's indigenous contribution.

They emphasise that community development interventions should aim to empower communities to 'share equitably in the fruits of development through active processes' and that communities should be able to influence the direction of development initiatives rather than merely receive a share of the benefits in a passive manner.

Aiming for a community development approach can be both challenging and labour intensive. One of these challenges can be in overcoming the tensions that emerge in respecting and working with local hierarchies. Seeking the support of local community leaders is a key step in this process; however, this can lead to the perpetuation of unequal power and lead to some voices within the community not being heard. There may also be conflicting priorities between community members. As Hargreaves and Twine (2006, p.161) remind us 'reaching the most marginalised groups is a guiding principle for community development', but it can present challenges if their views are deemed to be irrelevant.

Gilchrist (2009, p.37) outlines seven processes that she argues underpin community development work and differentiate it from other forms of community work (see Box 5.2). Through these processes the community development worker supports others to organise activities and to take up issues.

BOX 5.2 GILCHRIST'S SEVEN 'ES' OF COMMUNITY DEVELOPMENT

- *Enabling* people to become involved by removing practical barriers to their participation;
- *Encouraging* individuals to contribute to activities and decision making;
- *Empowering* others by increasing their confidence and ability to influence decisions and take responsibility for their own actions;
- *Educating* people by helping them to reflect on their experience and to learn from others through discussion;
- *Equalising* situations so that people have the same access to opportunities, resources and facilities within communities;
- *Evaluating* the impact of these interventions;
- *Engaging* with groups to increase community involvement in partnerships and other forms of public decision making

ACTIVITY 5.7

Reflecting on Gilchrist's seven 'Es' in practice
The following case study (Restless Development, Tanzania) is an example of development work in Tanzania. While reading through this case study try to identify where and how you might apply any or all of the seven 'Es' outlined above.

CASE STUDY 5.2

Restless Development (Tanzania)

Restless Development is a youth led international development agency currently working in Africa, Asia, Australia and the UK. Restless Development (Tanzania) runs a rural peer education programme (*Kijana ni Afya* – Youth is Healthy) in the Southern Highlands region and in the urban areas of Dar Es Salaam and Iringa. This approach uses peer-to-peer education (using young people to mentor other young people) and youth volunteering to achieve their aim of placing young people at the forefront of change and development. Their approach has been praised by both government officials and the international community and in 2007 they were awarded the STARS Impact Award for Education in recognition of the impact of their youth-led approach and the transparency of their management systems. You can read more about Restless Development on their website: www.restlessdevelopment.org/tanzania

Young people in Tanzania face many different challenges that include poor reproductive health, limited resources and opportunities, and a perception that young people are 'simply targets for services rather than essential components of the national response to development' (AMCA, 2011, p.21). The majority of the population of Tanzania are heavily reliant on agriculture for their livelihoods, and employment opportunities are limited. Key obstacles in these areas have been identified as: considerable distances to access health facilities; inadequate and unaffordable transport; lack of access to affordable health information services; and unrepresentative governance and accountability structures (AMCA, 2011, p.21). Young people are further hampered by low retention rates within education and rising HIV rates.

To address these issues Restless Development works with young people to empower them to improve their own lives and encourage them to engage in decision making on the policy issues that concern them. Key to their philosophy and approach is the need to work alongside and with existing community structures to build on what is already in place. They have found that this approach ensures local ownership by community leaders and stakeholders and leads to greater sustainability, capacity building and independence.

Kijana ni Afya

The rural youth peer education model involves pairing urban and rural community young people and building their capacity as volunteer peer educators in effective public health and sexual health practices. In turn, these young people are then expected to communicate this information to their peers and to their community. They work in the community by training and building the capacity of teachers in peer education methods. The teachers then go on to train students in their school who become the local peer educators. Trained volunteers (both national and local) then provide mentoring and on-going support to both the teachers and the student peer educators. This is seen as a successful and sustainable approach to building the capacity of the community.

Through the peer-to-peer approach used by Restless Development, young people in rural villages are empowered to advocate for their own rights. The advocacy initiatives and methods are designed so as to be appealing and understandable to the young people's own communities and local service providers. The community-based approach has enabled young people in rural villages to advocate for their rights with service providers and policy makers.

One successful approach used by peer educators is a process known as *edutainment* (AMCA, 2011, p.42), a form of entertainment designed to educate as well as entertain, where young people are taught how to convey their health and empowerment messages through song, dance, drama and sport. It has been noted that young people involved in edutainment activities could, more successfully, remember what they had learned on that day. Another initiative is to encourage the establishing of community libraries/resource centres in local villages where the community can access them, rather than in schools where access is more difficult for the wider community. This has been shown to encourage the culture of reading among young people and a greater awareness of issues taking place around them.

The urban youth development programme *(Afya Bomba)* builds on the experience the national volunteers have gained as peer educators in the rural villages and supports these young people to develop a range of capacity building interventions aimed at supporting urban young people living in low-income estates in urban areas to access employment opportunities. They do this through the setting up of youth groups that include establishing commu-nity resource centres and libraries and holding careers fairs. A recent report (AMCA, 2011) concluded that participation in income generation activities by the young people involved in these youth groups had led to an increase in young people's individual and household income and that involvement in associative activities had led to increased employability and entrepreneur-ship. Restless Development have found that initial youth groups set up by the young people around a particular focus, such as local community radio or producing community newsletters, develop over time into wider community-based organisations with young people involved as active participants in decision making.

As a result of Restless Development's on-going initiatives, young people's participation in policy making has become embedded, rather than being seen as a tokenistic one-off event and young people have been supported to actively participate in a range of consultations.

ACTIVITY 5.8

Reflect on the Restless Development case study

What methods are being used here to foster community energies and release capacity?

What definition or definitions of community can you identify?

What examples of underpinning theory, covered so far in this book, can you find in this case study, such as social capital, civil society, voluntary association, citizenship and empowerment?

What do you think might be the key factors for success in the Restless Development approach?

How many of Gilchrist's 'seven Es' for community development did you identify in practice in this case study?

You might have noted in the Restless Development case study the importance that their model of practice places on valuing local knowledge. Eversole (2012, p.29) has argued that 'culturally and geographically situated knowledges (often referred to as local knowledge, indigenous knowledge, community-based knowledge) have become increasingly visible in development studies over the last three decades'. She goes on to stress the importance of this 'situated knowledge' for development work, emphasising how 'the community and its members know and respect the particular constraints and possibilities of a geographical or cultural value system'. Eversole (2012, p.33) also argues that 'Outsiders seldom have this deeply placed knowledge and may too easily suggest solutions that are inappropriate, unsustainable, or, from a local perspective, clearly ignorant.'

Smith (2011, p.17) has argued that youth work, such as that embodied in Case Study 5.2 is 'fundamentally part of a civil society', since it is at heart about relationship and association 'and the good that can flow from this'. Spence et al. (2011) demonstrated how youth work in local communities can aid personal and social development, encourage friendships and relationships to develop and enable access to local knowledge and credible role models, all of which increase young people's social capital. A recent, UK-based, report by Ofsted (2011) found that the most effective programmes for engaging young people included those where young people were encouraged to develop their own projects. They found that allowing young people to take genuine responsibility helped those young people to build their self-esteem and sense of purpose. Some of the young people in their research had come to their own realisation that this approach was a means of building their capacity and confidence in seeking employment. The report concluded that volunteering activities support young people's learning and development and provide a means by which they are able to engage constructively in civil society. The most effective settings found creative ways of integrating volunteering within projects enabling young people to take on greater levels of responsibility rather than seeing voluntary activity as an 'add on' to mainstream learning. Effective providers recognised the need for young people to have skills, confidence and credibility in undertaking volunteering roles and so invested time in training the young people, especially those with responsibility for others such as in mentoring, or in relation to management and governance.

Chapter summary

This chapter has explored the developments in thinking that have informed community development practice from early philanthropic approaches to the more recent emphasis on empowerment and collective transformation. The chapter has noted how, this historical overview, enables us to develop a conceptual framework that helps to critique recent and current initiatives and practice. Through exploring these concepts and approaches the chapter has reached a concluding analysis identifying the key principles of community development. These principles include the premise that community development work is *with* not *for* communities, that participation is *voluntary and bottom-up*, and that the outcome is to achieve a *sense of empowerment* for all of those involved.

We have argued that the language of community capacity building and the contested themes associated with that are not easily separated from the debates that surround, and sometimes seek to hijack, community development as an approach. However, community development practice should always be focused on releasing, or restoring the capacity of communities and service users. Community development is about supporting structures that are sustainable and that can enable a continued response to issues of local concern. Community development practitioners, working from within a Freirian framework, seek to foster the development of networks and links between individuals and community groups within localities that enable mutual care and support.

In Part III we explore, in more depth, some of the methods and tools commonly used by community development workers. Brief reference has been made to some of these methods within Case Study 5.2, such as advocacy, mentoring and 'edutainment'. In Part III we will explore and discuss the theoretical frameworks that underpin these methods and you may wish to return and reread this case study at that point. Before that, in the following chapter, we will close section two by examining some of the personal tensions and challenges that working with service users and communities within this participatory paradigm can give rise to for the practitioner.

USEFUL RESOURCES

CDX (Community Development Exchange) CDX was an independent UK-based organisation working to ensure community development is understood by practitioners, funders and policymakers. Following withdrawal of funding CDX announced its closure in 2012. A wealth of useful resources, produced by CDX are now available on the IACD website (see below). These include research reports, case studies and tools for community groups and practitioners on themes such as empowerment and evaluation.

Community Capacity Building The website for Education Scotland has pages on the theory and practice of Community Capacity Building and includes examples of what capacity building can involve: **http://www.educationscotland.gov.uk/ communitylearninganddevelopment/communitycapacitybuilding/**

Community Development Foundation (CDF) is a social enterprise that is passionate about helping communities. They say they have unique expertise in using community development to strengthen local voices, improve people's lives and create better places to live. There are many useful resources on their website including one on starting up a community group that discusses how to overcome some of the common challenges you might face when trying to get locally-driven ideas off the ground: **http://www.cdf.org.uk/**

International Association for Community Development (IACD) is a global network of practitioners and activists working towards social justice through community development approaches. Their aims are to promote community development across international policies and programmes, to network and support community development practitioners and to encourage information and practice exchange: **www.iacdglobal.org**

United Nations Committee of Experts on Public Administration (CEPA) is responsible for promotion and development of public administration in connection with the implementation of internationally agreed development goals, including the UN Millennium Development Goals. It particularly focuses on the themes of human capital development, participatory governance, capacity development in crisis and post-conflict countries, and innovations in public administration and governance, among others: **http://www.unpan.org/cepa.asp**

FURTHER READING

Brent, J. (2009) *Searching for Community: Representation, Power and Action on an Urban Estate* (Bristol: Policy Press).
This book presents an extended case study of issues of power and capacity in communities. Set on a UK housing estate it examines ways to understand and engage with the concept of community and challenges simplistic policy solutions that aim for community empowerment.

Craig, G., Mayo, M., Popple, K., Shaw, M. and Taylor, M. (eds) (2011) *The Community Development Reader; History, Themes and Issues* (Bristol: The Policy Press)
This book develops some of the themes and issues introduced in this chapter in more depth offering a wide ranging collection of readings. Chapters in the book offer critical analyses of current policy and emergent approaches to community development.

Freire, P. (1972) *Pedagogy of the Oppressed* (Harmondsworth: Penguin)
Freire's work has been very influential to community development practitioners. We refer to his work in this chapter and in others. In his classic text he introduces the notion of banking education, highlights the contrasts between education that treat people as objects rather than subjects and explores education as cultural action.

Gilchrist, A. and Taylor, M. (2011) *The Short Guide to Community Development* (Bristol: The Policy Press)
This book offers a good basic introduction to the origins of and the trends and challenges in community development and is written by two of the leading writers on community development in the UK.

CHAPTER 6

Exploring Boundaries

CHAPTER OBJECTIVES

By the end of this chapter you should have an understanding of:

- a range of professional boundary issues when working with communities and service users;
- the nature of dual relationships;
- the impact on professional identities of working in communities with service users;
- how to manage ethical and power issues in relation to working with communities and service users.

Introduction

Koubel and Bungay (2012, p.1) suggest that, in their experience, 'the situations in practice that give people the most stress and cause the most tension and anxiety are those that involve the struggle to achieve an acceptable balance between often conflicting rights and risks when engaging with service users'. In Chapter 5 we began to discuss some of the tensions and challenges facing people who work with and alongside communities. In particular that discussion focused on the conundrum of power and empowerment. In this chapter, our aim is to take this analysis further and to explore in more depth a range of ethical and power tensions that might be encountered when working alongside people and within communities to release their capacity.

Some people who work alongside communities believe that their practice can be enhanced by being seen and accepted as 'part of the community' with whom they work. The feeling is that this closeness can provide a better insight into the locality and a less professionally distanced relationship with their service users. However, these connections can raise some complex issues that do not have straightforward solutions and community practice with service users can lead to tensions around issues of professional identity and accountability. Banks (2010, p.2170), for example, has highlighted the finding that 'over one-third of the conduct cases heard by the GSCC (the professional body for UK Social Workers until 2012) since its inception are reported as relating to "crossing professional boundaries and inappropriate relationships with people who use services"'. In such cases, it has been argued, practitioners need to ensure that they protect themselves and the people with whom they work from inappropriate intrusions by setting clear limits and boundaries (Cooper, 2012). In this chapter we do not seek to provide 'hard and fast' solutions or guidelines for managing these dilemmas. However, through consideration of some recent literature and research we aim to highlight a set of principles that can support reflexive, resilient and accountable practice. Consider this short case study.

CASE STUDY 6.1

Working in the community

Sheila is a community development worker who has been working with a local community group to support them in establishing a community resource centre in their neighbourhood. One Saturday she attends, with her partner and children, a large Community Festival, outside that local neighbourhood. She is sitting on the grass, with her family, enjoying the music and the food when, Mike, a member of the community group she works with approaches, recognises her and sits down with her family to talk to her.

Out of politeness, Sheila introduces her family to Mike and they engage in some 'small talk' about the music and the weather. Mike then continues to talk about developments in his neighbourhood and a recent disagreement in the community resource group that had been the focus for discussions the last time Sheila had met with the group. Sheila realises that she is starting to feel uncomfortable that she has been 'pulled' into a conversation about work. She notices that her partner and children are beginning to look uncomfortable and have become quiet. However, she is not sure how to extricate herself from Mike without appearing 'rude'.

- What would you do in this situation?
- What might Sheila have done differently?

What are professional boundaries?

The nature of community practice and the approaches we may use in seeking to empower service users can sometimes, also, lead to a blurring of professional/private boundaries and to the development of what have been referred to as 'dual relationships' (Pugh, 2007). Cooper (2012, p.13) has suggested that managing boundaries of this nature is a bit like 'walking a tightrope' and that the skill is in learning where to draw the line between maintaining a close trusting relationship while achieving a suitably professional perspective.

Doel et al., (2010, p.1867) have defined professional boundaries as 'the boundary between what is acceptable and unacceptable for a professional to do, both at work and outside it, and also the boundaries of a professional's practice' for example, whether complementary therapies can be undertaken by the professional as part of their work. It should not, they suggest, be confused with 'boundary disputes between different professions, namely inter-professional boundaries'. However, Banks (2003) draws attention to the ethical tensions that can arise in community practice and includes within these 'conflicts of culture and accountability'. We have also included this definition within our discussion of professional boundary issues in this chapter. As we will note later, the nature of 'client dilemmas' (Lindsay, 1995) involves the tension that can arise between practitioners in different agencies when it is perceived that both are not always working from a value base that seeks to empower communities and service users.

In many cases the difficult professional boundaries that we will encounter are caused by what Banks has called 'ethical dilemmas'. Banks (2003, p.103) offers a helpful definition of an 'ethical dilemma' that illustrates the nature of the issues under discussion. An 'ethical dilemma' arises, she suggests, 'when someone faces a choice between two equally unwelcome alternatives and it is not clear which choice is the right one'. The very nature of an ethical dilemma, therefore, means that there is not necessarily a right or wrong answer. Banks also defines 'ethical problems' as being different from dilemmas and which we prefer to define as *ethical tensions*. These occur when the situation may involve a difficult or ethical decision 'but it is clear what decision is the right one' (Banks, 2003, p.103). As community practice becomes more common across a variety of disciplines and professions, these tensions may increasingly arise and they serve to highlight the range of boundary issues that can face the community practitioner.

Reflexive practice

It is likely that you will be aware of when a professional boundary issue has arisen in your practice because you will probably feel uncomfortable or out of your depth. Schön (1983) refers to this as being in the 'swampy lowlands' of practice referring to the messy, confusing problems of professional practice that cannot be solved through the use of research-based theory and technique. It is because professional practice has this unpredictability that we need to develop the skill of being reflexive practitioners. As Ledwith and Springett (2010, p.18) remind us 'reflexivity is central to the process of becoming criti-cal' and to being able to reflect on our own attitudes, assumptions and preju-dices 'in order to open ourselves to new insights and understandings'. Being a reflexive practitioner involves being able to reflect on what is going on 'in the moment'.

Cooper (2012, p.115) has suggested that 'possible warning signs' that should 'make you stop and think' include:

- thinking or talking about service users when you are not at work,
- prioritising a particular service user,
- allowing your sessions with a service user to 'run over' their allotted time,
- allowing your relationship to become more and more social,
- sharing more personal information than is strictly necessary with a service user,
- sharing worries about issues and difficulties at work with a service user,

- finding it difficult to hand a service user over to other services,
- a service user 'hanging around' or waiting for you and
- flirting

It is important to reflect regularly on our work and to be alert for warning signs and feelings of discomfort. Once a boundary has been crossed, by worker or by service user, it becomes far more likely that further boundary crossings will follow. Codes of practice and associated guidance usually take the stance of advising that the key to managing difficult or grey areas is openness and transparency and that any dilemmas surrounding relationships with service users should be discussed with a line manager or supervisor as early as possible. The opportunity to explore your feelings and issues with someone else can be invaluable and it is for this reason that many health and social care professionals have regular supervision at work. However, this is not always readily available to workers, especially in community settings.

Developing the skills of regularly reflecting critically on your practice and maintaining a reflective diary, therefore, become very important in the context of practice of this nature. Banks (2010, p.2171) refers to the process of 'continuous reflexive sense-making' as an important aspect of what she refers to as 'professional integrity'. Practitioners, she argues, need to be able to 'develop the capacity to be reflexive and to talk of themselves and their work in ways that are plausible and credible to themselves, colleagues, employers, other professionals and the wider public' (p.2181). Banks suggests, therefore, that practitioners need to develop and practice the skills of 'debate and dialogue'. Taylor (2008, p.361) refers to this process as 'developing a moral compass'. He argues that community development practitioners need a greater understanding of ethics and reflective practice and that by developing a 'moral compass' through reflection and dialogue we become more conscious 'not only of what we ought to do or should do, but also what we can do'.

Doel et al. (2010, p.1871) take a similar position, arguing that codes of practice or professional frameworks are not necessarily helpful to practitioners who cannot expect to remember or be familiar with an increasingly lengthy list of things they should and should not do and that making boundary decisions requires 'ethical competence rather than following a framework of instructions'. They suggest that codes of practice can produce the unintended consequences of leading practitioners to feel they need to 'disguise their errors and not make accurate reports' (p.1873). In this way, 'professional' behaviour and integrity comes to be seen as being 'compliant with the code' rather than developing the skills of 'ethical sensitivity and decision making'. Doel et al. (2010) argue that, in order to be able to respond appropriately to the complexity of community practice, practitioners need to own, reflect on, question and debate practice dilemmas collectively with others.

To illustrate the nature of the issues that we are discussing we invite you to reflect on the following activity and the sorts of tensions that these scenarios cause you to experience (if any).

ACTIVITY 6.1

Professional tensions and dilemmas

Reflect on the following situations? What would your reaction be? How might you resolve the dilemma?

(a) You have worked very closely with a service user through a particularly emotional period in their life. He says that it is great to have a friend like you who he can rely on.

(b) A young woman in your community arrives at your home asking if she can come in and talk about a difficulty she is having with her parents.

(c) You go out for an evening with friends and meet one of the members of a support group you run who offers to buy you a drink.

(d) A member of the community group you work with invites you to a party at her home.

(e) You bump into a client you used to work with. They are now working with a different practitioner. The service user tells you that the new worker is not as supportive as you were and asks for your help with something.

The scenarios in the activity highlight a number of common *grey areas* that can arise in work with service users and communities. It is not uncommon that the relationship will feel like friendship when we have worked very closely to support people and have come to know them well. It is not necessarily only the service user who might experience the relationship like this; practitioners also can develop feelings for those with whom they work that make them want to pursue a non-work relationship. Mickel (2008) has suggested that practitioners who live and work in the same community, or who work closely with service users or members of the community, can find that 'life can be become claustrophobic' and can lead practitioners to feel they can never escape from the people with whom they work. 'Simply telling clients to wait until you see them in work time is more difficult than it sounds' (Mickel, 2008).

In thinking about your response to the scenarios above you might want to reflect on any professional guidance that is offered by the professional body that you belong to. Prior to the closure of the GSCC, guidance offered to UK Social Workers (GSCC, 2011, p.8), for example, reminded practitioners that if they were to encounter a client in non-working time 'there is still a power imbalance' and that they should 'act professionally – as if they were at work regardless of the age of the person'. Clearly, any requirement to continue to act 'professionally' in one's own time can place a burden on practitioners who can feel that they do not have any time when they are not at work. This is an especially significant issue where a practitioner lives in the community in which they work. In November 2011, research involving the Clinic for Boundaries Studies concluded that a definitive list of acceptable and unacceptable behaviours would not be helpful given the grey areas encountered by community practitioners. Accordingly, guidance on professional boundaries for social workers in England, launched in 2012 by the Health Care Professions Council (HCPC), sets out a framework of guiding principles intended to help practitioners make 'informed, reasoned decisions' about practice without 'dictating' how one should meet pre-defined standards (HCPC, 2012, p.4).

Dual relationships

Cooper (2012, p.52) has argued that in order to keep one's relationship with service users unambiguous workers should 'ensure that they have only one relationship with a client'. However Pugh (2007, p.1405) has pointed out a range of tensions that emerge for practitioners who find themselves in situations where they have 'dual relationships' with service users. Such relationships commonly arise, he suggests, when workers live and work in the same community that they serve. What he calls 'out of hours connections' can raise some complex issues about how workers conduct their practice 'and comport themselves socially within the wider community'. Furthermore, in some small communities 'the normative style of relating to others may be one in which it is expected that daily life is conducted in a friendlier way and this is less narrowly circumscribed by a neutral, "professional" style of engagement' (p.1406). Pugh goes on to argue, however, that rigid sets of guidelines are not always helpful in these situations and that the practical realities of community practice often 'challenge absolutist conceptions of confidentiality and undermine assumptions of objectivity and neutrality in professional stance'. In smaller and close communities confidentiality can potentially be compromised 'by existing knowledge and relationships' as well as through informal contact and associations with other people that can result in the worker hearing 'unsolicited and informal information about community members' (Pugh, 2007, p.1415).

Pugh (2007) illustrates a range of examples of tensions that can arise for practitioners who live and/or work in small communities. These include the dilemma about how to behave in relation to service users outside the professional encounter. This dilemma not only involves decisions about whether to accept invitations to family parties, weddings and funerals but also how to behave if attending other local events at which people known to the worker will also be present: 'While [the decision to opt out of local social activities] runs the risk of being thought stand-offish ... it can be an effective though somewhat isolating strategy' (Pugh, 2007, p.1414).

A further tension is discussed by Kvarnström et al. (2012, p.130) who highlight the 'multi-dimensional' nature of the relationship with service users in inter-professional and participatory practice where the 'service user can be regarded both as a member of a team and as the recipient of its services' a role that Kvarnström describes as being a 'co-actor'.

As we discuss in Chapter 8, one approach to working alongside service users to increase their capacity to engage independently is that of informal education. In that chapter we discuss the growing body of practice associated with informal education known as social pedagogy. A key principle within social pedagogy is that the people with whom we work are in charge of their own life, and the social pedagogue aims to work *alongside* them rather than telling them what to do. Practitioners working within a social pedagogic framework aim to work with 'the whole person as emotional, thinking and physical beings, promoting their active engagement in decisions about their own lives and as members of society' (Cameron et al., 2011). It is a discipline that takes account of the complexity of different social contexts and practitioners often operate in a way that makes it difficult to separate the personal and the professional. Social pedagogic theory therefore makes a distinction between what are called the *three Ps of practice*: the professional, the personal and the private (see Figure 6.1).

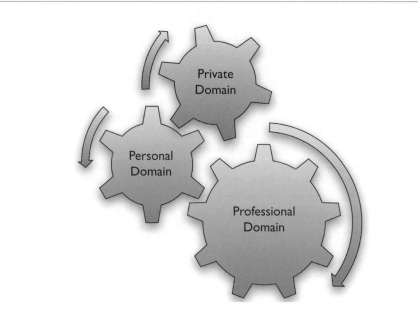

Figure 6.1   The three Ps of practice

- The *professional* domain draws on legislation, policy, research and theory to help explain, reflect on and understand practice.
- The *personal* domain represents what the practitioner brings to the developing relationship with service users. This is often based on an approach to practice known as being *authentic* and may involve some carefully considered self-disclosure to help build trust and develop a relationship.
- The *private* domain aims to set the personal boundaries of what should not be shared with those one works with and should not form part of the relationship. The private domain relates to who you are with those closest to you, and the experiences you have had that may have shaped who you are but which you should not share with a service user.

According to social pedagogic theory, the three Ps are constantly in play during practice and practitioners need to understand the impact their relationship with an individual may have on them and be able to reflect on this in supervision in order to improve practice and at the same time protect their private life.

Beginnings and endings

The nature of community practice and work to build relationships with service users is, by its very nature, complex, multi-layered and will very often involve an emotional component with strong attachments being formed by both sides. The beginning and end of a relationship can, therefore, have a profound impact on the service user or community. Unlike personal relationships and friendships, professional relationships will almost always have an end point. A badly managed ending can be emotionally damaging to the service user and can cause problems for future engagements. Many people, not just vulnerable service users, experience difficulties with ending relationships appropriately. Endings can often involve a process of grieving for both the worker and the service user or community. As Cooper (2012, p.90) cautioned 'Don't underestimate the impact that the ending of a relationship may have on either you or your clients'.

Lombard (2010) discusses the difficulties with knowing how to end a working relationship with a service user with whom you have built a strong relationship based on empathy and respect. Handled insensitively or abruptly, endings can lead to the service user feeling emotionally damaged, abandoned, disillusioned or disempowered. On the other hand, maintaining contact with people one is no longer working with could lead to a blurring of professional boundaries and could foster a culture of dependency. Lombard (2010) offers guidelines on how to manage a relationship with a service user or community in a way that is always working towards an ending (see Box 6.1).

BOX 6.1 MANAGING ENDINGS (LOMBARD, 2010)

Establish a contract – establish a contract with the service user from the beginning of any relationship. Make it clear that this is not an open-ended relationship and it will be focused on clear objectives within a limited time frame, with the ultimate aim of helping the service user take control of their own life.

Don't make promises you can't keep – it is important for practitioners not to make promises or false reassurances to service users about what you can deliver. This can lead to a blurring of professional boundaries and unrealistic expectations.

Open communication – ensure communication with the service user is transparent throughout the relationship. Do not assume they understand how long you will have contact with them. Review the progress of your relationship regularly and recognise the service user's progress.

Plan the ending – plan with the service user how they will access support after your relationship ends and ensure a smooth and sensitive transition if required.

Saying goodbye – be prepared for a host of different responses as your work nears termination phase. Do not underestimate the part you have played in someone's life

and accept that some resistance, challenge, fear, distress or confusion may go
alongside the process of saying goodbye.

Be aware of your own feelings – understand how personal experiences of endings may
affect how you work. For example, a difficult ending in your life may lead you to
rescue service users rather than assisting them to help themselves.

Cooper (2012, p.92–93) offers a further set of guidance in relation to maintaining the boundary after the relationship has ended:

Do not establish a personal relationship with the service user – once you
have had a professional relationship with a service user it is unethical to
continue to have a personal relationship with them, whether friendship or
a sexual relationship, and can undo the good work done within the professional relationship.

Do not continue working with the service user formally or informally – if
you have ended the relationship, it is not appropriate to continue to provide
support. If you do, there is a strong likelihood of increasing dependency on
you as an individual (as opposed to you the worker).

Do not maintain contact with the service user – if they do contact you regularly, you need to let them know that it is not appropriate and refer them
to other more suitable support. It may be tempting to keep in touch to see
how they are doing. However, this can open the door for them to start
contacting you and implies you wish the relationship to continue.

Do not establish a different professional relationship with the service user
– if your service user is a plumber or car mechanic or pensions adviser, for
example, it can be tempting to make use of their services. This can lead to
complications.

ACTIVITY 6.2

**Revisiting Swindon Family LIFE Programme and Restless
Development**

Thinking about these guidelines offered by Lombard and Cooper above, how easy
would it be for you as a community worker working within a community or as
student on placement in a project like in the Swindon Family LIFE case study
(Case Study 3.1) or the Restless Development case study (Case Study 5.2), to
follow this guidance? What do you foresee might be some of the dilemmas and
tensions that could arise for you in following such guidance?

Power and empowerment

The role of being 'the professional' in relationships with communities and
service users inevitably imbues us with power in many scenarios. These may
be both perceived and real. The practitioner may, for example, be the 'gatekeeper of resources that the service user needs' (Melville-Wiseman, 2012,
p.123). Some service users will be in need of support and may be vulnerable.

Even if they are not vulnerable in other settings, the power dynamic in the professional relationship can mean that they are placed in a vulnerable position in relation to you the worker. Experience and/or training might mean that the practitioner has some greater knowledge about how the system works or about what resources are available. The practitioner may have personal information about the service user, whereas the service user does not have access to that information about the practitioner. As Cooper (2012, p.12) reminds us this relationship 'puts you in a position of power and control and with this power comes responsibility'.

One of the reasons why a consideration of professional boundaries is important in the context of work with service users is that boundaries can serve to help the service user develop skills to manage their own boundary issues. Relationships between service user and worker can be dynamic and fluid, and setting (and keeping) appropriate boundaries can help to set limits so that both understand their role in the relationship. Many service users will have had previous experiences of being let down or abused and people in this situation may be vulnerable to victimisation in the face of inappropriate boundaries by a professional. It is likely that such people find it hard to trust and may need to test where the boundaries are in their relationship with the practitioner. Work with vulnerable service users makes the issue of maintaining appropriate boundaries an important part of helping the service user to understand how to manage their own relationships and boundary issues. It is also an important part of encouraging and empowering service users to become independent.

In Chapter 5 we explored the contested concepts of power and empowerment. We also began to explore notions of professional knowledge, situated knowledge and expertise. When considering complexity and tension within community practice those debates also bring into focus consideration of what it is to be 'a professional' and the challenge to the concept of 'being the professional' through the increasing significance placed on the concept of 'expert by experience'. Traditionally, workers in health and social care settings have engaged in 'paternalistic' type relationships where the practitioner has been seen as 'the expert' who decided the nature and appropriateness of the treatment or care. Such an approach to practice tended to confirm a view of service users as both dependent and passive. In that approach, the focus tended to be on problems, failings or inadequacies rather than the service user's abilities, strengths, resources and capacities. Furthermore, as Banks (2003, p.106) has pointed out, community practice can raise dilemmas for community practitioners about their role and identity within the work and can lead to difficult judgments about when 'parentalism is justified' in order to protect service users from being exploited or 'set up to fail'.

As we noted in Chapter 1, the move towards service user inclusion has witnessed a shift in the service user–worker relationship with a greater emphasis being placed on the rights and abilities of service users to define and understand their own situation. The recognition that worker and service user possess different knowledge and skills has led to an increasing willingness by professionals to see service users as active and equal partners. Thompson

(2007, p.55) refers to this as the 'emergence of new forms of professionalism' based on an ethos of partnership. Rather than viewing the professional as 'the one who knows best' practitioners are now thinking about the contribution they can offer to a partnership with the service user. This shift in conceptual thinking has led to gradual changes in the language, reflecting the principles of 'user-led' services or 'user-centred' services wherein practitioners engage in a partnership process of 'agreeing what the problems are, what the potential solutions are and how best to move forward' (Thompson, 2007, p.55).

Doel et al. (2010, p.1872) discuss the difficulties that the concept of professional boundaries raises for practitioners who aspire to practise from a relational or participatory empowerment model. They argue that the drive to professionalise or 'proceduralise' relationships with service users could be seen as leading to a 'strengthening of the patriarchal model' and to an approach to practice that sees service users as 'a different caste, others from whom professionals must be resolutely separate' (p.1881). They point out that there is very little research into the views of service users in relation to professional boundaries and where there is evidence (Nelson et al., 2004) this tends to suggest that service users have a preference for practitioners who are flexible with boundaries and who go beyond a strict interpretation of the professional's role. Where a practitioner adopts the approach towards working with service users that sees them as 'fellow citizens or co-actors in inter-professional practice' (Kvarnström et al., 2012, p.130) hard and fast rules about 'professional' boundaries become more complex. Doel et al. (2010, p.1884) argue that 'because complaints come to light in the way that compliments do not' it is difficult to evaluate the positive outcomes for service users when practitioners 'are prepared to cross hard and fast lines'. However, they suggest that 'there is evidence that boundary crossing can be something to celebrate rather than suppress' and that more research into service users' opinions about professional boundaries is needed.

ACTIVITY 6.3

Boundary crossing

Reread Case Study 3.1 in Chapter 3 (The Swindon Family LIFE Programme). In this approach, families were able to pick their own multi-agency team; workers act as *co-actors* helping with practical tasks such as gardening, decorating, cooking and budgeting and are expected to develop their own skills alongside the family. It is argued that this approach gives the families and the workers an opportunity to really get to know each other, and a chance to talk about their lives in an informal setting, creating the basis for a purposeful relationship.

What potential boundary dilemmas do you envisage might arise for the workers involved in this project?

What could be the benefits to the sorts of professional boundary crossing that they are exploring?

In thinking about your answers to Activity 6.3 you might find it helpful to reflect on Batsleer's (2008, p.100) discussion of what she calls the 'dilemmas of friendship' in relation to community practice. She suggests that one of the most notable features of an approach, such as that in Case Study 3.1, to working with families and communities is its 'friendliness'. Batsleer points out that this view of 'practitioner as friend' has been considered as 'contentious'. However, she argues that 'classical definitions' of 'friend' construed this relationship in terms of 'friendship as usefulness ... as one who produces and provides really useful knowledge' (p.103) and in terms of 'friendship as enjoyment' and pleasure in mutual enthusiasms. This latter aspect of the relationship with service users, in her view, should be celebrated and promoted and not confused with personal friendships and intimate relationships. 'Recognising when and how those relationships shift' is the important issue: 'It is in the confusion of roles and in particular in the confusions about power in relationships that the potential for harm lies' (Batsleer, 2008, p.104).

Professional accountability

Banks (2003, p.104) argues that there are 'certain features' of community practice that tend to give rise to ethical dilemmas. One of these features is that community practice is essentially about the values and principles of 'empowerment, participation, collective welfare and social justice' and that such 'value-based activity' can lead to misunderstandings or conflict with other professionals. Working in communities involves considerable inter-agency and inter-professional work. This results in a range of organisations, interest groups and individuals with different organisational systems, cultures and values being brought together. We have discussed elsewhere (Oliver and Pitt, 2005, p.180) how differences in professional cultures and values can lead to complex accountability dilemmas for practitioners working in communities or with service users. This can lead to what Lindsay has called the 'client dilemma' (Lindsay, 1995, p.493) where a tension arises between wishing to make ethical decisions on behalf of the individual service user and one's professional accountability and responsibility. Oliver and Pitt (2005, p.175) refer to the case of a youth worker in the community who is required to choose between maintaining the trust and respect of the young people who attend her drop-in centre and co-operate with other professionals who are organising a local truancy sweep. The police and education welfare officers wanted to work with the drop-in centre and use it as a 'neutral territory' to which they could bring young people they 'picked up on the street'.

> The dilemma ... was that she was more interested in why young people play truant rather than who or how many, and she thought that the trust relationships with young people could be undermined if the centre was used in this way. (Oliver and Pitt, 2005, p.175)

The practitioner in that case example, therefore, made the decision to maintain relationships of trust with the young people and let them know the week, but not the day, that the centre was to be used in this way. As Lindsay (1995) argues, the intention of ethical guidelines and professional codes of practice is to guide us towards high professional standards. However, community practitioners and those seeking to engage and empower service users will also be guided by a set of principles that frequently lead us to want to put the service user at the centre of decisions. Other examples of 'client dilemmas' could be spending too much time on a case because you find the company of a particular service user rewarding; failing to challenge a service user; colluding with service users against your own agency; or watering down difficult messages because you fear it could upset them. As Lindsay points out, when looking at the direct application of ethics in our decision making it becomes clear that there is a tension between ethical decisions for the individual and ethical decisions within professions or even society at large. Consider the Case Study 6.2.

CASE STUDY 6.2

Practitioner dilemma

Rachel, a development worker working for a voluntary agency, works with Lara, aged 14, who had gone missing from her children's home about 80 times in one year. Lara had become involved in sexual exploitation, and alcohol and substance misuse. She was seen as being very much a loner who did not want to engage with support workers.

The dilemma for Rachel was to find a way to build a relationship with Lara in order to advocate for her and to support her through child protection procedures, while at the same time share some information with other professionals without alienating Lara.

It was a long process that required honesty and transparency. For example, when a police officer wanted to talk to Lara, Rachel acted as an advocate and represented her views. Lara did not want to attend some of the child protection meetings so Rachel met and talked with her first, represented her views at the meeting and then told her what had happened. The idea was to keep her informed and offer her support. Being 'totally upfront' meant being clear with Lara as to the limits of what Rachel could do. This meant telling her that sometimes Rachel might have to breach her confidence, but explaining why she would have to do this. A confidentiality sheet was provided that Lara read and signed, which explained that if she committed a serious crime or was found to be being harmed or abused, other professionals would have to be told.

Rachel, the worker in this case, believes that one of the factors helping to prevent young people being alienated is her agency's open-file policy whereby any young person can read their file at any time. The key factor in Rachel's view is 'to always keep the young person informed'.

Banks (2003, p.107) refers to the 'multiple accountabilities' that community practice of this nature entails. She has argued that 'the principles of community practice are essentially contested' and that, because it can often be a value-based area of work, practitioners will inevitably 'get caught up in value disputes' (Banks, 2003, p.105). These differences in values might be caused by, for example, different interpretations of the process of participation and empowerment. A further example is offered by Pugh (2007, p.1409) who points out that where workers act as advocates for 'unpopular causes or people such as substance abusers, ethnic minorities, travellers and gypsies', they may find that their own social position becomes 'a reflection of the status of those whom they seek to help'. Banks (2003, p.117) describes the approach to managing tensions such as these as 'acting with professional integrity, competence and honesty'. In a later paper (Banks, 2010) she explores the concept of professional integrity in more depth, arguing that it is 'becoming increasingly topical' but also suggesting that it is a contested concept with no definitive definition. Banks argues that there is a need to 'reinvigorate dialogues and debates about the ideals and core purposes' of professional work with service users and communities (p.2181). Practitioners, she suggests, need to engage in regular critical reflection and to explore boundary dilemmas and tensions with colleagues and with the wider public.

Ambiguous boundaries

Doel et al. (2010, p.1880) have argued that 'the very word 'boundary' is full of ambiguities' and that rather than there being a clear cut consensus about what is acceptable or not, boundaries are actually 'more like no-man's land or a disputed piece of territory that is capable of being claimed by many sides'. From this perspective, crossing a boundary is not necessarily a violation or a transgression since the 'boundary areas are fluid'. Those individuals or agencies that see boundaries as fixed lines, they argue, are more likely to see the need for a highly prescribed code of conduct. Those who view boundaries as 'shifting areas of shadow' will be more inclined to follow a set of guidelines based on general principles.

In 2008 the publication *Community Care* surveyed nearly 300 practitioners to try to understand the full extent of the confusion surrounding professional boundaries (Hayes, 2008). Their findings highlighted some differences in opinion on whether, and to what extent, it was appropriate for practitioners to have relationships with clients. The survey revealed that while 98 per cent of the respondents considered it 'never acceptable' to have a sexual relationship or 'go on a date' with one of their 'clients', when it came to friendships or relationships with former clients, 'the waters become murkier'.

Doel et al. (2010) followed up this survey with some further, more in-depth research and found that practitioners actually make very little use of regulatory guidelines when trying to determine how to navigate complex professional boundaries. They found that the majority of practitioners relied on their 'own sense of what is appropriate or inappropriate, and made their judgements with no reference to any formal guidance'. The reasons for this, they concluded, was that existing guidelines 'tended to ignore the ambiguous areas of practice and seemed to act as an insurance policy, brought out and dusted off when something goes awry'. As a result they caution against 'ever-increasing bullet points of advice and prescription', and recommend, as a way forward, a system of ethical engagement in which professionals are supported to 'avoid transgressions' through regular 'ethical hill climbs' (p.1884), considering and discussing scenarios that explore professional boundary dilemmas with others in teams.

> A long list of principles or standards risks losing sight of the wood for the trees ... would it not be better to learn how to navigate through the wood rather than to count, map and identify all the trees? (Doel et al., 2010, p.1885)

A strategic approach to embedding professional boundary issues in the reality of daily practice, argue Doel et al. (2010), should be developed by an 'ethically engaged workforce' in partnership with service users, adopting a bottom-up rather than top-down approach. This approach should not view boundaries as always 'problematic; some service users appreciate professionals who can cross boundaries, but this must be approached in a transparent and considered manner' (p.1885). Cowden and Singh (2007, p.5) support this perspective, arguing for an approach in which user perspectives are neither privileged nor subjugated, but are situated in a process of creative critical dialogue with professionals, and which is linked to the development of a concept of welfare that is 'driven by emancipatory rather than regulatory imperatives'.

Chapter summary

In this chapter we have explored and discussed a range of professional boundary tensions that might be encountered when working to support and empower communities and service users. As we have noted, working in this way can raise some complex issues for practitioners that do not have straightforward solutions. Our discussion has highlighted the importance of regularly reflecting on our work and of being alert for warning signs that a boundary has been crossed. We support the argument that practitioners need to develop and practice the skills of critical 'debate and dialogue' (Banks, 2010) in order to develop 'a moral compass' (Taylor (2008) so that we might become more conscious of and accountable for the reasons behind the decisions that we make.

Part III includes three chapters that aim to engage you in debates about some of the methods and approaches commonly used by practitioners who aim to work from an empowering, participatory and enabling paradigm. As we have identified in this chapter these informal approaches, based on partnership and relationships of trust and mutual respect often give rise to dilemmas and tensions about the boundaries of practice. We hope you will keep in mind some of the issues we have explored in this chapter as you read and engage with the following chapters.

▬▬ USEFUL RESOURCES ▬▬

Professional Boundaries (an online self-assessment tool) is an interactive resource on the GSCC website aimed at social workers and students and is designed to complement their guidance by providing hypothetical examples of possible professional boundary dilemmas. It offers the opportunity to compare your answers with those of others and makes interactive links to relevant parts of the GSCC's codes of practice: **www.gscc.org.uk/professional-boundaries-assessment-tool/**

Community Care magazine has an online quiz aimed at helping you to think about yourself and the professional boundaries that underpin your work: **www.communitycare.co.uk/blogs/social-work-blog/2011/02/professional-boundaries-in-soc.html**

Visual Ethical Decision-Making (VED) Project aims to develop a computer-based package that presents versions of Seedhouse's Ethical Grid in a format that allows the graphical images to be manipulated and recorded. It aims to offer a pictorial and written record of deliberations and enable practitioners to fully involve service users in decisions. The case examples are used as starting points for reflection around professional boundaries issues. See: **www.aut.ac.nz/study-at-aut/study-areas/ health-sciences/research/national-centre-for-health-law-and-ethics/decision-making-tools/ethical-grid**

FURTHER READING

Cooper, F. (2012) *Professional Boundaries in Social Work and Social Care: A Practical Guide to Understanding, Maintaining and Managing Your Professional Boundaries* (London: Jessica Kingsley).
This book is a practical reference guide to professional boundaries offering practical advice and suggestions on how to judge boundaries and how to manage a situation when boundaries have been crossed. It includes a selection of practical activities and self-assessment tests.

Doel, M., Allmark, P., Conway, P. Cowburn, M. Flynn, M. Nelson, P. and Tod, A. (2009) *Professional Boundaries Research Report* (Project Report. General Social Care Council/ Sheffield Hallam University).
The research that informed the work by Doel et al. (2010) referred to in this chapter can be accessed from the Sheffield Hallam Research Repository and provides further discussion of professional boundaries issues: http://shura.shu.ac.uk/1759/

Koubel, G. and Bungay, H. (eds) (2012) *Rights, Risks and Responsibilities: Interprofessional Working in Health and Social Care* (Basingstoke: Palgrave Macmillan).
This is a very helpful, practice focused collection of chapters that explores the complexity of balancing issues of power and empowerment with service users from a range of professional perspectives. It includes some good reflective case studies and challenges to encourage engagement with the issues raised.

Seedhouse, D. F. (1998) *Ethics: The Heart of Health Care*, 2nd edn (Chichester: Wiley & Sons).
This book offers an introduction to ethical analysis and offers a model for practical decision making: The Ethical Grid. The book includes case studies and exercises and explores a range of complex ethical issues.

PART III

Methods

CHAPTER 7

Supporting Engagement through Advocacy and Mentoring

CHAPTER OBJECTIVES

By the end of this chapter you should have an understanding of:

- contexts, aims and purposes to engaging service users and communities through advocacy and mentoring;
- definitions and a range of forms of advocacy and mentoring;
- critiques of models of practice in relation to advocacy and mentoring;
- the impact of advocacy and mentoring on individuals and communities;
- examples of initiatives in relation to advocacy and mentoring.

Introduction

In this chapter we focus on advocacy and mentoring, which we argue can be effective methods to support participation, engagement and empowerment of individuals, service users, groups and communities. There are different forms of advocacy such as *citizen* or *peer advocacy* with similar aims and underpinning principles. These offer support in enabling voices to be heard or being empowered to make decisions to improve the lives of, for example, children, young people, older people, and people with learning disabilities or mental health issues. We present different forms of mentoring such as *classic* or *befriending* that provide support and role models, often to young people by adults. The impact of mentoring can be to counter any feelings of marginalisation, increasing a young person's confidence and putting them on a path to social inclusion and re-engagement with wider communities.

We present advocacy and mentoring separately in this chapter using a framework that offers definitions, types and models, and evaluates their impact using case studies. We introduce examples of initiatives throughout the chapter to give you insights on the developing methods in the UK and the US. The chapter concludes with some discussion about similarities, differences and current ideas about advocacy and mentoring. Activities, additional reading

and useful resources offer you signposts to extend your understanding in relation to supporting engagement in a range of contexts.

What is advocacy?

> When people are denied or unable to gain access to a fair share of what's on offer
> in society ... then it becomes necessary in a caring society for more powerful people
> to act with integrity on their behalf or wherever possible to enable them to move to
> a point where they can retrieve control for themselves. (Advocacy in Action, 1990,
> cited in Boylan and Dalrymple, 2009, p.83)

> Advocacy is the process of acting on behalf of another person to secure services or
> rights which they require or are entitled to. (Scottish Executive, 2001, p.1)

> Advocacy promotes equality, social justice and social inclusion. It can empower
> people to speak up for themselves. Advocacy can help people become more aware
> of their own rights, to exercise those rights and be involved in and influence deci-
> sions that are being made about their future. (Lee, 2007, p.7)

These definitions offer a range of interpretations of what advocacy is, what it
can do and who does it. We can see then that the purpose of advocacy is not
limited to ensuring people gain control and a voice by which to secure their
rights or access to services. It is also, as stated above, about principles of
'equality, social justice and social inclusion' (Lee, 2007, p.7). Beyond this there
is recognition that independent advocacy can 'add weight to a person's (or
group's) ideas, hopes, ambitions and opinions' (Advocacy 2000, 2002, p.50).
Those who advocate may be more 'powerful' people advocating on behalf of
someone in a weaker position or those self advocates who are able, supported
or empowered to 'speak up for themselves'.

Advocacy is about getting something stopped, started or changed
(Barnardo's, 2012). For organisations like UK children's charity Barnardo's
and the National Youth Advocacy Service (NYAS) it can play an essential part
in ensuring the voices and views of children and young people are heard when
decisions are being made about their lives such as when leaving care. From a
wider perspective that brings in, for example, people with learning disabilities,
advocacy provides support where people have their own voice and speaks for
them where they have no voice. Advocacy is about representing others' views,
wishes and needs to decision makers, and helping them to navigate systems.
Advocacy services aim to be independent and confidential to help people make
informed choices.

Advocacy is a practical skill where those who advocate refer to working
with their *partner* rather than using other terms such as a *service user* or *client*
that we introduced in Chapter 1. There are recognised skills and personal
qualities to performing the role of advocate such as: listening to understand
their partner's needs and wishes; negotiating so that their partner is heard
within decision-making processes; ability to develop trust within the relationship; and offering practical help and correct information to help the partner

make choices. The advocate works in a way that is anti-discriminatory and empowering by building the confidence of their partner.

With or on behalf of their partner the advocate may be stating a case or challenging assumptions, protecting them from abuse or securing better services, or influencing decisions to ensure inclusion and equal treatment. Advocacy can be viewed as involving a rebalancing of power through the exercise of rights and having access to information. It thereby has the potential to empower both the advocate and their partner.

ACTIVITY 7.1

Speaking up for someone
Think about an occasion when you have spoken up for someone, either with them or on their behalf.

- What was the occasion and background?
- How did you prepare and present?
- What was the result or outcome?
- What feelings and emotions do you recall?

This activity is making the point that we are all advocates and will need advocates at some times in our lives to help us find or give voice, to empower us in circumstances where a case needs to be stated or to protect us from those misusing or abusing their position of power. In summary the meaning of advocacy varies according to its different aims or purposes that determine how it operates in practice.

Historical and policy context

Bateman (2000) observes how early writing on social work as a professional activity refers to social workers in the role of advocates addressing social injustice. Both *citizen advocacy* and *self-advocacy* as distinct movements can be seen developing in the US in the 1960s in relation to people with learning disabilities. Citizen advocacy became established in the UK in 1981 with the Advocacy Alliance, a coalition of five major voluntary agencies (Mind; Mencap; One-to-One; Spastics Society, renamed Scope in 1994; and the Leonard Cheshire Foundation). This spread to other groups such as Age Concern, the Volunteer Centre and the Coalition for People with Disabilities. Self-advocacy took off in 1984 with the People First movement leading to the establishment of projects and organisations such as My Life, My Choice (see Case Study 7.1). Other fields such as mental health have developed a similar timeline for self-advocacy with increasing numbers of self-help groups of survivors and the formation of the Survivors Speak Out project from a MIND conference in 1985.

A further growth in advocacy projects in the UK followed the NHS and Community Care Act 1990 (Great Britain, 1990) that required consultation in assessment and producing community care plans. Article 12 of the UN Convention on the Rights of the Child (United Nations, 1989) 'encourages adults to listen to the opinions of children and involve them in decision-making'. The Advice, Advocacy and Representation Services for Children (now the National Youth Advocacy Service) project was set up in 1992, after the UK ratified the UN Convention, to help young people who felt their voice was not being heard. Advocacy projects aimed at helping partners to articulate their needs and ensure their rights were upheld and respected.

'Objective 3' of the learning disability White Paper *Valuing People* states the intention to:

> enable people with learning disabilities to have as much choice and control as possible over their lives through advocacy and a person-centred approach to planning the services they need. (DH, 2001, p.26)

In 2002 the Department of Health published national standards for children's advocacy services available to all children and young people 'in need', as defined by the Children Act 1989 (Great Britain, 1989), and those in the looked-after system. The standards see advocacy for children and young people as being about speaking up for them and empowering them to ensure that, according to Standard 1: 'Advocacy is led by the views and wishes of children and young people' (DH, 2002, p.3). The Adoption and Children Act 2002 (Great Britain, 2002) gave local authorities the duty to provide advocacy services for children wishing to make a complaint under the Children Act. In the UK advocacy can be seen as developing from a rights perspective concentrating on securing civil, political or social rights towards a greater emphasis on the rights of service users as consumers of welfare services. Teasdale (1998) saw self-advocacy developing more in the US while the UK embraced wider definitions that include citizen advocacy, collective advocacy and professional advocacy. Before offering more detail on these different forms of advocacy it is worth considering some of the principles that underpin the concept.

Principles of advocacy

Boylan and Dalrymple (2009) focus on advocacy with children and young people. They highlight the legislation that requires social workers to act in the 'best interests of the child' as set out in the Children Act 1989 (Great Britain, 1989). They recognise the limitations and challenges legal duties place on professionals when they act as advocates according to this principle of 'best interests'. For example, where they make a professional judgement that may not be what the child wants or are required to breach confidentiality in some cases such as child abuse.

BOX 7.1 THE ADVOCACY CHARTER

The Advocacy Charter was launched in 2002. Over 75 organisations in the UK contributed to the development of a set of core principles used as a tool to guide the work of advocacy organisations in the UK. The principles include:

- clarity of purpose,
- independence,
- putting people first,
- empowerment,
- equal opportunity,
- accountability,
- accessibility, and
- confidentiality.

Source: www.actionforadvocacy.org.uk

In relation to advocacy for older people Dunning (2005, p.8) identifies four common over-arching principles within the literature:

- *Independence*: 'to ensure that the needs and interests of the older person remain paramount'.
- *Empowerment*: where 'advocacy should enable older people to find and use their own voice wherever possible, as well as being about speaking up on their behalf if needed'.
- *Inclusion*: where 'older people should have equal opportunities to be involved in managing, developing and delivering them [services]'.
- *Citizenship*: where 'older people may need to be informed, advised or represented in order to secure and exercise their rights and entitlements as citizens'.

Dunning refers to older people being 'advised'. This is unusual in advocacy services that mostly operate under the principle that advocacy is *user-led* and the advocate does not give advice but rather explains choices so that the partner comes to their own decision.

Principles of advocacy may be summed up as follows: where people have their own voice advocacy means making sure they are heard, for example, by establishing a youth forum for young people. Where people have difficulties speaking out it means providing help, for example, an interpreter or signer. Where people have no voice, due to communication difficulties, it means speaking up for them.

Advocacy is a duty or responsibility for some practitioners or professionals, for example, independent mental health advocates. It becomes a necessary skill for others such as social workers or nurses as a consequence of working with those experiencing marginalisation, exclusion, discrimination or disadvantage such as asylum seekers, travellers or older people. The issue may be about legal redress or claiming certain rights, such as the right to vote or marry. However, there is a common theme: to help another person obtain something from someone with the power to give or withhold that service or right.

Forms of advocacy

While some advocacy, such as *legal advocacy*, is short-term, there are unpaid volunteers such as *citizen advocates* who make a long-term commitment to individuals. Advocates present their partner's view of their best interests, even when this conflicts with the advocate's own views or professional judgement. Advocacy may be for oneself or someone else, or for a group or community. Commonly it is seen in work with children and young people, older people such as those with dementia, people with physical or learning disabilities, and people with mental health issues.

In exploring the meaning of advocacy we have introduced a number of different forms. Dunning (2005, pp.10–11) presents a range of some forms or models of advocacy:

> *Self-advocacy*, which essentially means 'speaking up for yourself' to represent your own needs, wishes and interests.
> *Collective advocacy*, self-advocacy groups and organisations that provide mutual support, skill development and a common call for change.
> *Peer advocacy* takes place where one person advocates for another who shares a common experience, difficulty or discrimination.
> *Citizen advocacy* is a one-to-one, long-term partnership between an independent, unpaid 'ordinary person' and a disadvantaged 'partner'.
> *Professional advocacy* may refer to the partial advocacy role of staff in health, social care and other settings.
> *Legal advocacy* is the most established and widely recognised form of advocacy and is undertaken by trained lawyers.

We go on to offer further detail on some of these forms likely to be used or experienced by practitioners working in health, social care and education.

Legal and professional advocacy

These forms involve trained and paid advocates who generally provide short-term issue-based advocacy for individuals. Legal advocates such as solicitors represent the interests of the individual client. While they offer specialist services they generally operate within an adversarial system that due to financial costs can limit access for many people. It is also a system where the individual client may have difficulty in understanding and controlling the process. Professional advocates are increasingly used rather than unpaid volunteers, for example, within Independent Mental Health Advocacy (IMHA) Services as they have specialist training and knowledge.

A rights-based approach to advocacy such as one that emphasises the rights of the child under the 1989 United Nations Convention on the Rights of the Child will be valuable in some situations where, for example, the child is not present or there are difficulties in obtaining their views, but not all. Where professionals are encouraged to work with families then there may be conflicts and tensions created around who exactly the advocate is representing. In such cases it may be unclear as to how the role of the advocate is any different to that of, say, a social worker or family support worker. Knight and Oliver note that taking a rights stance can make the boundaries clearer between the role of an advocate and other professionals. However, they point out that 'the question remains whether it is better that the young person receives support from an advocate ... or does not receive a service at all' (2007, p.424). The questions are does advocacy make a difference, and if so then how?

Citizen advocacy

Citizen advocacy services developed in the UK during the 1980s and 1990s to work mainly with people with learning disabilities. This can be linked to discussion in Chapter 4 about the nature of citizenship and rights or entitlements. Some professionals were increasingly acknowledging that people with learning disabilities should be able to exercise the right to vote, to live more independently, to marry or have their own family. Citizen advocates are independent of both the setting and the agency that provide the service for the advocate's partner. Citizen advocacy is primarily a one-to-one relationship where the advocate offers time, effort and loyalty to their partner. It is a means of working in a long-term relationship with people unable to advocate for themselves and can often lead to friendship. Citizen advocacy seeks to involve people from different backgrounds and experiences to help their partner develop the skills needed to get the most out of life. It works to empower and support those who are devalued, discriminated against, excluded or marginalised. The long-term nature of the relationship is seen as a positive aspect by enabling the partner to develop trust and communicate their views. Citizen advocacy offers more practical support in daily aspects of life and is not primarily issue-based.

Challenges within this form of advocacy may arise in the matching of the citizen advocate to their partner, around recruitment of the unpaid ordinary person, and their motivation and abilities to deliver support. Citizen advocacy involving a befriending element with people with learning disabilities could be regarded as both disempowering and patronising. In addition citizen advocacy has been seen as introducing conflict and challenge to service providers where citizen advocates voice concerns about attempts to control behaviour, medication and neglect (Simons, 1993). Simons has noted 'resentment towards citizen advocates from some professionals who feel an important part of their own role is being usurped' (1993, p.29).

Peer advocacy

In this approach advocacy is done by someone who has experienced or is experiencing similar difficulties or discrimination such as bullying in school or mental health issues. Peer advocacy can be challenging to professionals as in this approach the advocate's partner keeps ownership of the issue or problem so advocacy is done not on their behalf but in partnership. The advocate is likely to ask 'what is it that you wish to stop, start or change?' and 'how will you achieve this?' This approach is more about researching information and providing support for the person and whatever they want to do about an issue even if the advocate disagrees. The advocate never takes action or speaks for their partner without careful thought and their agreement. This form of advocacy supports the principle that the partner remains in control of the issue. While mostly individual issue-based advocacy this form can be used in a collective systemic model with a group or community. It can produce productive relationships due to peers having common understandings with their partners and the ability to draw on personal experiences.

In peer advocacy the idea of taking ownership of a problem can be difficult where the partner feels too weak and vulnerable to tackle an issue them self, such as facing racial abuse or harassment. A further issue, made also in relation to citizen advocacy, arises in trying to match the advocate to their partner. While a mental health survivor may advocate successfully for someone in a similar situation, how well can a 14-year-old advocate for another 14-year-old experiencing bullying at school? Issues of age, gender, ethnicity and culture are likely to arise in the recruitment and matching of advocate and partner. Problems may continue in providing on-going motivation and support for the peer advocate who is being asked to return to previous difficult experiences such as bullying or substance misuse.

Self-advocacy

Self-advocacy is 'do-it-yourself' advocacy where individuals speak up or stand up for themselves on issues, represent their own interests, make choices and take responsibility. This benefits the individual as it gives them a voice, enhances personal identity, raises self-esteem and empowers through self-determination. It can be seen as a successful end to other types of advocacy as the advocate is no longer needed where their partner attains the knowledge, skills and confidence to advocate on their own behalf. Developing the ability to self-advocate could be seen as an example of the process model of empowerment as outlined in Chapter 5.

Challenges to the use of self-advocacy might include having sufficient ability and experience to present your case and be listened to thereby avoiding tokenistic involvement in decision-making meetings where others set the agenda. There may be concerns about a self-advocate being able to access impartial and correct information alongside tensions with professionals claiming expert knowledge or with others who feel they understand the individual's 'best interests', such as parents or carers. An individual may need support while developing skills of self-advocacy. Finally self-advocacy may not always be appropriate or beneficial in circumstances where an individual is under stress or where, for example, a patient is suffering from illness.

Collective advocacy

Self-advocacy is also evident in *collective advocacy* that represents a social movement where groups or organisations seek to influence policy and practice or promote a cause. An example of a self-advocacy group is People First (http://peoplefirstltd.com/), an international civil rights movement campaigning for people with learning disabilities to be treated equally and fairly. Local groups run by members promote self-advocacy and link to a UK national network to form a collective voice to campaign for change. A further example is illustrated in Case Study 7.1.

CASE STUDY 7.1

My Life My Choice

My Life My Choice (MLMC) is a self-advocacy organisation in the UK run by and for people with learning disabilities. It invites individuals with learning disabilities to become *champions* 'acting as consultants and experts to help improve services and the quality of life for people with learning disabilities'. *Champions* consult, meet, lobby and research with local and central government, the police authorities and universities.

MLMC provides a team of trainers with learning disabilities who offer training for professionals such as health workers, GPs and dentists to inform and change attitudes, and to improve health and social care for people with learning disabilities.

(See: http://mylifemychoice.org.uk/)

Boylan and Dalrymple (2009) see problems with collective advocacy arise where groups, such as MLMC in our case study, become part of systems and bureaucracies that they originally set out to challenge. Within these systems it can be easier for professionals to manage and manipulate groups to act against their own 'best interests'. Where those groups consist of children and young people self-advocating then there may be reliance on supportive adults, for example, to support those who are looked after within the local authority care system. The tension lies in the extent to which the role of the supportive adult can be determined and controlled by the children and young people themselves.

For people who cannot express their feelings and wishes effectively due to, for example, their age, learning disabilities or dementia then gaining a 'voice' through advocacy remains problematic. Voice may be expressed through non-verbal means and this is the challenge for advocates working with those without speech. As Knight and Oliver (2007) observe this 'can result in the tension between putting someone else's views across or acting in their "best interests"' (p.421).

Non-instructed advocacy

A further form of advocacy gaining recognition and acceptance in practice is *non-instructed* or *non-directed* advocacy. This form is determined by the capacity of the person requiring an advocate. It has added to debates since the Mental Capacity Act 2005 (Great Britain, 2005) that provided a statutory framework for independent mental capacity advocates working to safeguard vulnerable people. Where a person is unable to communicate their views or wishes due to, for example, learning disabilities, dementia or a temporary incapacity resulting from an accident, then an advocate may use non-instructed or non-directed advocacy. Action for Advocacy has adopted a definition of non-instructed advocacy proposed by Henderson (2006, p.7) as 'taking affirmative action with or on behalf of a person who is unable to give a clear indication of their views or wishes in a specific situation'. Its key principles are set out by the UK's Office of the Public Guardian (OPG):

- The client does not instruct the advocate.
- The advocacy is independent and objective.
- People who experience difficulties in communication have a right to be represented in decisions that affect their lives.
- The advocate protects the principles underpinning ordinary living which assumes that every person has a right to a quality life. (OPG, 2007, p.9)

Non-instructed advocacy is seen where an advocate responds to a request from a key person in the life of the person who is unable to communicate their views. A framework is used whereby the advocate considers how a person's life will be enhanced or detracted by any decision being proposed for that person. It is not using the principle of 'best interest' as the advocate is not offering an opinion or view on a course of action. The advocate may act as a 'watchdog/negotiator' to ensure the partner 'has access to appropriate services and support', or as an 'articulate friend' to check the partner 'is healthy, happy and feels, to the extent that it is possible, in control of their own life and circumstances' (Henderson, 2006, p.6).

Activity 7.2 gives you the opportunity to apply your understanding of different forms of advocacy we have outlined so far.

ACTIVITY 7.2

Choosing forms of advocacy

Which form of advocacy would you use in the following examples?

- An older person with a hearing loss who wants to go to the theatre.
- A young man with learning disabilities seeking to marry his fiancée and live independently.
- A group of travellers wanting literacy and numeracy classes for their children.
- A neighbourhood group wanting the police to introduce a night curfew to combat vandalism and substance misuse by young people in its area.
- A group of young people (under 16) facing the introduction of a night curfew in their neighbourhood.

How would you proceed? Refer to some of the forms of advocacy outlined above.

What would you regard as a successful outcome?

What principles of advocacy did you consider or apply from the Advocacy Charter presented in Box 7.1?

In some examples you will be using a model of individual issue-based advocacy in the form of legal or professional-based advocacy, perhaps in the case of the travellers where you need to ascertain the statutory duty of local authorities to provide literacy and numeracy classes. For some you may need to combine this approach by establishing a long-term relationship through citizen advocacy, perhaps with the young man seeking to marry, or even develop a wider systemic collective advocacy on behalf of all those with learning disabilities who may wish to marry and/or live independently.

You might have noted that the advocate would need to research information carefully and to keep their partner properly informed about relevant legislation and their rights, as for example, the older person with the hearing loss in Activity 7.2. They would need to act impartially in the face of both personal and professional views in, for example, the case of a neighbourhood group wanting to impose a curfew on young people where the advocate may disagree with their solution to a problem. Also they would need to act in accordance with their partner's instructions and carry out those instructions with diligence and competence in the example of the group of travellers. The community curfew example gives you the opportunity to compare a collective advocacy approach to the same issue from different sides. Reflect on what this tells you about your ability to advocate, according to some of the principles stated by the Advocacy Charter, such as with 'clarity of purpose' and 'independence' while showing that you are 'putting people first' and demonstrating 'empowerment' of your partner.

Impact of advocacy

The nature of advocacy and the role of the advocate mean that advocates are neither neutral nor indifferent in working with the partner. Intrinsic to the process is that the advocate actively supports a person once they have made their views and wishes known. This may result in advocates being required to adopt a position that brings them into conflict with other people including professionals and 'experts', and with whom they disagree at a personal level. This is recognised by some who refer to advocates feeling isolated and to 'the inevitable loneliness of personal advocacy' (Kendrick, 2006, p.8). Kendrick understands that some advocates will be prepared to go further than others and they 'can be ahead of their peers on many issues' (2006, p.9).

Other advocates will recognise limitations and constraints that can lead to accusations of them colluding with service providers rather than acting in their partner's best interests. Advocacy services in general can face problems with staff caring for children, young or older people who may regard confidential and independent services as threatening to those working in, for example, residential homes. Some professionals may dislike the child or young person-centred and rights-based approaches in the belief that they work primarily for their organisation and all service users rather than for the individual. A UK review of advocacy services suggests that some practitioners view advocates as 'challenging, even irritating and inappropriate' (Newbigging, 2012, p.9).

Case Study 7.2 focuses on the impact of advocates working with disabled young people.

CASE STUDY 7.2

Advocacy for disabled children and young people

Knight and Oliver (2007) draw on the findings of a wider research study of the role of advocacy for looked-after children and children in need carried out by the University of London between 2003 and 2004. They recognise that while traditionally children have been excluded from decision-making processes affecting their lives this is even more the case for children with communication difficulties. This vulnerability makes it more important that they have access to independent advocates.

The most challenging aspect identified by advocates was exploring the wishes of young people without speech. Working through non-directed advocacy created uncertainty and tensions about whether they were acting in the best interests of the young person. On the other hand working to a rights-based approach offered positive outcomes. Drawing on the Children Act 1989 (Great Britain, 1989) or the UN Convention on the Rights of the Child (United Nations, 1989) helped some advocates to argue for services to which the young people were entitled.

The study also raised an issue for advocates by asking 'who is the client?' This acknowledges there are potential conflicts between the different wishes and interests of the young person, parents or carers, and other professionals. Advocates spoke of parents taking a *best interest* approach to their child making them 'less likely to keep the child or young person fully informed and allow them to express their own views' (Knight and Oliver, 2007, p.423). The effect of this can have an impact on advocates who may become parent or carer led. The paper describes some social care professionals working with disabled children and young people as arguing 'advocacy needed to be more assertive in supporting disabled children rather than their parents' (Knight and Oliver, 2007, p.423).

Knight and Oliver conclude that the quality of the advocate–young person relationship is 'the most significant component in enabling disabled young people to participate in decision-making' (2007, p.424). Spending time in establishing rapport may mean that the advocate can be directed even where the young person is severely disabled. This would be enhanced through training in communication skills for working with people with learning disabilities.

Working as an advocate with children and young people in particular 'is about creating the space to listen and put forward the views of the young person' (Boylan and Dalrymple, 2009, p.81). It is a role that is about 'more actively fighting' the young person's corner, being independent of service providers so there is no potential conflict of interest and understanding the importance of truth and confidentiality in the developing relationship. The advocate must be aware that the child or young person may be experiencing marginalisation or oppression that makes it difficult for them to control their lives. The advocate needs to give clear and accurate information as well as support the individual to speak for themselves.

It might be helpful for you, at this point, to revisit the discussion about empowerment in Chapter 5 and to reflect on some of the parallels between the models of empowerment presented there and the forms of advocacy discussed in this chapter. We agree with the view that advocacy enables children and young people to 'come to voice' rather than the notion of 'giving voice' to them that assumes this is in the gift of adults (Boylan and Dalrymple, 2009). Where dominant groups represent oppressed, marginalised or excluded groups then this can have the effect of erasing *voice*. This reminds the adult advocate in particular that they not only work with the child or young person to enable them to speak in their own voice but for the advocate and adult audiences to learn to listen, hear and understand.

In summary the impact of advocacy in a particular setting and with a specific partner will depend on the form and model in use, and the principles followed. Effective advocacy to benefit both parties requires adequate practical skills, knowledge, time and resources. Having explored advocacy we now turn to mentoring as an alternative method for supporting engagement with individuals and communities.

What is mentoring?

> Mentor: an accomplished and experienced performer who takes a special personal interest in helping to guide and develop a junior or more inexperienced person. (Gibb, 1994, p.32)

Despite the reference to inexperience Gibb regards mentoring as 'a distinctive relationship – not just a "substitute" for what is lacking' (1994, p.32). Gibb noted a key characteristic of those mentoring young people was that they came from the world of work. Words describing what mentors do refer to actions such as 'support', 'guide' and 'facilitate' using skills of 'listening' and 'questioning' underpinned by principles of building 'trust' and 'enabling'. Parsloe and Leedham (2009) note the increasingly wider definitions of mentoring since the 1970s, when mentors were prominent in staff and management development in organisations, using words such as 'coaching', 'counselling', 'networking' and 'advising' (p.197).

Writers have observed different models of mentoring operating internationally. Clutterbuck (2004, cited in Parsloe and Leedham, 2009) views academic literature on mentoring in North America as demonstrating and emphasising the power differential between the 'senior' (mentor) and the 'subordinate' (mentee or *protégé*). The UK, Europe, Australia and New Zealand take a broader view that incorporates mutual learning and encouraging mentees to do things for themselves.

Philip (2000) has noted how mentoring can bridge boundaries between generations and describes a way of working with young people regarded as 'socially excluded'. She found that mentoring relationships contribute to young people developing a form of cultural capital to deal with challenges they face in their daily lives. She outlines the mentor role as being an older experienced guide offering support and challenge to ease a young person into adulthood (Philip, 2000). It is a relationship based on the sharing of information and advice from mentor to mentee. Crucial within the relationship is that the older guide is acceptable to the young person. Philip sees the appeal of inter-generational mentoring as reviving the idea of young people and elders finding common ground through large extended families and friendly neighbourhoods.

Historical and policy context

Philip (2000) has argued 'the effects of globalization in combination with general social, demographic and economic trends have had a powerful impact' on young people in Northern Europe. Within the UK policy changes in housing, education, employment and access to benefits have extended the transition from adolescence to adulthood as young people remain dependent on their families. As we noted in Chapter 3, there are on-going 'moral panics' (Cohen, 1972) about youth, evident for example, in responses to the disturbances in Tottenham and other cities and towns in the UK in August 2011 presenting the young people as both a threat and as being vulnerable.

In the US experience reference to 'natural mentoring' describes traditional intergenerational contacts between adults and adolescents arising from extended families, schools and neighbourhoods (Rhodes, 2001). Change and loss of those traditional sources of caring adults led to a proliferation of volunteer mentoring programmes during the 1990s. These programmes appeared in response to a perception of 'poor' family support. Rhodes estimated that five million US youth were involved in school- and community-based programmes. One example is the 'Big Brothers Big Sisters' mentoring programme.

CASE STUDY 7.3

Big Brothers Big Sisters mentoring programme

Big Brothers Big Sisters (BBBS: see www.bbbs.org) traces its historical roots in the US back over 100 years. The programme vision is that all children have the ability to achieve success and thrive in life. It promotes itself as 'the nation's largest donor and volunteer supported mentoring network'. It matches adult volunteers and children aged six to 18 in communities across the US to develop positive relationships with lasting effect on the lives of young people. The aim of BBBS is for each child in the programme to achieve higher aspirations, greater confidence, and better relationships; avoid risky behaviours; and experience educational success. It refers to a 1995 research study (Tierney et al., 1995) as evidence of that direct impact with participants measured as more confident in their schoolwork, getting on better with their families, less likely to begin using illegal drugs or alcohol, and less likely to truant from school.

Philip (2000) considers that 'UK interest in youth mentoring programmes has drawn heavily on the US experience'. In the UK mentoring schemes for young offenders and those excluded from school has seen 'an exponential growth' (Greenop, 2011, p.35). School and community-based after-school programmes are seen as offering 'safe havens from the pressure of the streets' (Rhodes, 2001) that can protect young people from negative peer pressure, promote learning and offer opportunities to develop caring relationships with non-parent adults. Benefits of mentoring programmes include providing a support network that offers access to opportunities, advice, guidance, listening and understanding to help build self-esteem and self-worth. The mentor offers support to an individual young person that may be missing elsewhere in their lives (Turner, 2012).

An example of inter-generational mentoring to work with young offenders has been piloted in the UK. Community Service Volunteers initiated a new mentoring scheme for young offenders in 2010 by recruiting volunteers to act as grandparent-style mentors or *grandmentors*.

CASE STUDY 7.4

Grandmentors

Grandmentors work in north London to support young people to find work, stay on in education or take up training. Those supporting the scheme see older volunteers as strong role models, detached from the pressures faced by the younger generation and offering an untapped resource capable of transforming young lives. They argue young people respect the life experience of older people and are more likely to trust them.

Other voices see this idea as fitting in with the aims of *Big Society* (see Chapter 2) but warn it should be regarded as an extra service and not used as a cheap alternative to state support. They also recognise that success will rest on ensuring a good match between mentor and mentee (Lepper, 2010).

The Department for Education and Employment introduced the Excellence in Cities Initiative in the UK in 1999 in order to raise standards and tackle failure in schools. Part of the plan was to achieve the aims by use of professionally trained *learning mentors* who would focus on removing barriers to pupil's individual learning both inside and outside the classroom. In particular they would provide a complementary service to teachers, pastoral staff, special needs and other services, with a particular focus on reducing truancy and school exclusion rates. Government guidance suggested those likely to benefit from a learning mentor included pupils experiencing low attainment, poor motivation, non-attendance, behavioural difficulties and poor relations with staff and other pupils. In our view this is an example of what Smith (1999) has called 'the continued trend to individualization' with 'an increasing focus upon targeting interventions at named individuals rather than working to enhance the readiness and capacity of groups and communities to better meet their members' needs'.

It is apparent in searching the literature for titles on mentoring that the term is not straightforward and unproblematic. Reference to the 'art of mentoring' (Allen, 2004) suggests it is more than just about technical skills. Titles of publications indicate those who receive mentoring include 'disaffected' young people, 'young people leaving care', 'students', 'social workers' or 'nurses'. They also highlight where mentoring happens, for example, in schools or communities (*community mentoring*), and who delivers it, such as learning mentors or peers. The description of the mentoring holds clues about its purpose and process, for example *inter-generational, dialogic, structured, power* and *motivational mentoring* or *social mentoring* and *befriending*. An exploration of the different forms of mentoring, underpinning principles and then the practice of mentoring will develop our understanding of the term.

Forms of mentoring

There are three broad categories of mentoring programmes for young people: one-to-one adult mentoring, one-to-one peer mentoring and youth mentoring groups. Philip and Hendry (2000) have produced a typology of mentoring in relation to working with young people that recognises other forms with distinct characteristics within those broad categories.

- *Classic mentoring* is 'a one-to-one relationship between an adult and a young person where the older, experienced mentor provides support, advice and challenge'. The adult is a role model offering support through a shared interest or hobby.
- *Individual-team mentoring* is where 'a group looks to an individual or small number of individuals for support, advice and challenge.' This form is found, for example, in youth work settings where the mentor has respect for and understanding of the peer group and is recognised as having previous relevant experience
- *Friend-to-friend mentoring* is 'a "safety net" especially for some young people who may be mistrustful of adults'. This can be seen as 'a testing ground for disclosure' where the young person may rehearse revealing information, values and beliefs in a safe environment prior to further action.
- *Peer group mentoring* is 'where an ordinary friendship group takes on a mentoring role at a specific time'. The peer group is both arbiter and a resource to determine appropriate strategies in certain situations or on common issues such as relationships.
- *Long-term relationship mentoring* is similar to *classic mentoring* but with 'risk-taking' adults where the mentor may have 'a history of rebellion and of challenging authority' (Philip and Hendry, 2000, pp.216–217).

Looking beyond mentoring with young people there is community mentoring that 'happens between individuals who are based in different organisations' (Skinner, 1997, p.26). Skinner distinguishes between two forms according to whether the mentor comes from the business sector or from well-established voluntary or community organisations. Community mentoring can have a variety of aims such as: increasing the skills and confidence of individuals; sharing of knowledge, skills and experience; improving effectiveness of organisations; or facilitating networking links. The community mentor 'acts as a friend, expert adviser or counsellor to individuals in a wide range of situations where the individual may be disadvantaged'. (Parsloe and Leedham, 2009, p.27)

According to Parsloe and Leedham (2009) four distinct forms of community mentoring are shown to be emerging within the UK:

- Befriending – 'to describe the role of volunteers who provide informal social support.'
- Employment mentoring – in schools by volunteers from local businesses 'to increase the pupils' appreciation of what companies expect of future employees.
- Positive action – 'to offer positive role models' to people from oppressed and minority groups 'where the mentor is expected to make influential introductions, open doors and remove organizational barriers'.
- Social inclusion – where 'engagement mentoring targets those people considered to be disaffected with society or who are socially excluded'. (Parsloe and Leedham, 2009, pp.46–48)

Elements of these four forms are apparent in the example of the 100 Black Men mentoring organisation (see Case Study 7.5). The concept of 100 Black Men comes from the US where a group of African-American men met in New York in 1963 to explore ways of improving conditions in their community that included a focus on youth development. The organisation today consists of 116 chapters of over 10,000 members. The first international chapter was established in the UK in 1997. 100 Black Men of London was formed in 2001 as 'a charity dedicated to the education, development and uplifting of our youth and the wider community' (see: www.100bmol.org.uk/about-us.html).

CASE STUDY 7.5

100 Black Men of London

We have a saying: 'What they see is what they will be'. We understand that young people are most influenced by the images that they see most often and are more likely to aspire to become the kind of role models that are most presented to them.

Our flagship mentoring programme is delivered under the trademark 'Mentoring the 100 Way Across a Lifetime'. It is our aim to support and help develop young people in our charge from their youth into adulthood and then to continue to act as their mentor throughout their lives.

The 100 Black Men of London believes that through the process of mentoring, we can help endow our youth with the life skills they will need to become positive contributors to society and develop into the leaders of tomorrow.

We have developed a unique method of mentoring, known as 'Mentoring the 100 Way Across a Lifetime' which has been carefully designed to address the most pressing issues relevant to young boys and girls living in London in a group mentoring setting.

We offer a 'Group Mentoring' programme, which means that our mentoring is primarily delivered in weekly or bi-weekly sessions with a number of men and women mentoring a group of young mentees.

> We call all mentees, who join our programme our 'Diamonds'. This is because we recognise that every single child has a light and sparkle inside of them and it is our job to uncover that light and help it to shine. We will always be there on time for every single session, no matter what, whether our Diamonds turn up or not. We have a passionate commitment to what we do that will not waiver.
> Extracts taken from 100 Black Men of London, n.d.

The forms of mentoring introduced mostly present individualistic models of mentoring where information and advice is passed from the mentor to a relatively passive mentee. Such constructions of mentoring emphasise fitting the mentee into existing structures and ignore deeper structural issues of inequalities or 'historical, environmental and cultural problems' (Greenop, 2011, p.51). References to supporting young people through transitions to adulthood and 'challenge' (Philip, 2000) as examples of some types of mentoring are far more likely to be about getting the mentee to engage with school or the world of work. Mentoring does not appear to offer opportunities, in the same way as advocacy, to challenge existing structures that could impact on the mentee's life chances in education and employment. Failure to address structural issues can mean mentors and programmes set unrealistic goals and create false hopes.

Impact of mentoring

Mentoring on the basis of the mentee lacking something, for example, a role model, two parents, friends, employment, or skills and knowledge, constructs the mentee as 'in deficit' and reinforces the notion of them as a passive recipient of a mentor's wisdom and experience. For Rhodes (2001) 'mentoring programs are not a substitute for a caring family, community support, or a concerted youth policy agenda' to redress that deficit.

The individualistic nature of much mentoring carried out in private spaces makes it difficult to judge and evaluate 'good' mentoring. We may make a judgement by acknowledging principles followed within the mentoring process such as: developing trust and mutual respect; supporting, challenging and empowering the mentee; not using an authoritarian approach; long-term commitment; and both sides gaining benefits from the process. In any of these criteria there is the recurring problem of how you measure or observe elements such as trust, mutual respect or benefits of the process. The most thorough review of research evidence in the US published in 1997 by the National Institute of Justice 'found that community-based mentoring programmes could, at best, be described as only "promising"' (Shiner et al., 2004, p.1). A meta-analysis reviewing 55 evaluations of the effects of youth mentoring programmes found evidence of 'only a modest or small benefit of program participation for the average youth' (DuBois et al., 2002, p.157). An example of evaluating a mentoring programme in the UK is presented in Case Study 7.6.

Mentoring Plus

Mentoring Plus refers to a series of projects established in the UK in the late 1990s by Crime Concern, an independent national charity. The projects aimed to reduce youth crime and help young people labelled as being 'at-risk' back into education, training and employment. Mentoring Plus included a focus on black and minority ethnic communities. Programmes recruited 15- to 19-year-olds who were interviewed and selected, usually following referral from statutory and community agencies. Programmes ran for 10 to 12 months and consisted of an education and training programme alongside one-to-one mentoring and residential courses to build trust between young people and mentors.

Shiner et al. (2004) carried out an evaluation study between 2000 and 2003 using quantitative and qualitative methods. They gathered the experiences of young people, staff and volunteer mentors in order to assess both the process by which the programme was implemented and the outcomes achieved. The research concluded that 'positive interventions can be made that help to bring about fairly substantial changes in the lives of even the most disaffected young people' (p.71). The programme 'recruited and engaged actively with a large number of young people who were at considerable risk of social exclusion' and 'was also reasonably successful in encouraging these young people to (re)engage with education and work' (p.71).

The researchers note that Mentoring Plus presents a specific model of one-to-one mentoring alongside a programme of education and training that made it difficult to see if one part was more successful than the other. They conclude that 'on balance' it was 'likely that the two main components of the programme tended to reinforce one another' while acknowledging the possibility that mentoring on its own 'does not provide an effective way of working with disaffected young people' (p72).

The researchers in the example described in Case Study 7.6 acknowledge that studying a mentoring programme around youth crime and offending can present a partial focus on a negative aspect of young people's behaviour. The sample was based on referrals and selection by professionals who decided on the suitability of individuals for the programme rather than a random selection of young offenders. While some measures of impact may be relatively easy to quantify, such as reoffending rates, problems in applying other criteria of success are evident, for example in measuring *engagement*. Projects themselves provided information by classifying the level of a young person's engagement as 'not engaged', 'minimally engaged', 'moderately engaged' or 'highly engaged'. This self-reporting using criteria open to different interpretations would affect the overall validity and reliability of responses. In conclusion the researchers question whether any changes in behaviour were due to Mentoring Plus or other influences. The study notes that while levels of offending fell 'fairly substantially among the young people who participated in Mentoring Plus, similar, and in some cases more marked, reductions were evident among non-participants' (Shiner et al., 2004, p.70).

Evidence remains 'mixed and inconclusive' on the effectiveness of mentoring with excluded young people (Greenop, 2011). In evaluating what worked well in a mentoring project in a Welsh town Greenop applied attachment theory. John Bowlby developed this theory arguing that the earliest bonds formed between a child and their caregiver has an impact that continues into adulthood. So, 'young people who have experienced care givers as unreliable therefore often find it difficult to trust others, particularly authority figures, in times of distress' (Greenop, 2011, p.42). This recognition stresses the need for the mentor to build trust and to be reliable. It requires careful selection and training of mentors who can offer time and long-term commitment alongside other personal qualities. Greenop's evaluation concludes mentoring is 'a hybrid relationship providing "professional friendship"' (2011, p.51). This resonates with the work of Keller and Pryce (2010) who argued that

> the relationship reported most rewarding by participants and judged most successful by researchers were those in which the mentor balanced youth-oriented efforts to build an engaging and enjoyable relationship with adult-oriented efforts to promote development-promoting structure (p.45).

ACTIVITY 7.3

Evaluating mentoring

A problem in evaluating any type of mentoring is how to measure benefits to both parties as mentor and mentee work together through a transition from, for example, exclusion to inclusion, offending to non-offending, or education to work. How would you measure the impact of having a mentor? Think about measuring the contributions and outcomes of the mentoring as well as the costs. Gibb (1994, p.34) suggests 'mentoring outcomes can be expected to manifest themselves as changes in skills, knowledge and attitudes'. You may find this a useful starting point.

In reflecting on this activity you might follow Gibb's suggestion and use interviews and questionnaires to collect data about the mentor and mentee's skills, knowledge and attitudes at the beginning of the relationship and then at intervals until the end of the programme to identify changes.

Choosing advocacy or mentoring

Advocacy and mentoring have been presented as methods that support engagement and participation. Practitioners need to decide which method and form or model to use in particular settings and situations. Advocacy would be used where the engagement involves listening, supporting, consulting and active dialogue to get something stopped, started, changed or someone heard. If the purpose of the engagement is to develop confidence, to value and draw on experience or to inspire, motivate and encourage then mentoring could be the starting point. The practitioner may shift from one method to the other and back depending on the nature of the support required at the time. On occasions the roles may be interchangeable, for example, either an advocate or mentor could help people make informed choices or advise, assist and support them.

ACTIVITY 7.4

Understanding the differences between advocacy and mentoring
Look back through the case studies in this chapter and note key differences between these two methods of engagement. Revisit Activity 7.2 and consider whether mentoring might be used in any of the examples listed. If not, why not? If so, what form of mentoring might be appropriate?

The case studies show advocacy can be carried out by an individual or organisation on their own behalf and does not require a partner (self-advocacy). Advocacy is evident in social movements where groups and communities use it to assert their rights and challenge structures of power and decision-making (collective advocacy). Advocacy is often issue-based and useful in the short-term (legal and professional advocacy). Mentoring programmes have expanded in response to a deficit model perspective that regards an individual as lacking something or someone. The mentor becomes a substitute for a parent, grandparent or friend. The mentor may be regarded as a role model who seeks to develop a long-term positive relationship with their mentee (classic mentoring). Mentoring is more individually focused with a two-way exchange of knowledge, skills and attitudes between mentor and mentee. Activity 7.2 offers some examples where mentoring might work alongside advocacy, for example, with the group of young people facing the introduction of a night curfew or the young man with learning disabilities seeking to live independently.

In this chapter we have shown the potential of advocacy as a useful method for 'enabling those who have previously been ignored or silenced to come to voice' as well as providing 'a possible force for change and the promotion of social justice' (Boylan and Dalrymple, 2009, p.90). Advocates may campaign on wider issues and collaborate with other professionals. We see potential for advocacy to be carried out by and for communities through coming together in collaboration. Communities of interest such as My Life My Choice (Case Study 7.1) advocate for themselves to regain or retain control in order to shape services and to challenge the professional power of organisations and practices.

We introduced the meaning of advocacy as being in general about: empowerment by ensuring rights are respected; information and support provided to make choices; and views and wishes are heard and properly represented to decision makers. How effectively these aspects are addressed may be considered by an advocate asking some key questions.

- What rights does the individual, group or community have to services and to participate in decision making?
- Is information provided properly researched and correct?

- Where, when and how do you listen to and hear the service user or community voice?
- How do you ensure all voices are heard or represented within a community? Who is left out, excluded, marginalised or forgotten?

Mentoring is similar to advocacy insofar as it has the potential to be a mutually empowering two-way process depending on the type of mentoring used. The evaluation of Mentoring Plus (Shiner et al., 2004) suggests that mentoring is more successful when offered alongside an educational or training programme. References to 'modest' and 'small benefits' or 'positive effects' of mentoring acknowledge these advantages increase over time (Greenop, 2011). Further, they 'are enhanced significantly ... when greater numbers of both theory-based and empirically-based "best practices" are utilised and when strong relationships are formed between mentors and youth' (DuBois et al., 2002, p.157).

Theory is important in helping us to understand what makes good or successful mentoring. A key problem is that 'work with young people is under theorised' and there is 'an absence of any explicit model of change' (Shiner et al., 2004, p.72). There is a need for better understanding of both individual change and 'the impact of the personal attributes of mentors and mentees in the process of change' (p.73). This suggests a useful line for future research that could help in the matching of mentor to mentee while noting two points made by Gibb (1994) that remain relevant. First, the myth that mentors are 'all-wise and wonderfully patient individuals' (1994, p.38) and second, in the context of public spending cuts and emphasis on policy drives for volunteers 'mentoring should not be seen as a low-cost option for avoiding commitment to the use of specialists' (1994, p.36).

Chapter summary

In this chapter we have presented advocacy and mentoring as two key methods used in supporting engagement with service users and communities. We described the historical and policy contexts behind these methods and explored a range of meanings and forms of advocacy and mentoring in different settings illustrated with examples. A number of research studies were referenced to outline the impact of the methods. Case studies helped to demonstrate how current ideas about advocacy and mentoring are being applied in practice. Reflective activities offered opportunities to think about some of the challenges of advocacy and mentoring in order to work out ideas for good practice.

In Chapter 8 we continue considering practical methods and approaches for working with communities and service users and explore an approach known as informal education. We will explore the theory and practice of social pedagogy and offer insight into debates in relation to the use of conversation and dialogue that build on some of the themes and frameworks covered in this chapter.

USEFUL RESOURCES

Advocacy Charter defines and promotes key advocacy principles:
www.actionforadvocacy.org.uk

Advocacy Resource Exchange is a UK national organisation supporting the provision of independent advocacy. The site offers definitions, principles and models of advocacy: **www.advocacyresource.org.uk/Advocacy-Introduction**

Community Service Volunteers (CSV) website gives details of the Grandmentors project: **www.csv-rsvp.org.uk/site/grandmentors.htm**

Foundation for People with Learning Disabilities influences policies and raises awareness of learning disability issues. Its website has many useful resources including a link to a publication on citizen advocacy: **www.learningdisabilities.org.uk/publications/ citizen-advocacy-people-severe-ld/**

Mentoring and Befriending Foundation website has useful links and guidance on mentoring: **www.mandbf.org/**

My Life My Choice is a self-advocacy organisation run by and for people with learning difficulties in England: **http://mylifemychoice.org.uk/**

National Youth Advocacy Service provides advice, advocacy and legal services for young people: **www.nyas.net/**

Older People's Advocacy Alliance is a national UK organisation that supports, promotes and develops provision of independent advocacy services for older people: **www.opaal.org.uk/**

People First is run by and for people with learning difficulties to raise awareness, campaign for rights and support self-advocacy groups in the UK: **www.peoplefirstltd. com/**

TimeBank is a UK national volunteering charity. It designs and runs mentoring programmes, and supports individuals, corporations or small businesses to find rewarding volunteering: **http://timebank.org.uk/**

FURTHER READING

Allen. T.D. and Eby, L.T. (eds) (2007) *The Blackwell Handbook of Mentoring: A Multiple Perspectives Approach* (Chichester: Wiley-Blackwell).
This book presents a multi-disciplinary approach to theory and practice of mentoring across fields including social work, education, sociology and psychology.

Clayden, J. and Stein, M. (2005) *Mentoring Young People Leaving Care: 'Someone for Me'* (York: Joseph Rowntree Foundation).
This report explores long-term mentoring for young people leaving care by describing their experiences of mentoring relationships and the outcomes.

Colley, H. (2003) *Mentoring for Social Inclusion* (Abingdon: Routledge).
This book offers detailed case studies with accounts of mentoring through the voices of participants.

CHAPTER 8

Learning through Conversations

CHAPTER OBJECTIVES

By the end of this chapter you should have an understanding of:

- approaches to working with service users through informal education;
- the theory and practice of social pedagogy;
- an insight into debates in relation to conversation and dialogue;
- useful resources to improve knowledge and practice.

Introduction

One way to engage with communities and service users is through a process known as informal education. Many of the case studies, throughout this book, have drawn on this approach to achieve their aims. We have frequently found, however, that practitioners can find it difficult to articulate the intention and the outcome of their interventions when working informally within communities and alongside service users. The view has often been expressed by practitioners with whom we have worked that they can feel (and be seen as) 'just talking' with people and that it is difficult to explain or critically analyse what it is that they are doing and achieving. The aim of this chapter, therefore, is to provide a theoretical framework for analysing this approach.

In this chapter we build on some of the theoretical frameworks already covered in this book. In particular, the discussion will build on the concepts and values explored in Chapter 5. Van der Veen (2003, p.581) has described community development as a form of 'citizen education' and that as such it has three forms: 'education as training; education as consciousness raising; and education as service delivery'. According to Van der Veen, the practice of consciousness raising can be something that takes place in a course or discussion group. This approach to community development starts with learning and the goal 'is an active act'. Informal education is an approach that is embodied by this framework. In this chapter we will analyse approaches to working with service users and communities through this process of informal education, within which conversation, dialogue and relationships are central themes.

Informal education

One way of thinking about educational practice is within a framework of formal, non-formal and informal education (see Table 8.1). Formal education can be characterised as an approach to learning within which the learners have very little control over the content, timing or setting of the intervention. This is the sort of education with which most of us are familiar from our days at school, college or university. It tends to take place in an institutional setting, has a structured curriculum and a timetable that can mean that if the learner is not emotionally, intellectually or physically ready or present to learn that particular topic at that particular time, there is little opportunity to 'catch up'. This approach to education is usually typified as the 'empty vessel' (Freire, 1972) approach whereby the learner is assumed to not know the things that the 'expert' or educator does know and the role of the educator is to impart their knowledge to the learners. Many learners are capable of engaging with most aspects of this approach, most of the time. However, it is well recognised that a large number of people are not engaged and thereby miss out on many further economic, social or educational opportunities.

Engagement in formal education tends to be measured through attendance and the attainment of results. Increasingly, around the world, governments have concerns about both attendance in and achievement from formal education. At the same time there are a large number of young people who, while attending education, and achieving sufficiently so as not to raise concerns, are in fact not reaching their true potential because they have not been effectively engaged in the learning process. Many adults who return to education, whether formal or informal, commonly express the view that they did not perform as well as they could have done when they were at school for a range of reasons including boredom, not really understanding adequately, being bullied and not liking the teacher.

Watts (2001, p.163) has noted that some 'traditional' educational approaches to working with young people have 'paid little if any attention to their informal economies and that if practitioners or educators' were to be able to form 'meaningful relationships' with young people who had dropped out of the formal system or were at risk of doing so, they would need to understand – and be prepared to work to some extent within – the subjective frame of reference of these young people. Such an approach would involve working with young people to explore how and where they may flourish and to encourage them to develop their own strategies for growth.

Non-formal education recognises that learning at school or other formal settings is not necessarily a positive experience for everyone. Non-formal approaches attempt to remove the barriers to engaging with learning such as environment, pace, timing and controlled content. Typically, non-formal education will take place in local community venues where people feel more comfortable and the learners tend to have more control over the curriculum or content and with the pace at which they are expected to learn. In recent years, a tension has been introduced into the context of non-formal learning as funding structures have required an increasing focus on accreditable outcomes.

Table 8.1   Formal, non-formal and informal education

Education	Location	Content	Outcomes
Formal	Formal institutions such as schools	Predetermined by educator	Accreditation; achievement against set targets
Non-formal	Community education settings; libraries; colleges	Semi-predetermined but flexibly paced to meet needs of learners	Increasingly accreditation; achievement of personal goals
Informal	Anywhere	Emergent depending on needs of learners/ community; unpredictable.	Personal growth; engagement with learning; positive relationships

This tension has often been experienced as the moving of a formal education approach into community venues and has been resisted by many practitioners and development workers who view their practice from a more 'informal' standpoint: 'Community groups tend not to think of people as "students" or their provision as "classes"' (Oliver, 1994, p.5).

Informal educators stress the importance of maintaining informal and unstructured routes back into education that aim at increasing confidence and raising aspirations. Informal education frequently takes place within non-formal community settings. It is also an approach often associated with building on the 'here and now': working with the concerns, preoccupations, activity or interests of individuals or groups 'in the moment', rather than expecting the learner to engage with the preoccupation or interests of the educator. In this sense, the approach is learner centred and serendipitous. As Batsleer (2008, p.5) has argued informal educators start 'where people are, with their own preoccupations and in their own places' and that learning occurs because it is of 'immediate significance ... rather than derived from a pre-established curriculum'. Informal education, therefore, does not have preconceived ideas concerning outcome, rather it is unpredictable and is used as a methodology for building relationships that value respect and reciprocity. Brewer (1993, p.165) has defined this approach as being 'about people learning together to improve the quality of their lives as individuals and for the communities in which they live and work' and Coats (1994, p.3) as being 'about the growth of the individual as well as developing the spirit of the community'.

ACTIVITY 8.1

Reflecting on your learning experiences
Reflect on your life and your educational and learning experiences.
Can you think of examples where you have engaged in formal, non-formal and informal learning?

Where were you when each of these took place?

Who else was there?

What use have you made of the learning from each of those examples?

Conversation and dialogue

Jeffs and Smith (2005) argue that 'conversation' is a central methodology to the informal education approach. For Smith (2005) the skill of informal education is to 'catch the moment' in conversations with people in order to 'deepen their thinking or to put themselves in touch with their feelings' with the aim of 'exploring or enlarging' their experience. Importantly, the concept of conversation embodies the principle of 'dialogue', which is contrasted with the major form of speech or instruction in formal schooling: that of monologue. Part of the role of the informal educator is to keep the conditions for conversation alive. Ledwith and Springett (2010) offer a helpful explanation of the difference between conversation and dialogue.

> Dialogue is more than conversation; it is at its best an interactive process of learning together whereby mutual value is enhanced through the process of meaning making. It is a relational exchange process that allows interplay in trusting and respectful ways, to explore new understandings through the language of feelings, ideas, facts, dissent, opinions and plans. (Ledwith and Springett, 2010, p.128)

It is through dialogue that individuals and groups of people may be enabled to 'discover what is within their grasp and what is outside their power' (Batsleer, 2008, p.9). Central to a theoretical understanding of this approach as a method of engagement are the ideas and contribution of the Brazilian educationalist, Paulo Freire. Freire's work was mostly devoted to raising awareness about oppression and empowerment. His contribution to and influence on informal pedagogy has been most profound. According to Freire there is a symbiotic relationship between the oppressed and the oppressor, with each dependent on the other. The emphasis is on enabling the oppressed to act to change their own and their oppressor's situation (Cotterell and Morris, 2012, p.60). To Freire the concepts of dialogue and reciprocity are key to effective learning. Education, to his way of thinking, should involve mutual respect and be carried out in dialogue *with* people and not *on* or *to* them. His work has been very influential in developing a theorised approach to informal education. This approach is about 'listening to the narratives of people ... paying respectful attention to the story being told and taking it seriously' (Ledwith and Springett, 2010, p.135).

ACTIVITY 8.2

Informal education and social capital

Revisit the discussion about social capital in Chapter 3. In what ways do you think that the Freirian approach to informal education, outlined above, might assist with the development of *bridging* and *linking* social capital?

Informal education from a Freirian perspective is about teaching people to question the issues affecting their lives. It is about working to uncover the many truths and many ways of experiencing and making sense of the world. The process of questioning helps to develop a critical awareness of the root sources of social issues. In creating the conditions for dialogue we are aiming to create the structures and conditions for collective learning. Freire advocated the importance of taking aspects of everyday life experience as the focus of dialogue and reflection. Dialogue, he argued, should be about respectful communication and deliberation and should be about listening as much as talking. It is through dialogue that educated and educator work together, equally, on 'their knowledge raising journey' (Cotterell and Morris, 2012, p.60). This has led Batsleer (2008, p.5) to conclude that 'learning through conversation and through dialogue is the most important method of informal learning' and that the concept of 'conversation' is important for conveying 'a sense of the mutual learning'. In this sense 'conversation' is something more than that which may take place between friends over a dinner table. Batsleer (2008, p.7) describes conversation as a methodology within informal education as 'an art' that enables the development of knowledge and understanding: 'Conversation is a vehicle of enquiry, which opens up new ideas and new ways of understanding the world' (Batsleer, 2008, p.7).

The skill of the facilitator, educator or animator is to 'get the discussion to go as deeply as possible, from surface reaction towards the root causes of the issue, simply by asking questions' (Ledwith and Springett, 2010, p.18). To this end, as Jeffs and Smith (2005, p.31) suggest, informal educators may at times need to 'teach some of the protocols that underpin the art of conversation ... sensitively devising opportunities for individuals to learn how to listen and participate in dialogue and conversation'.

Informal educators also aim to engage people in a range of activities and as Robertson (2005, p.18) has argued aim to 'foster environments for learning' or as Packham (2008, p.73) suggests 'create spaces for critical dialogue and debate'. In whatever situation or environment informal educators work, they seek to build a relationship of trust, to understand and respect the context of that person's experience, and to engage that person in a conversation that helps them to both deepen their understandings and to act on them. The informal approaches discussed in this chapter draw on this notion of 'everyday activities' as the medium through which to build relationships and develop dialogue and understanding. You will probably observe the many similarities in the approaches discussed in this chapter with the *bottom-up* community development approach explored in Chapter 5. These methods of working with individuals and communities are all informed by a Freirian theoretical framework that seeks to explore with people their current and 'real life' preoccupations, concerns and everyday narratives.

Informal education and voluntary participation
You might at this point wish to reread Chapters 1 and 3 where the conceptual frameworks of voluntary participation and association were discussed.

Why do you think informal education stresses the importance of voluntary participation?
In your opinion, or in your experience, how does this affect the type and quality of the learning that takes place?

You will recall from your reading of Chapter 3 that Brodie et al.'s (2011) research focusing on the factors that can help support participation in community activity highlighted the importance of participation being voluntary. Participation, they argued, can be encouraged, supported and made more attractive, but it should inherently be about a free choice. A report (Ofsted, 2011) investigating the most effective programmes for engaging young people concluded that the most effective settings did not just see volunteering and community activity simply as an 'add on' to mainstream learning but found creative ways to enable young people to take greater levels of responsibility for what they learned.

As we have noted in our discussions about the rhetoric of 'participation' and 'empowerment' in previous chapters, opening spaces for dialogue and inviting people in is by no means sufficient to ensure their active engagement. As Cornwall (2008, p.275) has noted, much will depend on the processes that help to build capacity, nurture voice and enable people to empower themselves. The ability, capacity and willingness of people to engage in dialogue in spaces that are created through invitation are often in stark contrast to those that people create for themselves and it is for this reason that informal education approaches are more effective when employed in places where people feel comfortable. Spaces that people create for themselves tend to consist of people who come together because they have something in common and 'these kinds of spaces can be essential ... as sites in which they gain confidence and skills, develop their arguments and gain solidarity and support' (Cornwall, 2008, p.275).

Social pedagogy

Social pedagogy draws on similar origins, values and approaches to informal education but has its historical roots in Germany and other Western European countries. Like informal education, social pedagogy draws on the ideas developed by Paulo Freire (1972) that individual and community learning and development should be about liberation from oppression and marginalisation and about the sense of empowerment, or coming into a sense of one's own power, as discussed in Chapter 5. Social pedagogy is an approach to care and education that takes a socially embedded or holistic approach. That is, it is an approach to care and education that does not see them as separate. Well-being is a central aspect of this approach as is an emphasis on group work. It draws on the reflective and communicative abilities of the practitioner and aims to ease social difficulties by providing people with the means to manage their own lives.

Mathiesen (1999) defined a social pedagogy approach as one that identifies the ways in which values, psychological, social and material resources may further or hinder a person's personality development or growth. Cameron et al. (2011, p.13) concluded that social pedagogy is 'both person centred and socio-political: it provides opportunities for personal development towards inde-pendence, but also has a socialising function in reinforcing social solidarity and interdependence'. Eriksson (2011, p.407) refers to Natorp (1904) as 'the father of social pedagogy' and argues that the key principle in his teachings was that learning and development should not separate the individual from their community: the individual and the community are each other's prerequisites and people learn through interacting within a social environment.

Social pedagogy, therefore, typically involves sharing the same 'social life spaces' with those with whom we work (Stephens, 2009) and places a high value on associative life (Petrie et al., 2006). People learn in interaction with others and in the interchange of perceptions about the world. 'Liberation' (Payne, 2005, p.215) comes through engagement in conversation and dialogue with others in the group or community. Learning is seen in terms of dialogue and the practitioner (or the pedagogue) is seen as being on a journey with the service user, learning together. Petrie et al. (2006) conclude that a social peda-gogue should be able to use their heart, head and hands in a delicate balance involving caring, rational decision making and creative and practical activities. Social pedagogues therefore place a strong focus on engaging in practical activities with those with whom they work. In common with informal educa-tors, social pedagogues try to move away from feelings of 'us' and 'them' and aim to work in dialogue with community members and other colleagues 'believing that different perspectives make for richness and creativity' (Cameron, et al., 2011, p.15).

ACTIVITY 8.4

Learning activities
Refer back to your answers to Activity 8.1.

In the three examples of learning that you identified, what were the differences in the nature of the activities that you engaged in?
In which of the activities was your learning influenced by the other people around you?

Common third

Social pedagogues refer to the useful concept of the *common third*, that is, using a third element to build relationships and foster learning. This approach involves practitioner and community member or learner using an activity to create a commonly shared situation around which they can develop their rela-tionship and build new skills. For example, they might choose to work on a project about which neither of them have any prior knowledge, such as putting up shelves, planting a garden, repairing a bike or making soft toys. Together they would find out what they need to do and which resources they might need. In learning together it could be that the community member or learner would understand sooner than the practitioner and then they would lead the practitioner in the task. This process enables them to explore new dimensions of their relationship, giving them the chance to get to know each other and each other's needs better.

This approach aims to put learner and educator on an equal footing and encourages independence and empowerment. Sharing an activity and having something in common implies being equal; on equal terms, with equal rights and dignity. The challenge is in finding an activity in which the social peda-gogue and the community member/learner are both genuinely interested and this requires a person-centred and participatory approach at each stage. In order to be successful the service user or learner has to be involved on equal terms in all phases of the project.

Smith (2012, p.1) has discussed a phenomenon, common in her own prac-tice, where she noticed that children and young people with whom she works often 'feel safe enough to reveal intimate details about themselves' when trav-elling in her car. She suggests that this 'magical space within a tin box' is created because 'you are not staring at them'. Instead, with your focus on other activities, such as driving, the weather, getting somewhere on time, the young person feels more at ease, they feel more able to reveal personal infor-mation 'because the attention is not on them'. Furthermore, Smith observes, the car often provides an opportunity for the young person to connect to the personal life of the worker because there are frequently personal artefacts, such as your choice of music, evidence of family members or pets that 'draws them nearer to us'. In a process similar to that created by a common third activity, the car provides a distraction and a glimpse into your private space that significantly enhances their trust and feelings of safety.

ACTIVITY 8.5

Revisiting Swindon Family LIFE Programme

At this point you might find it interesting to revisit Case Study 3.1 – the Swindon Family LIFE project.

What examples of a social pedagogic approach can you identify in that case study?

What examples were given of using a *common third* to engage the community members?

What were the outcomes for the community members as a result of engaging in that approach?

What do you think might be some of the boundary dilemmas for the practitioners in working in that way?

The Family LIFE project uses an approach based on co-building of capabilities in which families and workers work together to release innovation and resource in the family. The practitioners and families work together on practical tasks such as gardening, decorating, cooking and budgeting. There is no key worker in the team, and practitioners are expected to develop their own skills alongside the families. This approach is very similar to a social pedagogic approach and gives the families and the workers an opportunity to really get to know each other in an informal setting, creating the basis for a purposeful relationship. Outcomes included: sufferers of mental health issues engaging in social activities and work opportunities on which they had previously given up; parents developing skills in how to support themselves and their children emotionally; children choosing to return to school after long periods of exclusion; and adults seeking employment and/or training after long periods of unemployment.

Taylor (2008, p.363) refers to this approach as 'emancipatory education' and to the people involved as 'co-learners' concluding that 'transformative learning occurs when we see our old ways of understanding are not working well for us' (p.364). The challenge for practitioners, he argues, is to 'learn how to facilitate and support transformative learning and consciousness in others and within ourselves'. According to McGonigal (2005) 'the transformative educator' needs to learn how to 'strike a careful balance between support and challenge' and that often this will involve encouraging and supporting critical self-reflection by the learner or learners. This might involve the educator or facilitator in acting as a 'visionary, a motivator, and a catalyst: enabling people to discover what it is they want to explore and to help them decide what they might need for that exploration' (Packham 2008, p.73). These ideas are illustrated further in the next case study in which Burgess (1998, p.145) describes a project with young Bosnian survivors of torture and trauma who fled to and settled in Perth, Australia.

CASE STUDY 8.1

Saplings in the forest

Burgess (1998, p.145) describes a project with young Bosnian survivors of torture and trauma who settled in Perth, Australia. The young traumatised men did not dare speak of their experience, believing they had to be 'as tough as their fathers' and as a consequence some resorted to heavy drinking 'to block out their memories'.

In order to begin to engage these young men in conversation the project workers organised a barbeque 'solely for the youth' where they would not feel silenced by having to keep up a front in the presence of their parents. Through informal conversation at the barbeque the young people not only outlined some of their issues, but developed ideas for solutions that included 'time out from their parents and the heavy atmosphere at home; the chance to be young again because they felt cheated out of their youth; to do some fun activities; and learn about the Australian culture and meet some Australian people'. The group came up with two activities that would meet most of their immediate needs: soccer matches and a retreat.

They arranged to spend four days in a country town, away from their families. The young people owned the project from the start, including deciding all the activities. Burgess writes about how inspiring it was to watch the young people grow together over the few days and mix socially with the local community.

Watching the members of the Rotary club dancing Bosnian dance and singing romantic Bosnian ballads will be remembered by all who participated, as well as the sharing of tongue-twisters and jokes. This is what community work is all about: gaining a sense of shared understanding and a sense of belonging (p.148).

The young people said that they had had fun 'for the first time in years', and began to talk for the first time about their futures. They continued to meet up after the retreat and support each other. This was not 'just a camping trip' but part of a process of re-engagement for the young people.

You can read the full article about this intervention in Burgess (1998).

ACTIVITY 8.6

Reflecting on this case study

The workers in this case used a holistic and empowering approach to help the young people determine for themselves what they needed to be able to feel they could move on and begin to build a new community for themselves.

In what ways does this case study illustrate the approaches of informal education and social pedagogy discussed in this chapter?
What examples of the use of a *common third* can you identify?
How did the workers use *conversation* to engage the young men?
How did they use this methodology to *knit* (Wilkinson, 2012) the young people into a new community?
What type of social capital would you say this illustrates?

The *common third* in this example could be the use of the camping retreat or the use of the folk dancing activities. Batsleer (2008, p.131) devotes a whole chapter to the importance of 'silence, spirit and solidarity' in informing the resources we might use for informal education practice. She suggests that young people 'who have experienced acute trauma or loss' can find what she refers to as 'peak experiences' very helpful in 'giving access to a counter-experience of joy'. The tradition of what she calls 'outdoor education' has, in her analysis, the capacity to encourage discovery, exploration, conversation and sharing and can lead to a renewed spirit of joy and solidarity.

Animation

While Packham (2008, p.73) argues that conversations can be 'constructed', it is generally agreed that for informal education to be successful, conversation cannot be required or coerced. It must be freely entered into when 'people are interested and involved in a topic' (Batsleer, 2008, p.7). However, the role of informal educator frequently involves the creation of 'an activating event' (Taylor, 2008, p.363) that provides an opportunity to foster a learning environment within which to engage in an exploration of particular issues through purposeful conversation and enable informal learning to take place. We might seek to do this through sport, arts events and activities, theatre, excursions or similar activities, such as the camping trip and barbeque discussed in Case Study 8.1. Such approaches enhance conversations and can help to promote mutual respect and open-mindedness. However, as Petrie (2011, p.80) reminds us 'the spirit in which creative activities are approached' should always be that of 'joint exploration and dialogue'.

In France and Italy, informal educators are known as *animateurs*. This approach to informal education draws on play and imagination and other arts-based approaches such as theatre, dance, music and the visual arts. Smith (2005, p.7) has described this approach to working with communities as 'using theatre and play as a means of self expression'. Practitioners who use this approach aim to 'breathe life into situations' and help to build environments and relationships where people can grow and participate. Such approaches can be a valuable method of enabling conversation as they introduce that *common third*, an addition to a relationship that makes the interaction, disclosure or engagement feel less threatening or difficult. The practice of using *animateurs* as informal educators has transferred to the UK in the areas of theatre, dance, music and the visual arts, as for example in designated roles within orchestras, the UK music industry and dance such as with the Rambert Dance Company. Involvement in arts-based activities can enable participants to experiment with alternative choices in a depersonalised way. As Ledwith and Springett (2010, p.89) have illustrated 'it was found that conversations about sensitive issues, such as depression, were able to take place more easily when the participants' eyes were focused on a creative activity'.

The arts have been widely embraced as a medium for engaging communities in health education and health promotion, particularly in developing countries. Sloman (2012) has argued that international community development is increasingly using participatory theatre as such a tool. However, the role of *animateur* has moved beyond arts-based projects into social care and youth work. For example the Salvation Army uses *animateurs* to motivate people in their centres to develop self-belief, learn new skills and make a difference in their local communities through activities such as drama, sport, gardening, and painting and decorating. In Europe the role is extending into health work with *animateurs de prévention* and *animateurs de santé*.

As we have discussed in Chapter 5, recent years have witnessed an increasing international community development practice away from non-governmental organisations (NGOs) and other development organisations making decisions about and for communities towards a more 'bottom-up' approach where communities have responsibility for making their own decisions about how they want to develop. Alongside this shift in thinking and practice more participatory methods are being developed 'that focus on visual, collective, community-based means of working and theatre has been embraced as one of these tools' (Sloman, 2012, p.43).

We noted in Chapter 5, in the case study about Restless Development, how the use of, what they refer to as *Edutainment* (AMCA, 2011, p.42) has impacted on the communities with whom they work. Practitioners and community members in Tanzania found that young people could remember what they had learned on a particular day when there had been an edutain-ment event (entertainment, sports, song, dance and drama) organised. Studies (Bryant, 2006) have shown that community theatre can help audiences retain information and support informal discussion and dialogue about change. Participatory community theatre provides a forum to put across a message and address issues in the same way that conventional theatre might, but also provides 'an active way for the audience and community to become involved in the issues explored and form a sense of ownership' of the issues and how to address them (Sloman, 2012, p.44). When the community provides the songs, dances and scenarios for the theatre, messages are expressed in locally under-stood terms and as a consequence are more accessible and encourage greater participation.

Sloman (2012) describes the range of ways that participatory theatre can be used in informal education and community development. These include: being directly made with a community to explore issues related to their lives; discus-sion theatre where the audience is encouraged to have active discussions during the performance; forum theatre where the audience is invited to enter the action and change or challenge what is happening; and through the use of theatre-based techniques in monitoring and evaluation or action research. It is frequently used as a tool for activating discussion, dialogue and engagement with taboo topics such as sexual health and domestic violence. In these contexts theatre works as a 'method of transitional space linking external real-ity and the internal world of emotions' (Batsleer, 2008, p.113).

Other media for arts-based informal education activity include dance, music, making videos, photography projects, woodwork and other craft activ-ities, cake decorating, quilt making and collage making. Ledwith and Springett (2010) discuss a range of examples of community arts engagement projects from around the world that they have evaluated. These include encouraging young people to become active and interactive participants, rather than passive recipients of health interventions by working with them to develop a play about the health and well-being issues that were at the centre of the young people's concerns. Another example used graffiti art and mosaics to work with young people of Asian ethnicity and facilitate their engagement in an exploration of issues of marriage. Batsleer (2008, p.114) argues that dance and movement offer 'possibilities for expression and communication in terms that go beyond words and intellect' and has been found to be especially valuable in 'building connections and communication between disabled and non-disabled participants'. However, as Ledwith and Springett (2010, p.88) point out, the type of arts medium selected should always be influenced by 'the local context and the enabling contextual factors. Creative arts need to be introduced sensitively to people who have spent the majority of their lives marginalised and who may see art as elitist and not for them. A formulaic approach does not work'.

My new friends

This innovative project worked with children aged 10 and 11 from two different communities in Bristol. The two communities are geographically separated from each other by a motorway. This had led to the creation of myths and stereotypes about each other, and increasingly to conflict and aggression. The project worked with the children to explore the idea of territory and boundaries, and highlight the similarities and positive elements of both communities.

The children were given instant cameras and over a period of six weeks they worked in paired groups to photograph each other's community and explore the perceived divide between their two communities They worked with community workers through conversation and dialogue about their images to explore the negative perceptions of their areas and cultures. An exhibition of their photographic images at the end of the project demonstrated the shift in their views and how quickly prejudices can be dismantled.

You can view a short video of the young people talking about what they learned from taking part in the project by following the Community Resolve YouTube link: www.youtube.com/user/CommunityResolveUK?feature=watch

Using visual media

Taking photographs and making videos can enable an exploration of dominant visual themes and representations and can be a very powerful informal education tool.

The activity of photography and image making, in this example, was the 'activating event' (Taylor, 2008) for informal education to take place. What other skills, methods and approaches did the project workers use to ensure that 'liberating education' (Freire, 1972) took place?

Can you think of other examples from your own experience of projects using visual media to work with communities?

What factors contribute to success in projects like this and what can get in the way of success?

Tensions in informal education

As we noted in the introduction to this chapter, practitioners can feel that they are 'just talking' with people when working in informal education contexts and find it hard to critically analyse what it is that they are doing and achieving. Unfortunately, it is also true that to an uninformed or untrained eye, the approach can appear 'easy' and simplistic. This can lead to some people setting up projects under the guise of informal education, or increasingly under the banner of community development, without having an appropriate understanding of what it is they are trying to achieve. However, as Ledwith and Springett (2010, p.88) remind us, a 'formulaic approach does not work'.

Drawing on Freirian principles, Young (1999, p.79) has argued that the purpose of informal education is to 'liberate as opposed to domesticate' and its purpose should be to enable and support people's capacity to take charge of themselves and their lives. It should not be used as an activity for inculcating 'rigid patterns of socially accepted behaviour'. However, it has been argued (Smith, 2002) that even within informal education there has been a recent shift from open and informal provision towards the targeting of provision on working with groups deemed to be 'at risk' in some way. Smith suggests the central principles of informal education should emphasise voluntary participation and relationship, committing to association, and being friendly and informal. Initiatives that focus on case management and individualised ways of working run counter to the 'key characteristics' of informal education (Smith, 2002, p.10). Bradford (2005, p.58) agrees that the underlying principles of this approach are a commitment to 'voluntary' and 'participatory' relationships and that these have become 'threatened' in recent years by policy developments that attempt to quantify the impact of interventions and to target interventions onto particular client groups. With the increasing focus on work with people considered to be 'at risk', many community and youth workers have become concerned that they are required to be 'agents of social control' rather than 'informal educators' seeking to engage collaboratively with service users 'on their own terms' (Bradford, 2005).

A further tension can be the requirement from funders to evidence outcomes that are difficult to quantify in the short term, such as a reduction in teenage pregnancies or incidents of domestic abuse. We will examine some of these tensions more fully in the next chapter when we consider the difficulties with finding appropriate ways to evaluate this sort of work, however, it is increasingly the case that practitioners can find themselves manoeuvring between servicing the aims and needs of funders and working in a way that respects the needs and agendas of the service users and communities with whom they work.

Ledwith and Springett (2010, p.138) discuss the 'fragile process' of trying to enter into equal conversations and dialogues with others. Inevitably practitioners will bring their own personal or professional agendas into their conversations and it is arguable that the imbalance in perceived power between informal educator and learner can lead to an unethical influencing of the views of those less powerful than ourselves. We noted in Chapter 6 a range of tensions and dilemmas that informal work with communities and service users can give rise to and we discussed Batsleer's (2008, p.100) analysis of the contested nature of 'friendship'. Later in her book, Batsleer (2008, p.136) goes on to raise awareness of the risks and dangers of 'manipulation and brainwashing' inherent in these close relationships when the practitioner is not sufficiently reflective about the impact of their power and influence.

Ledwith and Springett (2010) argue that dialogue only truly takes place where there is 'mutual regard' and where we are open to having our own ideas examined as well as examining the ideas of others. This can, however, be experienced as extremely challenging 'because we have to suspend our learning to unlearn and relearn' and as we noted in Chapter 6 this can force us to confront our identity as 'the professional'. As Ledwith and Springett (2010, p.138) point out, many organisations 'find it extremely hard to engage in dialogue because they often want an outcome that favours their view or interests'. They suggest that 'health promoters often engage with communities with the assumption that the latest health advice about lifestyle is the right one'.

As Batsleer (2008, p.105) has argued, what is needed is an 'understanding of the ethics of closeness' and insight by practitioners into the importance of their role in creating a 'professional boundary for a safe space in which learning can occur'.

ACTIVITY 8.8

Liberation or manipulation?

According to Ashton et al. (2010) the rate of tobacco use among people with mental illness is 'very high' and many workers 'believe that it is important to address tobacco use with their patients as part of routine care'.

If you were one of the workers in this situation, reflect on how you might seek opportunities to engage in informal education with these service users about this issue.

How might you ensure that you are 'educating for liberation' rather than manipulating people for your own professional agenda?

There are, of course, no easy answers to this question and this is the challenge of participatory practice. As Ledwith and Springett (2010, p.138) remind us pre-determined agendas stop true dialogue taking place. 'Fundamental to true dialogue is an openness to unanticipated outcomes' and any attempt to manipulate or direct the process towards a desired outcome 'kills it'.

> Our task as participatory practitioners is to engage vigilantly in a process that treads the line between liberation and domination (and) ... the reward for perseverance is the achievement of transformative, inspiring, unique and creative outcomes, sometimes out of polarised positions. (Ledwith and Springett, 2010, p.139)

Chapter summary

In this chapter we have discussed the informal education approach to working with service users and communities from a range of theoretical perspectives. These perspectives are all informed by a conceptual analysis of liberation, empowerment and participatory dialogue. We have noted how this approach to engaging communities and service users commonly draws on the notion of an 'activating event' (Taylor, 2008) and how this is increasingly in the form of community arts and other similar participatory activities. The chapter has encouraged you to make conceptual links with frameworks and case studies in other chapters and to begin to develop an integrated analysis. This approach is continued in the next chapter as we develop some of the tensions briefly explored at the end of this chapter and begin to think about how we can effectively evaluate this approach to practice.

USEFUL RESOURCES

Cypnow This web resource contains a range of very useful links to informal education resources to help *activate* situations for conversation and dialogue: **www.cypnow.co.uk/ youth-work-resources**

Encyclopaedia of Informal Education is a website maintained by the author Mark K. Smith and contains a wealth of interesting and relevant papers exploring informal education, lifelong learning, social pedagogy and social action: **www.infed.org.uk**

Nonformality is a website dedicated to the theory and practice of education, learning and critical pedagogy across the continuum and lifespan. It takes what it describes as a European view and with a youth bias. There are interesting contributions on the work of Paulo Freire: **http://www.nonformality.org/categories/learning/**

The website **socialpedagogyuk.com** is a good source of information, workshops and discussion about social pedagogy. You can sign up for regular email newsletters and find information on research, practice and training.

Another website that offers information on the theory and practice of social pedagogy is **social-pedagogy.co.uk**.

FURTHER READING

Jeffs, T. and Smith, M. (2005) *Informal Education: Conversation, Democracy and Learning* (Derby: Educational Heretics Press).
Cameron, C. and Moss, P. (eds) (2011) *Social Pedagogy and Working with Children and Young People: Where Care and Education Meet* (London: Jessica Kingsley)
Two very accessible and straightforward introductory texts on the topic of informal education and social pedagogy.

Ledwith, M. and Springett, J. (2010) *Participatory Practice: Community-based Action for Transformative Change*, (Bristol: Policy Press).
This is a more in-depth analysis together with a range of varied examples of informal community education in practice from a worldwide perspective.

CHAPTER 9

Evaluating Engagement and Participation

CHAPTER OBJECTIVES

By the end of this chapter you should have an understanding of:

- the meaning of 'evaluation' that distinguishes it from 'research';
- why we evaluate;
- recent policy context introducing some principles behind the provision of services and the importance of evaluation;
- models and methods of evaluation, including critiques of different approaches;
- examples where communities and service users get involved in evaluation, research and the co-production of knowledge.

Introduction

In this chapter we explore the meaning of evaluation, how it differs from research, and why we do it. We trace the recent policy context of underpinning principles such as *best value* in provision of local services with its commitment to greater efficiency and effectiveness, and getting user perspectives on the quality of services. Issues such as accountability mean that service providers are seeking more active engagement with service user or community representation. We outline useful models for evaluation in community development and community education and use examples of user involvement in evaluating services to measure and demonstrate how they may gain a sense of community, belonging and achievement. We discuss opportunities for communities and service users to be involved in wider aspects of research and the co-production of knowledge.

Defining evaluation

For Everitt and Hardiker (1996) evaluation involves the generation of evidence about a policy, programme or activity; and 'the process of making judgements about its value' (p.4). This view is supported by others who see evaluation as 'determining the merit, worth or value' (Clarke, 1999 cited in Hall and Hall, 2004, p.28) of a policy, programme or intervention; and 'a process to judge or assess the worth of a particular act or product' (Rose, 2010, p.160). For us the meaning of evaluation is neatly presented by Weiss who sums up what it is, how to do it and why:

> Evaluation is the *systematic assessment* of the *operation* and/or the outcomes of a program or policy, compared to a set of *explicit* or *implicit standards*, as a means of contributing to the *improvement* of the policy or program (Weiss, 1998, cited in Hall and Hall, 2004, p.28).

This definition tells us that evaluation is a process to assess or judge value of an activity. It should be carried out systematically using clear criteria to measure value with the overall purpose of improving the activity. Questions to ask of the activity, programme or policy include: is it worthwhile? Is it good? Is it 'good enough'? (Everitt and Hardiker, 1996, p.24).

Evaluation may be seen as a research activity so that the terms 'evaluation' and 'research' get used interchangeably. However, some see a clear difference and argue evaluation is 'a study which has a distinctive purpose; it is not a new or different research strategy' (Robson, 2011, p.176). Research is more a 'process of getting to know' about the practice. It is about finding out, documenting, scrutinising, asking questions, testing assumptions and being 'research-minded' (Everitt and Hardiker, 1996, p.21). Research asks 'does it work?' and produces evidence about the practice, policy or programme being evaluated. Hall and Hall (2004) see the difference as whether the emphasis is on investigation (research) or judgement (evaluation). That is investigation to know and understand how a programme works or evaluation of how well it works and its strengths, weaknesses and how to improve.

Key characteristics that recur in the meanings of evaluation outlined include the systematic collection of information and making a judgment about the value of a policy or programme. There is a focus on the aims of an activity or intervention to judge its worth or value based on the extent to which the aims are achieved and the impact on those involved in receiving or delivering it. In making judgements and assessing value the evaluator is interested in *inputs*, *processes*, *outputs* and *outcomes*.

ACTIVITY 9.1

Inputs, processes, outputs and outcomes

- *inputs*: the resources used to formulate or execute a policy, programme or project (people, buildings, equipment, funding and so on);
- *processes*: the manner in which the inputs are applied to achieve the intended outputs (how we go about it);
- *outputs*: the specific products of the process activities involved in a programme or project (what we actually do);
- *outcomes*: the effects of the outputs (the difference we make) (Barr, 2003, p.140).

Describe an activity to produce something in which you have been involved within your workplace or at home. What were the aims and processes?

> Distinguish between the inputs, outputs and outcomes. What is difficult in making those distinctions?

A common problem in using these terms is confusion between 'outputs' and 'outcomes'. Generally outputs are clear and observable at the time of the activity or intervention. Outcomes, such as gaining knowledge, skills or confidence, may not be immediately apparent. Evaluators face potential difficulties in measuring outcomes as they are more difficult to observe, determine and reveal than outputs.

Purposes of evaluation

We focus on three purposes of evaluation identified by Chelimsky (1997, p.10) as 'accountability, development and knowledge'.

> *Accountability* focuses on the inputs of material and human resources and on the outputs of the mainly intended results and short-term impact. The point of evaluation is to determine what adjustments need to be made where outputs fail to meet original aims. The emphasis is on outputs rather than on processes or outcomes that may be longer term, harder to determine and produce unintended results or benefits from the original aims. The evaluators may regard themselves as objective in applying criteria with which to judge results but they may also appear detached, remote and can have a negative impact on staff whose programme is being evaluated (Hall and Hall, 2004).
>
> *Development* recognises the importance of human interventions so places more stress on processes. The purpose of the evaluation is to develop the programme staff, hear the views of service users and improve service provision. There is a stronger potential for empowerment where the evaluator works with programme staff and service users. The problem here is that the evaluator may be too close to the programme leading to issues of potential bias in presenting results and impact. This raises the questions of whether evaluators should be internal or external to the organisation: 'insiders' or 'outsiders' as discussed in Chapter 5.
>
> *Knowledge* seeks to generate understanding, explanation and 'to explore the issues underlying social problems and to examine the appropriateness of program provision in dealing with these problems' (Hall and Hall, 2004, p.34). A key issue is how to report and disseminate that knowledge to the wider public and to influence policy and policy debates.

Chelimsky argues that 'one reason for the tensions in evaluation today may be the failure to recognise that all three perspectives exist' (1997, p.22). Cooper (2011) suggests that for evaluation to be an effective process then these three purposes need an equal focus, however, the concept has been corrupted by focusing on accountability. Other writers also point to the dominance of evaluation for accountability driven by 'a continuing political agenda that prioritises "economy, effectiveness and quality"' (Rose, 2010, p.156). This results in the generation of quantifiable targets, key performance indicators and measurable inputs, outputs and outcomes. Achieving that better balance between these purposes may be accomplished by more participatory forms of evaluation involving participants who are both 'providers and beneficiaries' of a programme (Hall and Hall, 2004, p.37).

In addition to defining evaluation and understanding its purpose, it is useful to have 'an appreciation of the socio-political context of the evaluation' (Hall and Hall, 2004, p.7). In the next section we look at the policy context within which evaluation has developed in recent years.

Policy context to evaluation

The expansion in evaluation developed from the 1960s with the growth in government funding in both the US and the UK in education, health and social welfare programmes (Hall and Hall, 2004). The growth raised concern about accountability and whether the funding was being spent effectively and offering value for money. To determine this initially required the collection of quantifiable data, usually statistics and numbers that represent outputs, impact and efficiency in delivering any benefits to service users. However, there has been increasing interest by practitioners and acceptance by governments in the processes and in the usefulness of qualitative data for evaluation of outcomes. That is evaluation needs to offer more formative or on-going assessments based on service user and community views and judgements for improvement in services.

Within this historical background different ideologies and policies have determined and shaped approaches to evaluation. For example New Right policy agendas from the 1980s sought to diminish the role of the state, control public expenditure and improve the quality of public services. Policies to achieve these aims led to the decentralisation of services and budgets and a new focus on user participation. As indicated in Chapter 2, that participation, was allied to the ideas of citizen choice and service users as consumers. The new language in social welfare of the 1980s and 1990s in the UK referred to 'value for money', 'performance indicators' and 'efficiency and effectiveness'. Governments were seen as increasingly using performance indicators, standards and benchmarks to evaluate work that they funded. This trend was challenged by Everitt and Hardiker who saw their task as 'to retrieve evaluation from being applied as a tool of social control to one that will contribute to the development of "good" practice' (1996, p.1).

Writing at the same time from an Australian perspective Dixon refers to the benefits of communities evaluating their own developmental work for change by becoming more skilled participants and exercising greater control in programme evaluations. She saw a further benefit was 'to enable community members' reflections on their own wins and losses to enhance the never-ending struggle to get resources' (1996, p.328). These were essentially calls for the need to attend to service user voices and to involve the recipients of policies and practice and participants in programmes and activities with any evaluation. An example of UK policy embedding user perspectives is *Best Value* aimed at evaluating the effectiveness and efficiency of services.

CASE STUDY 9.1

Best Value

Best Value was introduced by New Labour in the Local Government Act 1999 (Great Britain, 1999) to improve local services in terms of cost and quality. Local authorities 'are under a general Duty of Best Value to make arrangements to secure continuous improvement ... having regard to a combination of economy, efficiency and effectiveness' in Section 3 of the Act.

Best Value Performance Indicators were developed by government departments to measure the performance of local authorities with a focus on four areas: strategic objectives, service delivery outcomes, quality and fair access. Measuring the quality of the service delivered needed to reflect the experiences of service users. Originally a statutory set of 170 Best Value National Performance Indicators was developed by the Government and Audit Commission to cover local services such as health, education, social services, housing, environmental, cultural and emergency services. The indicators were revised and published annually until 2007/08 when they were replaced by the National Indicator set (see Activity 9.2).

From April 2011 the Coalition Government had a period of consultation about Best Value statutory guidance as part of its aim of 'freeing local authorities from targets, guidance and duties' (DCLG, 2011b, p.2). As a result of this 'light touch' approach in September 2011 it published a single page of new Best Value guidance. This sets out expectations for councils considering changing their funding or other support to local voluntary and community groups and small businesses. Within this it makes clear that under the 'Duty of Best Value' authorities 'should consider overall value including economic, environmental and social value, when reviewing service provision' (DCLG, 2011c).

> As a concept, social value is about seeking to maximise the additional benefit that can be created by procuring or commissioning goods and services, above and beyond the benefit of merely the goods and services themselves. (DCLG, 2011c)

This illustrates how political agendas change with governments along with the language and purpose of evaluation. It is left to practitioners, service users and communities to work out how, in this case, to demonstrate and measure 'social value' unless and until the Government produces a new set of definitions and guidelines.

The following activity is an opportunity for you to view and apply the National Indicator set that replaced the previous Best Value National Performance Indicators referred to in Case Study 9.1.

ACTIVITY 9.2

National Indicator categories

The National Indicator set listed indicators or measures under four separate annexes that included *Annexe 1: Stronger and Safer Communities*. View the outcomes and national indicators on pages 4–5 of the document available at: http://webarchive.nationalarchives.gov.uk/20090524203105/http://www. communities.gov.uk/documents/localgovernment/pdf/735115.pdf

- What do you notice about the list of indicators? What is missing?
- Highlight some indicators of interest to you listed under the outcomes of *Stronger Communities* or *Safer Communities*. Consider how effective these might be in measuring value or worth.
- How might you work with service users or communities to use or apply those indicators?

The policy drive to *Best Value* by New Labour continued a trend begun under previous New Right agendas of making professionals more accountable. Performance indicators were aimed at evaluating professional and practitioner interventions. This accountability purpose or model for evaluation focused on outputs more than process and assumed hierarchical management structures were in place where those below reported to those above. Critiques continued to emerge such as that by Barr who argued:

> Too often evaluation focuses on output performance. This is pointless because outputs are instruments for achieving outcomes. They are not ends in themselves. Their usefulness can only be assessed in terms of whether they produce the desired effects. (2003, p.142)

An example of the problem this accountability model presents to practitioners is demonstrated by Rose (2010) in relation to evaluating youth work. He observes that the ideology of the model is underpinned by systems that allocate funding based on meeting measureable outcomes. This enables funders, usually local or central government, to control delivery. In youth work there are requirements to count, for example, the number of young people not in education, employment or training (NEETs); attendance, retention and achievement in youth centres; and those young people involved in crime and anti-social behaviour. The problem for youth work lies in evaluating programmes that develop 'soft skills' and 'enhance emotional intelligence' (Rose, 2010, p.158). Further, the practitioner usually lacks knowledge of where the young person is at the point of intervention or start of a programme so there is no baseline established from which to measure change, 'distance travelled' or 'value added'.

Alongside trends for establishing professional and practitioner accountability is recognition that 'the public has a legitimate interest in the quality of service' (Barr, 2003, p.137). Cortis (2007) observes that not only in the UK but also in Australia, the US and 'other liberal welfare systems' performance measurement is required where there is increasing competition over allocating resources. She notes 'service user participation in this form of evaluation is not a common practice' (p.400). However, recent public service reviews in Australia call for performance indicators that reflect user perspectives. Cortis observes that such trends can be seen in the UK where child and family services such as Sure Start adopt participatory models of planning and evaluation that give specific guidance about involving parents in programme evaluation.

Service user involvement in evaluation and research

Service user involvement in evaluation is linked to wider aspects of UK and international health and social care research that recognise the importance of their participation. Alongside changes in government attitudes to include service users in policy or programme evaluation there has been a shift away from top-down research. That is from research done by academics and professional researchers on other people as objects for investigation to the idea of doing research with the people as co-researchers or co-investigators. As an example *community research* is 'the practice of engaging community members as co-researchers to research issues within their own communities with a view to accessing community specific knowledge' (Goodson and Phillimore, 2012, p.4). This approach involves collaboration between researchers, funders and those being researched that acknowledges the importance of 'local knowledge'. In Goodson and Phillimore's view community research is both 'a community engagement method, and a policy evaluation tool' (2012, p.10).

Barber et al. (2011) carried out a study evaluating the impact of service user involvement on research. They identify pragmatic reasons for involving service users in research. Service users can:

- Identify and prioritise research topics from a wider range of issues that are important to them.
- Develop more complex research questions and more ethically acceptable research design.
- Improve consent procedures and secure better recruitment rates of participants.
- Identify measures; collect, analyse and interpret data; and disseminate findings.
- Enhance the power and credibility of findings.

These advantages suggest involvement in research can be seen as empowering, strengthening voice and increasing the knowledge, skills and confidence of service users. However, a key test of the extent of any empowerment or strengthening of voice is to consider who initiated the research idea, the degree to which service users are involved in the analysis to identify themes, who has the power to create new knowledge, and what new knowledge is disseminated and to whom. Different types of knowledge may see professional knowledge being published in academic journals and taking precedence over 'situated knowledge' of people's experience to pass back to service users or communities. Situated knowledge 'is gained by service users in their struggle to resolve their issues' and offers 'a privileged insight' into particular situations and seeing the significance of data collected (Tew, 2008, p.276).

Disadvantages noted by Barber et al. (2011) suggest service users can lack experience and confidence as researchers or interviewers; and may feel over-burdened and relive distressing memories when interviewing other service users. In addition questions of access to, and participation of, service users and communities, power issues, and interpretation of new knowledge remain problematic. Service users may secure better recruitment rates but those involved in the research may not be representative of communities or other service users. In order to collect, analyse and interpret data the training of service users as researchers may not give them equal status to professional researchers in the eyes of some participants. This can have an impact on whether the research is therefore regarded as worthwhile. The interpretations of data by professional researchers may carry more weight with funders and policy makers than those by service users.

Within the Barber et al. (2011) study four themes emerged: trust and commitment; impact on the wider study; mutual learning; and timing of the involvement. Early negotiations to establish ground rules, openness, confidentiality and honest reflection helped develop trust and commitment. Involvement in the research design, analysis and dissemination reflected the knowledge and experience of service users. There was mutual learning with researchers developing knowledge of how to involve service users in research and service users gaining knowledge of research process. Timing, with early service user involvement, was found to lead to greater commitment and ownership of the research and the opportunity to influence design and methods. While Barber et al. (2011) note involvement mainly takes the form of collaboration and consultation with service users there are an increasing number of user-controlled research studies and UK initiatives. Case Study 9.2 focuses on an example of user-controlled research.

CASE STUDY 9.2

Involve

Involve is a UK national advisory group set up in 1996 to support public involvement in NHS, public health and social care research. It aims to bring together expertise and experience to make public involvement an essential part of the process for identifying, prioritising, designing, conducting and disseminating research. Part of its role includes providing details of research projects looking to recruit service users and service users offering to participate in research. Find out more at: www.invo.org.uk

---

Faulkner (2012) endorses the importance of service user involvement in research to change and improve mental health services. Service users can be involved directly in creating new knowledge as co-producers rather than using them as subjects of others' research. Faulkner sees the involvement on a continuum stretching from consultation through collaboration to user control of the research (see Figure 9.1).

Figure 9.1   A continuum of service user involvement in research

The key determinant of the levels within this continuum is power. Faulkner recognises an on-going power imbalance in relation to mental health service users or survivors 'in a world dominated by rationality and order' (2012, p.51) that sees them involved more at the consultation and collaboration end of the continuum. Service users need support to get involved and control research through adequate training, time and resources. You may notice that this continuum offers parallels with the ladders of participation models that were introduced in Chapter 1. For example Arnstein's (1969) ladder includes stages of *consultation* and *citizen-control*.

The idea of user control is evident in Tew's reflections on a collaborative study with mental health services users arguing for research where both the process and purpose are emancipatory. He has proposed that mental health research is judged by the extent to which it enables service users to 'have a greater awareness of their situation so that they can make informed decisions and choices'; 'have more control over the direction of their lives'; 'participate more in social, economic and political life'; and, with others, 'challenge stigma, injustice and social exclusion' (Tew, 2008, p.274).

We began this section by linking service user involvement in evaluation to wider aspects of health and social care research. Many of the advantages outlined of involving service users in research would also stand when involving them in evaluating programmes. We can apply Faulkner's continuum (see Figure 9.1) in relation to the evaluation of services provided for mental health survivors by asking:

- What was the level of service user involvement in the evaluation?
- What was the level of consultation?
- Was there direct collaboration in the study?
- To what extent did service users control the evaluation?
- Who had the power to decide what happened and when?

The following case study explores service user involvement in a different example of service provision: a drug treatment programme in Ireland.

CASE STUDY 9.3

Service user involvement in methadone maintenance programmes
This study found service users to be 'passive players in planning, developing, evaluating and delivering the services they received' (King, 2011). The study sought to understand the gap between policy recommendations on service user involvement and the reality of practice within treatment services.

King notes that harm reduction approaches have sought to make use of drug users' views and knowledge 'to improve services by encouraging their participation in policy development and service planning and delivery' (2011, p.277). Service providers and users over 18 years of age receiving methadone treatment for more than a year were recruited and interviewed. Findings showed that within the formal drug treatment services 'service users played only a minimal role in influencing their own care, in assisting each other's care and in shaping service policies and practices. Such involvement, as was identified, was deemed to be largely tokenistic' (2011, p.283).

Research participants agreed drug service users should participate in determining their own care needs and direct their treatment, yet power remained with the service providers. While practices had changed 'the underlying philosophy of the old drug treatment system had not shifted' and services users 'were still being viewed in terms of old stereotypes of pathology, deviance and helplessness, with lip service being paid to the ideals of service user involvement in the planning and delivery of services' (King, 2011, p.283).

- How would you involve service users in evaluating a drug treatment programme?
- With reference to your reading of this chapter so far indicate both the advantages and disadvantages of involving them.
- What principles lie behind your thinking?

In reflecting on Case Study 9.3 you could consider whether you would involve a service user in evaluation at the start, on completion or later. How are you involving them? Are you asking them questions or recruiting them as co-evaluators? Think about who is both determining and asking the questions. Advantages could be that service users identify issues that are important to them in evaluation or as co-evaluators they may secure better access to, and get more candid answers from, their peers. A disadvantage would be that by involving them at the start you overburden them as vulnerable individuals undergoing the treatment programme. Finally, consider the principles and purpose behind your ideas. Are you evaluating to develop the programme and your own skills and knowledge, to justify funding or to empower the service user?

The main difficulties in working with the individual service user as a co-evaluator in this case study lie in their vulnerability and power differentials with the service providers and practitioners. We need to consider a wider range of models or frameworks for evaluation that may be more appropriate to the individual, group or community in different settings or circumstances.

Models for evaluation

In describing the purposes of evaluation we outlined accountability and development approaches or models. The former emphasises impact, measurement and quantitative data. The latter focuses on process using on-going evaluation and qualitative data. There has been a shift towards more participatory evaluation such as 'empowerment evaluation' that gives control to practitioners, democratises the evaluation and empowers the participants (Hall and Hall, 2004, p.50). Fetterman states 'Empowerment evaluation is the use of evaluation concepts, techniques, and findings to foster improvement and self-determination' (1996, p.4)

In presenting the concept of 'empowerment evaluation' Fetterman (1996) argues we are more likely to adopt change and develop as individuals if we have some ownership of evaluation. Rather than taking on others' agendas participants take control to decide what is important. Hall and Hall note 'this can be emancipatory for groups, often from minorities, who are usually cast merely as users of services determined by others' (2004, p.51).

Empowerment evaluation can be applied to organisations, communities and individuals, but the focus is on programmes, empowering processes and outcomes. The model is designed 'to help people help themselves and improve their programs using a form of self-evaluation and reflection' (Fetterman, 1996, p.5). That is programme participants conduct their own evaluation through collaborative group activity. Thereby people empower themselves though often with assistance and support from professional practitioners.

BOX 9.1 FOUR PRAGMATIC STEPS OF EMPOWERMENT EVALUATION (FETTERMAN, 1996)

1. *Take stock* of the programme by using a rating scale of 1–10 with participants to identify strengths and weaknesses.
2. *Set goals* using the rating performance results to identify where you want to go in future.
3. *Develop strategies* to achieve programme goals and objectives.
4. *Document progress* determining what evidence you will use to show progress to achieving the set goals.

In empowerment evaluation participants 'negotiate goals, strategies, documentation, and time lines' (Fetterman, 1996, p.23) while data is gathered from the ground up. In summary empowerment evaluation offers a valuable approach for hearing voices of 'disenfranchised people and programs' and to address 'real problems' (1996, p.24). However, the problem remains, as shown in Case Study 9.3, as to whether it is appropriate to involve potentially vulnerable or inexperienced individuals with any certainty that they will experience empowerment. Supporting and guiding participants to design and evaluate programmes is a useful role for practitioners but they should also be mindful of the need to involve all stakeholders to include wider communities.

The term 'stakeholder' recognises there are 'a variety of participants who have a legitimate interest or stake in both what happens in communities and how it is done' (Barr, 2003, p.145). It is not just for reasons of policy that require user and community participation but to understand that 'the way in which stakeholders are engaged often determines the success or failure of community practice initiatives' (Barr, 2003, p.146). We require user involvement to monitor the quality of services, identify 'good practice' and 'what works'. Fundamentally evaluation is about value judgements and control. It is done to demonstrate value to funders in order to secure and control further funding. It is done by practitioners and organisations not just on behalf of, but increasingly in collaboration with, service users and communities.

Cortis (2007, pp.403–404) explores user involvement in the performance measurement of family support services in New South Wales, Australia. From this study she indicates five criteria, or 'domains', to demonstrate how users know services are working:

1. 'Feeling different' in themselves and in family relationships.
2. 'Putting learned strategies into practice'. Testing and adopting the learning demonstrated or acquired.
3. 'Transforming users' institutional status'. A changed status in relationship with institutions, for example, child protection proceedings closed.
4. 'Community and belonging'. Gaining a sense of community, belonging and achievement; forming bonds, gaining acceptance, overcoming isolation.
5. 'Feeling equal to other service users'. Feeling treated equally.

ACTIVITY 9.3

Evaluating your experiences

Think of a project in which you have been involved or about your experiences in education. Apply the five criteria listed above to those experiences. What insights does this give you into how well the organisation or institution works?

For example, if you took your experience at university the activity might highlight your increasing confidence in living independently away from home, provide examples of your application of learning in the classroom to practice in a workplace setting, taking on roles within the institution such as a student representative, feeling part of the student group and gaining new friendships, and being treated as an adult. Of course some of your experiences may be more negative but this activity is asking you to see if those criteria are useful ways of evaluating your experiences so far, understanding them and thereby improving them. Having considered this framework for use with individual service users we now turn to evaluation involving wider communities.

Two frameworks or models for evaluation involving communities are Achieving Better Community Development (ABCD) in relation to community development and Learning Evaluation and Planning (LEAP) in relation to community education (Barr, 2003). These models focus on both processes and outcomes. There are underlying principles that are common to both such as that community practice must be 'developed to address community needs' and 'evaluated in a participative manner for the purpose of learning for more effective change' (Barr, 2003, p.140). Each model offers useful steps and questions in evaluation to apply in other settings. For example, the LEAP Framework presents a series of steps and poses key questions:

1. *Outcomes*: what needs to change?
2. *Indicators:* how will we know change has happened?
3. *Inputs/Processes:* how will we go about it?
4. *Outputs:* how will we know we carried out planned activities as intended?
5. *Evaluation:* did we deliver planned outputs and intended outcomes? What next?
   (Adapted from Figure 8.1 in Barr, 2003, p.141)

Dixon (1996) presents two different approaches to the evaluation of community development programmes in Australia. First a 'community story approach' for evaluating community-led change, and second using co-produced indicators that reflect community values where work is driven by government or other outside organisations. She refers to the need for communities to acknowledge different actors, visions, records and memories through 'an insiders' story, or a community story produced by a group of people who could consider themselves to be co-researchers' (1996, p.329). As a formative tool for on-going self-evaluation by local activists and organisations, the 'community story' includes elements such as: local control; input from, and analysis by, as many stakeholders as possible; dissemination to influence further community development; and establishing a local archive for those stories.

Where programmes receive government or other external agency funding then evaluation is often concerned with looking for measureable results or outcomes to justify financial support. In these cases Dixon argues that 'the co-production of community indicators is essential for occasions where the community is not in control of the evaluative effort' (1996, p.333). Using examples from the health promotion field she notes 'a dual track strategy' whereby there is community-controlled evaluation of the process and 'expert-controlled' evaluation of the programme outcomes. There is a need for all stakeholders in a programme to negotiate an agreement on unambiguous and achievable standards and indicators to use in the evaluation. As an example Dixon offers the 'desired outcome' of 'enhanced citizen involvement in community problem solving' using such indicators as 'the extent of different interests represented on committees' (1996, p.334).

Within the following example of evaluating a programme using a specific toolkit there are further ideas on questions to ask about community involvement.

CASE STUDY 9.4

Assessing the Quality of Youth Peer Education (Y-PEER) programmes
The Y-PEER Programme was initially launched in 2001 in Eastern Europe and Central Asia to build the capacity of national non-governmental organisations and governments to implement, supervise, monitor, and evaluate peer education programmes to prevent HIV/AIDS and improve the reproductive health of young people.

The Youth Peer Education Toolkit was produced as an evaluative tool. It offers a series of checklists to use in rating the levels of involvement, co-operation and partnership within a peer education programme. *Checklist 7: Community involvement* (pp.33–35) is evaluated by rating from 1 (low) to 5 (high) on a checklist of statements that the organisations or decision makers, for example:

1. feel adequately informed of the programme's goals, philosophy, and activities;
2. experience benefits from supporting the programme; and
3. collaborate with the programme in planning and implementing activities. (Source: www.fhi360.org/sites/default/files/media/documents/Peer%20 Education%20Toolkit_Assessing%20the%20Quality%20of%20Youth%20 Peer%20Education%20Programmes_0.pdf).

What statements would you use to determine the level of community involvement in a programme, activity or policy?

In relation to children's participation, 'the *extent* of children's actual engagement can be assessed by considering the level of their involvement alongside the point at which they become involved' (Lansdown, 2010, p.20). Children's participation can be classified at three levels:

Consultative participation is where adults seek children's views in order to build knowledge and understanding of their lives and experience.
Collaborative participation provides a greater degree of partnership between adults and children, with the opportunity for active engagement of children at any stage of a decision, initiative, project or service.
*Child-led particip*ation takes place where children are afforded the space and opportunity to identify issues of concern, initiate activities and advocate for themselves. (Lansdown, 2010, p.20)

This is a useful framework for applying to levels of engagement with any service user or community. For example identifying where and how evaluators seek the views of service users; noting opportunities for, and evidence of, active engagement by communities at different stages of decision making within partnerships; and ensuring service users and communities have space to lead and challenge.

In our experience of youth work in the UK since the 1990s we have seen youth workers and agencies developing innovative evaluation systems. For example, Rose (2010) identifies three strands for measuring youth work:

1. Using organisation criteria such as attendance levels of young people, age and gender, types of activities undertaken including records of any achievements and qualifications gained.
2. By measuring how youth workers and agencies perform their role against job descriptions, organisational strategy or policy documents, or government-set benchmarks.
3. By evaluating the achievements and learning of young people in contact with youth work agencies and services through self-assessment, observation, reflection and recording.

The strength of youth work lies in its education role. However, therein also lies its weakness when its informal education approach does not match government policy imperatives for formal examination with a focus on results. Rose argues for the need to involve young people in alternative methods of evaluation from that used in formal learning by following principles of participation and empowerment. Case Study 9.5 uses a technique for evaluation that recognises the difficulties in measuring outcomes in certain areas of practice. The example used in the case study is from youth work viewed as 'a qualitative process ... concerned with personal and social development' (Cooper, 2011, p.55).

CASE STUDY 9.5

Most Significant Change (MSC) technique

The MSC technique is a participatory form of evaluation based on the collection and selection of stories from people about changes arising from development activities. The technique was developed in the mid-1990s to monitor and evaluate a rural development programme in Bangladesh. The technique was used in a recent study by professional youth workers in the south west of England to evaluate the impact of their work (Cooper, 2011).

The youth workers worked with young people to generate a number of Significant Change stories from which to select MSC stories for any given period. The youth workers asked an open question: 'Looking back over the last month, what do you think was the most significant change that occurred for you as a result of coming here?' (Cooper, 2011, p.60)

This was followed by prompts for the young person to explain the significance of any changes. The stories were passed on to a Youth Workers Group and a Management and Trustees Group for analysis, selection and feedback of the Most Significant Change stories. Further Reading at the end of this chapter details access to a guide on the use of MSC (Davies and Dart, 2005).

Cooper argues the Most Significant Change technique worked well because it is 'aligned to the ethos and values of youth work' and was akin to doing youth work as it enabled youth workers 'to re-engage with the process of evaluation in a meaningful way' (2011, p.67). It rebalanced the purpose of evaluation beyond accountability to funders and stakeholders and towards programme development and generating knowledge.

The technique helped to raise the youth workers' confidence, to develop an ability to assess the impact of their work, and to draw benefits from dialogue and time spent with young people. The technique shows commitment to local control where practitioners and young people collaborate to generate professional knowledge and improve service delivery, in addition to demonstrating accountability to external agencies.

Chapter summary

In this chapter we have explored definitions of 'evaluation' and indicated how the term is distinct from 'research'. We have emphasised the importance of understanding the socio-political context within which evaluation has developed since the 1960s in the UK and internationally. Developments in evaluation within the UK policy arena since the 1980s have been shaped by shifting ideologies presented by the New Right, New Labour and the Coalition government. The example of *Best Value* was used to illustrate some principles that underpin evaluation and to show how this continues to evolve.

We have outlined and discussed some key purposes of evaluation: for accountability, development and knowledge, and used examples from different areas of service provision or practice to show how service users may be involved. A range of models, methods and techniques have been described including examples from practice that could be applied by emerging and existing professional practitioners. The case studies and activities have attempted to get you thinking about why and how to use evaluation in your current or future practice involving service users, communities and all stakeholders. We have pointed out that in evaluation it is important to know who ask the questions and make judgements that put value on an activity, programme or policy as 'good' or 'worthwhile'. We also need a greater awareness of what we are asking in evaluation and why we are asking it.

USEFUL RESOURCES

CommunityNet Aotearoa is an Internet resource for communities in New Zealand offering access to useful guides on evaluation and research methods under the heading of 'Community Research': **www.community.net.nz**

Family Health International 360 is a global development organisation working worldwide to improve lives in areas of health, nutrition, education, economic development, civil society, environment and research: **www.fhi360.org**

INVOLVE is a UK national advisory group supporting public involvement in NHS, public health and social care research: **www.invo.org.uk**

Scottish Community Development Centre is recognised by the Scottish Government as the national lead body for community development. Its services include 'Community Research': **www.scdc.org.uk/**

FURTHER READING

Davies, R. and Dart, J. (2005) *The 'Most Significant Change' (MSC) Technique: A Guide to Its Use* (Cambridge: Rick Davies).
This guide outlines the technique used in Case Study 9.5. Available at: www.mande.co.uk/docs/MSCGuide.pdf

Driskell, D. (2002) *Creating Better Cities with Children and Youth: a Manual for Participation* (Paris/London: UNESCO Publishing/Earthscan).
This manual offers a good model of practice for engaging children and young people in community participatory action research.

Lansdown, G. (2011) *A Framework for Monitoring and Evaluating Children's Participation,* a preparatory draft for piloting, July. Available at: www.crin.org/docs/ M&E_%20frameworkJuly11.doc
Framework being piloted in a number of countries through interagency initiatives involving organisations such as Save the Children, UNICEF and local agencies.

Percy-Smith, B., Burns, D., Weil, S. and Walsh, D. (2003) *Mind the Gap: Healthy Futures for Young People in Hounslow* (Bristol: Solar).
Report on a project in a London borough to engage young people as peer researchers in exploring their health needs.

Percy-Smith, B. and Thomas, N. (eds) (2010) *A Handbook of Children and Young People's Participation: Perspectives from Theory and Practice* (Abingdon: Routledge).
This handbook presents a collection of accounts by key thinkers and practitioners from around the world working on children's participation.

SCIE (Social Care Institute for Excellence) (2007) *Developing Measures for Effective Service User and Carer Participation* (London: SCIE).
Publication presents ten key factors to consider when developing measures for evaluating participation.

Weiss, C. 1998 *Evaluation: Methods for Studying Programs and Policies,* 2nd edn (New Jersey: Prentice Hall).
Useful guide to evaluation studies that explores how research methods can be used in evaluating social programmes using examples from education, social services, public health and criminal justice.

PART IV

Conclusion

CHAPTER 10

Emergent Landscapes

CHAPTER OBJECTIVES

By the end of this chapter you should have an understanding of:

- emergent themes in the policy and practice of community and service user involvement;
- active approaches to engagement and participation;
- the significance of the concept of *space* in determining where engagement and participation happens and who is involved;
- principles that will help you to critically evaluate your own practice when working with service users and communities.

Introduction

At the beginning of this book we introduced you to a range of concepts and models that offered frameworks for beginning to understand and engage with the breadth of contested ideas covered in the chapters that followed. As we have pointed out throughout this book, it can be a challenge for all of us to get to grips with the complexity behind seemingly straightforward terminology. As a consequence, a range of different practices has emerged that all claim to have similar aims. In this final chapter, we look back at some of the key themes that we think have emerged from the discussion in the preceding chapters and draw some conclusions about where, in our opinion, all this has taken us. Our aim is to 'take stock', and to provide an overview of what we call *emergent landscapes* of practices revealed as a result of policy mandates and on-going interest in the meaning of engagement and participation. We explore what this might mean for practitioners who are striving to work with 'communities' and 'service users'.

The language used to discuss issues of engagement and community is frequently imbued with an assumption of agreement about their meaning (Braye, 2000). When examining, for example, engagement more closely we begin to uncover a confusion that suggests more support for rhetorical principles than for examining the reality of how to make it work in practice. Throughout this book we have discussed the nature of these contested themes and concepts and, in particular, the difficulties in arriving at shared definitions of constructs such as *community*, *service user*, *engagement* and *participation*. We hope that by this stage you will have an understanding of the problematic nature of the use of these terms and will be able to confidently question and challenge their use in policy announcements and practice initiatives. In this chapter, we would like to revisit some of the discussions about definitions and to take a view on where we think these debates have taken us.

The nature of engagement

While a clear, single definition of many of the concepts and terms used may be elusive, nonetheless we hope your understanding has developed sufficiently to critique any claims that engagement and participation is happening in communities, workplaces, or other public spaces. Key action words and phrases that we have explored in relation to engagement have included consulting, listening, dialogue, conversations, delegated decision making, empowering, encouraging and advocating to help you think about where and how engagement is happening.

> ACTIVITY 10.1
>
> **Practice and policy**
> At the end of Chapter 1 we set you a challenge to consider the extent to which policy drives practice or practice drives policy. Think about this now as you reread some of the case studies that we have used to illustrate themes and methods in the book. You might reflect on this question in relation to your own practice, or practice with which you are familiar. What would you say is the relationship between policy and practice in some of the examples of practice we have discussed? Check the 'key action words and phrases' outlined in the paragraph above. What would you say that politicians most often get wrong when seeking to engage with communities?

You might identify the rhetoric of politicians and policy makers in central government using words like 'empowering' communities and local people while adopting top-down approaches in setting regulations or guidelines or in allocating or withdrawing funding. Slocock (2012, p.6) has observed how successive governments have sought to 'empower communities and promote social action' through policy and you will have read about some of these in Chapter 2. Slocock refers to this desire by governments to find a way to re-engage people with their communities as 'the genie being out of the bottle' (p.6), indicating that we are unlikely to see a change in the foreseeable future to this direction of travel. In June 2012 the UK government (Cabinet Office, 2012) announced its plan to 'map out a social action journey' for young people, arguing that access to volunteering and community opportunities would enable young people to learn new skills which will 'reconnect them to their neighbourhoods and give them a sense of civic responsibility and pride for where they live'. It is unclear which young people suggested such a plan, or were even asked, or indicated that they want to be reconnected to their neighbourhoods through volunteering. This presents a further example of a new initiative that uses rhetoric and a top-down approach of doing things to young people. Slocock (2012) views this as one of many initiatives launched under the slogan of the 'Big Society' that have been greeted with 'cynicism and hostility and widespread controversy'.

In Chapter 3 we discussed the notion of 'manufactured civil society'. Hodgson (2004, p.160) argued that there needs to be recognition that 'authentic civil society is a complex, diverse, organically developing entity' that cannot be manufactured to suit the needs of government. Slocock (2012, p.8) reinforces this paradox: that without genuine voluntary engagement nothing will change and that 'much of the change that Government seeks cannot be led by the government'. Shaw (2011, p.137) draws similar conclusions from her analysis of the 'ideological confusion' surrounding the enthusiasm of government policy to embrace community development values. She suggests that too many government initiatives reduce community development 'to a set of programmatic principles and processes which can be applied in any situation' and which strip community development practice of its 'wider social purpose' and ability to make a difference (p.137). One of the features that have been identified throughout this book as helping to support the growth of people's involvement is the importance of participation being voluntary. Participation can be encouraged, supported and made more attractive, but it should inherently be about free choice.

The nature of community

In Activity 1.1 we asked you to think about the communities to which you belong and to try to categorise and group those in an attempt to arrive at a typology. In the chapters that followed we pursued the themes that have emerged from other attempts to devise typologies and how these can be observed in different strands of policy. An interesting issue to emerge is the increasing trend for people of all ages and backgrounds to be active on, and to feel a sense of belonging to, online communities and social networking sites such as Facebook, Twitter, LinkedIn, Mumsnet or other online blogs. While social networking sites such as Facebook started out with the aim of helping people connect with their friends, they have gone on to assume a far greater role in connecting individuals to organisations and interest groups. Facebook, for example has gone on to add the *Community Pages* feature 'dedicated to a topic or experience that is owned collectively by the community connected to it'. This allows members to connect with others who share similar interests and experiences enabling them to learn more about a topic such as cooking or a new language.

ACTIVITY 10.2

Online community
Visit the website of any community organisation or group that you know or to which you belong, or that you identified in Activity 3.2. Do they have the *join us on Facebook* facility?

> What are the advantages to the individual (you) and to the organisation to have this online version of their community? Can you identify any examples of attempts to embrace a *community spirit* through online postings?

Cunningham and Cunningham (2008, p.107) suggest that these types of 'aesthetic community' are about individual need rather than community goals and they do not necessarily always lead to the sort of values that develop a *community spirit*. However, we argue that some of these sites were instrumental in energising the groups of people who took part in the wave of protests that erupted across much of the world in the summer and autumn of 2011 as part of the Occupy movement. People took to the streets and occupied buildings and open spaces, such as Wall Street in New York and St. Pauls Cathedral in London, in a collective and international response to social and economic inequalities. The main aim was to challenge political, financial and economic structures and power relations using the 'We are the 99%' slogan in recognition of the concentration of wealth among the top 1 per cent of income earners. The role of social networking sites was highlighted in mobilising individuals during the riots in UK cities in August 2011 and in the aftermath to involve communities in clean-up operations. Such sites were found to be instrumental in engaging community action and in getting local people onto the streets with brooms and bin bags to clear-up (Allen et al., 2011). This could be seen as restoring *community spirit*, or at least community-mindedness. Case Study 10.1 offers an example of an online organisation seeking to promote *community spirit*.

CASE STUDY 10.1

Streets Alive

Streets Alive is a not-for-profit UK organisation that claims to 'promote community spirit at the street level through street parties and other neighbourly activities'. It provides online practical tips on organising street parties and estimates that about two million people took part in private street parties to celebrate Queen Elizabeth II's Diamond Jubilee in June 2012. This was in addition to the thousands of other public community events across the UK.

Streets Alive argue that with 'more independent and less localised lives' we have fewer chances to bump into people, so they try to fill that gap by providing an 'excuse to meet' in streets and a 'framework to build stronger communities'. Meeting in their street, they argue, means that 50 to 90 per cent of households can take part, including hard-to-reach households.

Streets Alive sees street parties as achieving 'community outcomes' and as being a method of 'community development'. They have been 'building community spirit' in the UK since 2001 and claim to help people make their street 'a friendlier, safer and greener place to live'. They also claim to contribute to the building of *social capital*, to reduce fear of neighbours, to provide a chance to talk about local issues and to 'support social cohesion between age groups and ethnic and cultural backgrounds'. They do this by methods that include:

- Providing a range of practical tools, training, events and advice designed for neighbours, and supporting organisations, to help them create more opportunities for social connection and inclusion in their street.
- Working with a range of different streets and communities, from leafy suburbs to inner city estates, to help access often overlooked reserves of pride, creativity, goodwill and trust in order to generate on-going resident-led action to improve streets and their neighbourhoods.
- Sharing practical learning about growing localism at the micro-level and how modern practices of neighbourliness can contribute to important policy goals, including social cohesion, crime, health and climate change.

Source: www.streetsalive.org.uk/about.aspx

ACTIVITY 10.3

Reflecting on street parties as community development
Streets Alive argue that street parties *are* community development as they are 'a good way for residents to meet their neighbours which is the rock on which communities are built'. To what extent do you agree with this statement about what street parties can achieve?

It would be interesting to consider the extent to which street parties reflect all of the types of community that we discussed in Chapter 1. You might yourself have had experience of being a part of one of these. You might have concluded that some of the ways people are using these sorts of approaches could be said to be developing *community goals* and *communities of interest* where members have opportunities to come together in a common commitment and achieving a *community spirit*. You might also, however, have questions about the extent to which such gatherings lead to the sustainability of a *community spirit* and on-going community development. You might also have questions regarding the limitations of a local entertainment event to establish neighbourhood watchfulness or a safe play area for children.

For us, it is not about the event or the gathering or about the online interface, but more about the ways people are using these sorts of approaches. A theme to emerge from discussions and case studies we have included in this book is the nature of what we call *space* and, in particular, who lays claim to that space. It is our view that the way in which people engage with the spaces they inhabit is the key to finding a way to work with and support them to find and release their capacity to be active. However, the challenge that arises when we begin to explore this notion of space is the tendency for us as practitioners to either invite people to participate in our space, or to encroach on their public, or even private, spaces without invitation. As we have noted above, without genuine voluntary engagement nothing will be achieved and the ability, capacity and willingness of people to engage in dialogue in spaces that are created through invitation are often in stark contrast to those that people create for themselves. It is for this reason that informal community approaches are more effective when employed in places where people feel comfortable. Spaces that people create for themselves tend to consist of people who come together because they have something in common and 'these kinds of spaces can be essential ... as sites in which they gain confidence and skills, develop their arguments and gain solidarity and support' (Cornwall, 2008, p.275).

As you will have read in Chapters 3 and 4, there has been much discussion recently about the lack of individual and community involvement in voluntary activity, or what politicians often call civil society. There has been particular concern voiced about the absence of young people from many established routes to voluntary activity and community engagement. In her 'audit of the big society', Slocock (2012) reported that participation in social action and community activism 'is focused predominantly in a small core of older people from higher socio economic groups'. Mohan and Bulloch (2012) also found that the social characteristics of members of what they refer to as 'the civic core' are predominantly the most prosperous, middle-aged and highly educated who live in the least deprived parts of the country.

Yerbury (2012) began to explore this concern with a group of young people in New South Wales, Australia. She found that to those young people a 'sense of community is formed when people keep in touch' and that their communal interactions 'can take place face-to-face or they can be mediated by some form of technology' (p.188). Among her participants only one young person had a 'very geographical notion of community'; most of the participants saw themselves as mobile and a sense of place was not significant to their understanding of community. The study found that participation in online communities had an influence on supporting and enabling young people to participate in civil society and to make a contribution as citizens. Yerbury identified a theme of 'action or process' in the vocabularies that young people used to talk about their sense of community, but also noted that their citizenship took place in a different arena than might be expected by those auditing civil society interactions. As one young person put it 'I'd much rather sit at home and write an informed argument than stand there with a placard' (quoted in Yerbury, 2012, p.190).

According to Yerbury (2012), 'the boundaries of community can be seen to stretch across time and space' (p.196). Community, she argues, can no longer be seen as an entity into which an individual is absorbed, 'but rather something that grows out from the individual and that is endlessly created and re-created' (p.196). To most of the young people in her study, the important contributory factors to developing a sense of community were 'discussion and dialogue and conversation that has reverberations' (p.189). Online discussion spaces were seen as examples of 'public spheres' where such discussion could take place.

ACTIVITY 10.4

Tensions in online communities

In Chapters 6 and 8 we discussed some tensions and boundary dilemmas that can arise for community practitioners when working informally within communities. What tensions have you experienced or might arise when interacting with groups in online communities? What guidelines can help us when working with those tensions?

Yerbury (2012, p.191) refers to 'a set of basic skills' that the young people she worked with claim exist to maintain appropriate social relations online. They discussed the importance of having a *moderator* in discussion forums to ensure that 'norms and standards of behaviour fundamental to the community' are maintained. According to Young (1999, p.79), however, the purpose of dialogue in informal education should not be for inculcating 'rigid patterns of socially accepted behaviour'. Consider, therefore, how you, as a practitioner, might work with an online community to 'liberate as opposed to domesticate' (Young, 1999, p.79) and enable and support people's capacity to take charge of themselves and their lives.

The nature of service user

In Chapter 1 we discussed the difficulties that many practitioners and policy makers struggle with in finding appropriate terminology to describe the people with whom we work. Coulter (2011, p.10) finds the use of the term service user 'clumsy' and that it 'implies a relationship with an inanimate object instead of an active partnership'. These debates about what to call people bring into focus consideration of what it is to be 'a professional' and the challenge to the concept of 'being the professional'. As we have noted, there have been past traditions for 'professionals' to place more emphasis on their own professional knowledge and judgments than on service user views and experiences. Such an approach to practice tended to confirm service users as dependent. In that approach, the focus tended to be on problems, failings or inadequacies rather than on the service user's abilities, strengths, resources and capacities. More recently there has been a nuanced development in the relationship between service users and professionals, with the terminology shifting towards embracing the concept of *expert by experience* in a challenge to the centrality of *professional knowledge*.

When introducing the term *service user* in Chapter 1, we acknowledged that defining people by their eligibility to receive services characterises them as passive recipients. This perspective and the experience of 'having things done to them' continue to be highlighted by service user organisations that emphasise the importance of active engagement in services. For example, when the UK organisation Shaping Our Lives, the National Network of Service Users and Disabled People, talks of 'service users' they conceptualise it as an active and positive term. The organisation notes in particular that 'being a service user means we can identify and recognise that we share a lot of experiences with a wide range of people who use services' including, for example, young people with experience of being looked after in care, mental health service users and older people. The network sees the shared experiences of using services as what 'makes us powerful and gives us a strong voice to improve services' (Shaping Our Lives, n.d.).

The trend towards greater inclusion puts more emphasis on the rights and abilities of service users to define and understand their own situation. An increasing willingness by professionals to see service users as active and equal partners derives from the recognition that practitioners and service users possess different knowledge and skills. This shift in conceptual thinking has led to other gradual changes in the language, reflecting the principles of *user-led services* or *user-centred services*. Barnes and Cotterell (2012b, p.2) describe the 'personal growth' of individuals and groups that has emerged from the development of these service user movements. Collectively, they suggest, these movements have challenged the ways in which the identities of people who use health and welfare services are seen by the rest of society. 'Claiming the right to identify themselves' has been an important objective and outcome (p.2).

Service users should be construed as 'ordinary citizens' who are empowered to work alongside professionals (Duffy and Etherington, 2012, p.3). In our view this offers a helpful framework for thinking about how we, as practitioners, could and should be engaging with service users and communities. In our conversations while writing this book we have been inspired by the notion of 'co-actors' (Kvarnström et al., 2012, p.130) where a practitioner adopts the approach towards working with service users that sees them as 'fellow citizens' alongside whom we are privileged to work. Evans et al. (2012) also describe an integrated approach based on co-production and mutualism. This is an approach where all parties are engaged collaboratively in negotiating how to proceed. Service users are not seen as passive but as active co-constructors.

This 'co-production model of care and support' is one that recognises that people who use services have 'assets and expertise' that should be valued and released (Carr, 2010, p.13). In this framework, practitioners need an approach of working alongside people to help build relationships and to identify common concerns. As Craig (2007) has observed for practitioners, or what he refers to as 'the powerful partners', this means recognising that communities 'have skills, ideas and capacities that are often latent or unacknowledged ... and listening to their demands and responding appropriately' (p.353).

Participation spaces

A co-production model of engagement requires practitioners to frame their interactions within communities as creating a 'participatory space' (Eversole, p.2012) that facilitates a meeting point between the knowledge and expertise of both the community and of the 'professionals'. Eversole emphasises the importance of practitioners ensuring that what takes place in this 'participatory space' does not become a one way journey and she suggests that community practitioners need to become what she calls 'translation agents who are comfortable in the circles of both the powerful and the powerless and who are able to facilitate the journeys of both' (Eversole, 2012, p.37). The requirement for this dynamic flow of dialogue between the 'insider' who lives in the neighbourhood with *situated knowledge* and the 'outsider' or trained practitioner who possesses *expert knowledge* is a significant point and is one that we have taken pains to emphasise throughout this book. Currently *knowledge exchange* is promoted as a dynamic process of interaction and flow of ideas between universities, colleges, businesses, and public and third sector organisations. The area to develop would be to actively secure meaningful interaction with local communities and groups where *expert knowledge* will also reside.

ACTIVITY 10.5

Revisiting the Swindon Family LIFE Programme

Looking back at Case Study 3.1, where do you see the potential for a dynamic flow of dialogue and knowledge between all insiders involved in the programme? What about between the insiders and outsiders including 'families in crisis' that may feel excluded or marginalised, may not see the programme as relevant or simply choose not to take part? How would you establish and maintain that flow? What barriers might present and how would you overcome them?

You might consider how the focus of the Family LIFE Programme on peer-to-peer learning offers opportunities to establish a flow of dialogue and knowledge between participant families and with practitioners. Participants tapping into their established social networks of families and friends might draw in other 'families in crisis' reassured that there is no stigma to presenting themselves on the programme.

Dialogue only truly takes place where there is 'mutual regard' and where we are open to having our own ideas examined as well as examining the ideas of others (Ledwith and Springett, 2010). This can, however, be experienced as extremely challenging 'because we have to suspend our learning to unlearn and relearn' and as we noted in Chapter 6 this can force us to confront our identity as 'the professional'. Ledwith and Springett point out many organisations 'find it extremely hard to engage in dialogue because they often want an outcome that favours their view or interests' (2010, p.138). However a co-production approach can create 'continuing mechanisms for dialogue and debate' that can help to continuously improve practice (Taylor, 2007, p.100).

There is a difficulty in distinguishing 'a clear line' between the autonomous actions of service users and 'official involvement initiatives' that invite 'organised users' to take part (Barnes and Cotterell, 2012b, p.1). This difficulty is due to the fact that many service users develop their confidence by taking part in their own group, and gradually move to a position where, supported by their peers, they are able to participate in 'officially led initiatives'. Barnes and Cotterell stress the importance of enabling service users to have the opportunity to 'develop their own analysis and ideas separately from service providers'. This can 'strengthen service users' capacity' to come up with alternative ideas, rather than simply respond to officially-determined agendas' (2012b, p.1). Self-organised groups that grow autonomously out of the community 'provide spaces in which people can experiment with their voices' (p.1) and plan to enter into dialogue with those who have power over their lives. Reflecting on the power of this process, Ledwith and Springett conclude that from such beginnings practice can 'connect with the everyday lives of people and reach out in collective action towards a global movement for change' (2010, p.208).

Our own experience of developing and supporting participation suggests that the process can be dynamic and unpredictable. We have noted throughout this book examples of practice that are complex and that suggest there is no easy checklist on how to facilitate participation and engagement. We have noted that the process needs to be gradual and that outcomes may be different for different people, depending on what other opportunities they have had. For the practitioner this can mean that we need to provide varying levels and types of support. Recent research tends to support this view. Brodie et al. (2011) 'found that people are involved to different degrees over the course of their lives in terms of the time spent participating, and level of responsibility they hold. Participation can develop and grow but it is unpredictable' (p.8). Being involved in a consultation, for example, can lead to greater participation for some, but not necessarily for all (Treseder, 1997).

Many successful outcomes depend on how people are supported and nurtured to take up and make use of what is on offer, emphasising that 'the contrast and the relationship between spaces that are created through invitation to participate and those that people create for themselves becomes especially important' (Cornwall, 2008, p.275). Cornwall is referring here to the problematic nature of what she calls 'invited spaces' and the need for community development workers to be careful not to raise unrealistic expectations. She suggests that different purposes require 'different forms of engagement by different kinds of participants' (2008, p.273). Participation in one activity may build up skills and confidence and lead to broader participation in other areas. In our own practice we have noted how people move in and out of different levels of participation and involvement throughout their lives. As confidence builds then expectations about an individual's capacity to be involved may also grow. This can of course, have a downside. With growing confidence Dinham (2007) observed that people's sense of cynicism and disillusionment, arising from the sorts of participatory activity with which they were expected to become involved, might also grow. For the practitioner this means being constantly responsive to the level of capacity or need in the individual and in the community or group through a process of listening, respect and dialogue.

In thinking about how we engage in participation spaces then analyses of who owns or lays claim to the space becomes important. Shier illustrated this in his work with children and young people in Nicaragua (Shier et al., 2012). In seeking to work with young people and to find ways to advocate effectively on their behalf to influence policy change, schools were used as 'the initial space for children and young people to organise and participate'. However, it was recognised that not all children in Nicaragua went to school and that numbers attending school generally fell during harvest time. Reflecting on the nature of participation spaces, Shier's team changed their approach and chose to reach out and engage the children by visiting them in their own homes, and in the fields – in other words, in their own spaces. From working with children and young people in this way they identified four 'spaces and ways of organising to achieve policy impact' (2012, p.9) that can be viewed as a spectrum of 'participation spaces' that builds on Cornwall's (2008) ideas about 'invited and popular spaces'.

1. *Children and young people's own spaces* – for decision making, planning and problem solving with adult support.
2. *Spaces for training and development* – to develop communication skills and knowledge about topics of concern and their rights.
3. *Lobbies, forums and assemblies* – established places or means to meet with politicians.
4. *Adult-dominated decision-making spaces* – closed spaces that exclude children and young people.(Shier et al., 2012, p.9)

Children and young people, as well as older people and others using advocacy services, need spaces to learn how to influence decision makers and access the 'adult-dominated decision-making spaces' as well as how to work, plan and organise together. These ideas about the use of different spaces are similar to those relating to the knowledge that parties bring to a co-constructed framework.

As we noted in Chapter 5, Eversole (2012) differentiates between 'expert knowledge' and 'situated knowledge'. 'Expert' knowledge is brought by the professional and 'situated' knowledge lies in the community. 'The community and its members know and respect the particular constraints and possibilities' (Eversole, 2012, p.33) in a way that outsiders seldom can. Situated knowledge is important because it is the contextual knowledge that is vital for enabling development activity to succeed. The recognition that practitioner and service user possess different knowledge and skills has led to an increasing willingness by professionals to see service users as active and equal partners indicating, according to Thompson (2007), the 'emergence of new forms of professionalism' based on an ethos of partnership. Rather than viewing the professional as 'the one who knows best' practitioners are now thinking about the contribution they can offer to a partnership with the service user. Principles of 'user-led' or 'user-centred' services suggest practitioners engage in a partnership process of 'agreeing what the problems are, what the potential solutions are and how best to move forward' (Thompson, 2007, p.55).

Active partnerships

Shier et al. (2012) concluded that one of the routes to success in enabling children and young people to advocate for change 'usually involves the support of equally committed adults who are themselves prepared and trained for this role' (p.12). In other words, the support of skilled adults and practitioners can ensure a greater degree of certainty in successfully supporting people to influence policy and decision makers and service providers. Research by Berridge et al. (2012) with young people in residential care found that the qualities in their carers that were valued by the young people were 'sensitivity and listening skills; reliability; a sense of humour; and relationships that felt akin to family' (p.88). In similar vein, Hambleton and Howard (2012) found that the characteristics of practitioners that are valued by people in communities include 'trust and authenticity' and that the 'essential skills and capabilities' needed to achieve 'transformative collaboration' with communities include 'emotional literacy and willingness to take risks on behalf of others' (p.35). Both Berridge et al. (2012) and Beresford (2012) argue that 'above all' service users value a relationship with practitioners based on warmth, empathy, reliability and respect. According to Beresford (2012) service users value practitioners 'who see them in their community, among their families and friends' and who take account of the broader barriers and difficulties they may face. Establishing such empathy and respect may challenge professional boundaries as discussed in Chapter 6.

Beresford (2012) found that service users sometimes talk of practitioners as 'friends', 'not because they confuse the professional relationship they have with them with an informal one, but because they associate it with all the best qualities they hope for from a trusted friend'. Service users reported how much they value being listened to and made to feel that they are valued and 'that their viewpoint has merit'. Beresford refers to this as 'the starting point for an approach to practice based on co-production', working with the service user to find out what will help. Listening is much more than a passive quality, it is the starting point for an empowering approach to practice.

In Chapter 8 we discussed the notion of friendship. Batsleer (2008) makes a case for the informal community practitioner to be seen as 'a useful friend' (p.103) who is able to provide 'really useful knowledge'. She argues that, crucially, her definition of 'friend' embraces the principles of being an ally and that it is not enough to 'be a friend', young people and service users 'must feel that we are their friend'. In Chapter 7 we presented the view of mentoring as a kind of 'professional friendship' (Greenop, 2011, p.49). As we have noted, this type of professional relationship can lead to a 'blurring of boundaries' and mentors need to 'be mindful of their limits and realistic in setting goals' so as to avoid creating false expectations.

We agree with the view outlined in Chapter 6 that the concept of *professionalism* has led to the creation of boundaries and accountability that can be unhelpful when trying to engage with communities and service users in a co-creation model of practice (Batsleer, 2008). As we discussed in Chapter 6, notions of what it is to be *professional* can impact on the ability and confidence of practitioners to adopt a relational, friendly approach to practice. We argue that first and foremost practitioners working with service users must see them as 'fellow citizens or co-actors in interprofessional practice' (Kvarnström et al., 2012, p.130) where hard and fast rules about professional boundaries are more complex. Hambleton and Howard (2012) came to similar conclusions and recognised that these 'new ways of working' might be perceived by some as 'risky'.

> Part of the risk involves engaging with service users as co-creators, reframing the relationship between professionals and residents from one of us/them and professional/problem to one of collaboration and mutual respect. Sharing information and decision-making with less powerful 'partners' means sharing power in real and meaningful ways. (Hambleton and Howard, 2012, p.35)

We are not advocating a cavalier attitude to boundary crossing but we do argue that boundaries need not always be problematic. As Doel et al. (2010) suggest crossing them can even be seen as 'something to celebrate rather than suppress' if 'approached in a transparent and considered manner' (p.1885). Doel et al. go on to observe that there has been very little research into the views of service users in relation to professional boundaries but limited evidence (Nelson et al., 2004) tends to indicate that service users have a preference for practitioners who are flexible with boundaries and who go beyond a strict interpretation of the professional role. Research by Hambleton and Howard (2012) came to similar conclusions and they argue that in order to work in a 'boundary-spanning way' then 'co-creative/collaborative' practitioners need to 'give new emphasis' to developing the skills and capabilities' that enable them to engage in 'greater dialogue and connectivity' with service users 'to share insights and experiences' (p.35).

Active practitioner

Finally we are in a position to consider what the practitioner should bring to the process of successful engagement with communities and service users. Community practitioners, we argue, need to become 'good facilitators and catalysts of development' assisting and stimulating energies and activity that is already emerging (Botes and van Rensburg, 2000, p.53). In our analysis, work with communities and service users should focus on releasing or restoring their capacity and assets. Practitioners need to be adept at identifying and respecting space for people to define their communities and determine the pace of their involvement. Community practitioners should foster the development of networks and links between individuals and community groups within localities that enable mutual care and support. In the 'well-connected community', community workers 'provide the "boundary-spanning mechanisms", brokering joint ventures between organisations or staying in touch through informal conversation' (Gilchrist, 2004, p.152).

Networked practitioners: We believe well-connected communities and service users need informed, knowledgeable and *networked practitioners*. Lack of knowledge and poor networking creates problems. For example, a recent UK review of advocacy services concluded that many practitioners have a 'troubling lack of knowledge and appreciation' of independent advocacy services and that 'resistance to advocacy remains strong in some quarters' (Newbigging, 2012). The report suggests that some practitioners view advocates as 'meddling amateurs'. Networked practitioners have both knowledge and understanding of services and organisations – what they do and how they work – that becomes a valuable resource to share and develop.

Translation agents: Community practitioners need to become *translation agents* by which we mean operating as brokers and 'acting as interpreters and mediators within communities, helping people to talk and work together when there are difficulties relating to language, assumptions and the occasional antagonism' (Gilchrist, 2004, p.152). Community practitioners should not simply be delivery agents who promote and implement top-down government policy at neighbourhood level. As translation agents they need to open dialogue on interpreting, evaluating and improving policy, building towards initiating policy from the bottom-up in 'powerful partnerships' forged with service users, groups and communities. Practitioners should work in these partnerships in a way where user perspectives are neither privileged nor subjugated, 'but are situated in a process of creative critical dialogue' (Cowden and Singh, 2007, p.5).

Policy drivers: We referred above to the example of Shier et al.'s work with children and young people to find ways for them to advocate effectively to influence policy making and change. The research identified participation spaces; preconditions, such as 'knowledge', 'capability' and 'leadership'; and ways of organising for effective advocacy. For practitioners the 'lessons from Nicaragua' (Shier et al., 2012) need not be confined to those working with children and young people. It is worth reminding ourselves that both people and practice can drive policy rather than the other way round. Involving those affected by a policy changes its nature from something done to communities and services users into partnerships of practitioners, project workers and community members as co-actors seeking to identify their own needs and improve the quality of life. Shier et al. argue that to be 'empowered' a child or young person 'must be in conditions that make it possible for them to effect change, must have the knowledge and capability necessary to do so, and above all must feel themselves to be able to effect change' (2012, p.5). The practitioner has a vital role to play in working with and supporting communities and service users to attain the conditions, develop the knowledge and capability, and gain the confidence to realise their own power.

The role of the active practitioner is to carve out a space to work alongside communities where they can be supported to formulate and articulate their own experience of 'a world in which their voice is too easily ignored or misrepresented' (Shaw, 2011, p.143). Throughout this book we have indicated the importance of identifying space where engagement happens. This includes physical space, for example 'communal buildings such as community centres or village halls provide space for casual interaction' (Gilchrist, 2004, p.153). There are on-going debates about where engagement is, is not or should be happening. For example, the UK government commissioned an independent review 'to breathe economic and community life back into our high streets' (Portas, 2011). Competition from out-of-town shopping centres and economic recession has resulted in a decline in the activities of central business districts accompanied by shop closures in town centres. The reason for seeking to reverse this decline is that high streets are seen as important places 'where we go to engage with other people in our communities as destinations for socialising, culture, health, wellbeing, creativity and learning' (Portas, 2011, p.14).

In this book we have noted others' references to different types of space, such as: 'participatory space' (Eversole, 2012) and 'transitional space' to link 'external reality and the internal world of emotions' (Batsleer, 2008, p.113); space 'created through invitation' (Smith, 2002); and space for advocacy (Boylan and Dalrymple, 2009) and for reflection in and on practice (Schön, 1983). In addition we have recognised the need for space for dialogue, conversations and informal education, that is 'an intellectual space, where people in a myriad of different groups and association can freely debate and discuss how to build the kind of world in which they want to live' (Howell and Pearce, 2002, cited in Crowther and Martin, 2010, p.265).

> **ACTIVITY 10.6**
>
> **Identifying spaces**
> What sorts of spaces would you use to connect communities and service users you know or work with to relevant local, national and international networks?
> How would you use the spaces?
> How would you sustain them?
> How would you evaluate their effectiveness?

Ledwith and Springett (2010) suggest the use of 'open space events' where representative groups or those who turn up on the day co-create the agenda that would be suitable to establish dialogue within local or national networks. Their idea of a *world café* is a way of working with large numbers of people where small dialogical groups have discussions at different tables and may move between tables 'for a series of deep participative conversations' (2010, p.144). This example could also work well online using *virtual cafés* to establish international networks. The useful resources at the end of this chapter include examples of online communities that provide space for dialogue, support and disseminating ideas. For example, TED is a non-profit organisation devoted to 'Ideas Worth Spreading' that started in 1984 to bring together people from three worlds: technology, entertainment and design.

Conclusion

One of the reasons that led us to write this book was the increasing requirement for students and practitioners working in health, welfare, housing and social care to involve the people and communities with whom they work in decisions that affect them. It had been our analysis that the resulting emergence of a patchwork of practices was leading to students and practitioners struggling to appreciate the complexity behind the meaning of concepts such as *involvement, participation, engagement* and *community*. We felt a desire to engage these practitioners in developing a stronger critical evaluation of successful approaches to engagement and to encourage reflection on a discourse that sets user involvement within a framework of *community engagement* rather than focus on a model of individual case management. As Brodie et al. (2011) have argued an individual's networked relationships are an important resource in determining how 'powerful' and successful they are in achieving their aims. Association with others can lead to new friendships, which encourage bridging social capital where other participants can provide a bridge between different activities, groups and communities through their many memberships.

Our aims, as stated in Chapter 1, included building a framework for understanding and analysing community practice and community engagement. We declared our intention to extend understanding of theories, skills and issues in practice to help students and practitioners articulate and evaluate their work. We hope our use of contemporary practice-based activities, illustrative case studies and signposting to useful resources have informed the development of your own analyses, critiques and reflective questioning.

We end by summarising what we see as the important ways forward for students and practitioners aiming for a more collaborative, transformative and democratic practice. The key factors, for us, underpinning this approach include reframing practice in a way that focuses on the *capabilities and assets* within individuals and communities. This takes us away from a deficit model focusing on problems towards ensuring a 'bottom-up' approach that emphasises *voluntary participation* on a pathway and at a pace determined by participants and the active development of *networks* and *bridges* between communities.

We strongly endorse the view of Brodie et al. (2011) that participation should be voluntary and call for vigilance and challenge to government initiatives such as the UK National Citizen Service for 16 year olds where participation may become formalised and increasingly used as a means of social control. Our experiences in developing and supporting people's participation suggest the process can be dynamic with no simple 'how to' checklist to their engagement. Brodie et al.'s research (2011) shows that people tend to participate to different degrees over the course of their lives and that levels of responsibilities develop and grow in unpredictable and not necessarily linear, ways. For the practitioner this means being flexible and differentiating the levels and types of support required over time.

In our view, the role of practitioner as *bridge* is an important concept. Bridges can play an important role, linking an individual to wider social networks and broadening their participation. In Chapter 1 we briefly examined the use of a bridge as a model for considering participation. Like John (1996) we see the bridge as a useful way to conceptualise the chasm between those with power and those without. In our view, following analyses developed through the chapters in this book, the *active practitioner* becomes this bridge, supporting the journey of the individual or community who is trying to cross it. Taylor and Upward (1995) have argued that there needs to be a flow across the bridge in both directions and we would support this analysis arguing that the co-creation of practice involves learning and reflection from both sides. The role for the *active practitioner* can be to: act as a guide to make the first step onto the bridge look inviting (from both sides); encourage engagement in activities and events and with other people along the way; help people navigate their way across in the face of obstacles; and celebrate their arrival at 'the other side'. As Yerbury (2012) observes community should no longer be seen as 'an entity into which an individual can be absorbed', instead it should be seen as 'something that grows out from the individual' (p.196). This is an important idea underpinning the frameworks in this final chapter and, in our view, is a significant aspect informing the practice of engaging with communities and service users.

USEFUL RESOURCES

CareSpace is an online community that discusses topics of interest to those working in social care: **www.communitycare.co.uk/carespace/forums/default.aspx**

OneWorld.net was founded in 1994 as an online civil society portal that aims to 'innovate people's media for a fairer, greener world': **www.oneworldgroup.org/**

Streets Alive offer downloadable resources for organising street parties and other resources to encourage residents of all ages to enjoy playing together to build community spirit: **www.streetparty.org.uk/resources/access.aspx**

TED is a non-profit organisation bringing together people and ideas from three worlds – technology, entertainment and design: **www.ted.com/**

References

100 Black Men of London (n.d.) Available at: www.100bmol.org.uk/mentoring.html accessed 12 February 2013.

ACSA (Aged and Community Services Australia) (2008) *Consumer Directed Care in Community Care: Discussion Paper for ACSA Policy Development* (Melbourne, Victoria: ACSA).

Advocacy 2000 (2002) *Principles and Standards in Independent Advocacy Organisations and Groups* (Edinburgh: Advocacy 2000)

Advocacy in Action (1990) *A Model for User Consultation* (Nottingham: Advocacy in Action).

Advocacy Resource Exchange (n.d.) *Advocacy Models*. Available at: www.advocacy resource.org.uk/Advocacy-Models accessed 12 February 2013.

Aked, J., Marks, N., Cordon, C., and Thompson, S. (2008) *Five Ways to Well-being: The Evidence. A Report Presented to the Foresight Project on Communicating the Evidence Base for Improving People's Well-being* (London: NEF).

Allen, J. (2004) *The Art of Mentoring* (Bristol: The Centre for Mentoring).

Allen, J., Stuffins, C. and Wilding, K. (2011) *After the Riots: Evidence from the Voluntary and Community Sector on the Causes of the 2011 Riots and Next Steps for Policy and Practice* (London: NCVO).

AMCA (2011) *Evaluation of Restless Development Tanzania Youth Peer-to-Peer Programme 2008–2010* (Dar es Salaam: AMCA Inter-Consult Ltd). Available at: http://www.restlessdevelopment.org/file/res-tz-amca-external-evaluation-2011-pdf accessed 13 February 2013.

Argyris, C. and Schön, D. (1974) *Theory in Practice: Increasing Professional Effectiveness* (San Francisco: Jossey-Bass).

Arnott, J. and Koubel, G (2012) Interprofessional Working and the Community Care Conundrum, in Koubel, G. and Bungay, H. (2012) *Rights, Risks and Responsibilities: Interprofessional Working in Health and Social Care* (Basingstoke: Palgrave), pp.159–178.

Arnstein, S. (1969) A Ladder of Citizen Participation, *Journal of the American Institute of Planners*, 35(4): 216–224.

Ashton, M., Lawn, S. and Hosking, J. (2010) 'Mental Health Workers' Views on Addressing Tobacco Use', *Australian and New Zealand Journal of Psychiatry*, 44 (9): 846–851.

Avis, J. (2005) 'Beyond performativity: Reflections on Activist Professionalism and the Labour Process in Further Education', *Journal of Education Policy*, 20(2): 209–222.

Ball, S. (1994) *Education Reform: A Critical and Post-Structuralist Approach* (Buckingham: Open University Press).

Ball-Petsimeris, S. (2004) Urban Policy Under New Labour: A New Dawn? *Dela*, 21: 171–181.

Banks, S. (2003) Conflicts of Culture and Accountability, in Banks, S. Butcher, H., Henderson, P. and Robertson, J. (eds) *Managing Community Practice* (Bristol: Policy Press), pp.103–120.

Banks, S. (2010) Integrity in Professional Life: Issues of Conduct, Commitment and Capacity, *British Journal of Social Work*, 40: 2168–2184

Barber, B.R. (1984) *Strong Democracy: Participatory Politics for a New Age* (London: University of California Press).

Barber, R., Beresford, P., Boote, J., Cooper, C. and Faulkner, A. (2011) Evaluating the Impact of Service User Involvement on Research: A Prospective Case Study, *International Journal of Consumer Studies* 35: 609–615.

Barber, T. (2007) Young People and Civic Participation: A Conceptual Review, *Youth & Policy*, 96: 19–39.

Barnard, H. (2010) *Big Society, Cuts & Consequences: A Thinkpiece* (London: Centre for Charity Effectiveness,).

Barnardo's (2012) Seen and Heard: Advocacy service. Available at: www.barnardos. org.uk/seenandheard/seen_heard_advocacy_service.htm accessed 13 February 2013.

Barnes, M and Cotterell, P. (2012a) From Margin to Mainstream, in Barnes, M. and Cotterell, P. (eds) *Critical Perspectives on User Involvement* (Bristol: Policy Press), pp.xv–xxvi.

Barnes, M and Cotterell, P. (2012b) Introduction: User Movements, in Barnes, M. and Cotterell, P. (eds) *Critical Perspectives on User Involvement* (Bristol: Policy Press), pp.1–5.

Barnes, M. and Sullivan, H. (2002) Building capacity for collaboration in English health action zones, in Glendinning, C., Powell, M., and Rummery, K. (eds) *Partnerships, New Labour and the Governance of Welfare* (Bristol: Policy Press), pp.81–96.

Barr, A. (2003) Participative Planning and Evaluation Skills, in Banks, S., Butcher, H., Henderson, P. and Robertson, J. (eds) *Managing Community Practice: Principles, Policies and Programmes* (Bristol: Policy Press).

BASW (British Association of Social Workers) (2012) *The Code of Ethics for Social Work* Available at: http://cdn.basw.co.uk/upload/basw_112315-7.pdf accessed 20 February 2013.

Bateman, N. (2000) *Advocacy Skills: A Handbook for Human Service Professionals*, 2nd edn (London: Jessica Kingsley).

Batsleer, J.R. (2008) *Informal Learning in Youth Work* (London: Sage).

Bauman, Z. (2001) *Community: Seeking Safety in an Insecure World* (Cambridge: Polity Press).

BBC News (2010) *David Cameron Launches Tories' 'Big Society' Plan*, 19 July. Available at: www.bbc.co.uk/news/uk-10680062 accessed 13 February 2013.

BBC News (2011) *Liverpool Withdraws from Government 'Big Society' Pilot*, 3 February. Available at: www.bbc.co.uk/news/uk-england-merseyside-12357450 accessed 13 February 2013.

Begum, H. (2003) *Social Capital in Action: Adding up Local Connections and Networks* (London: National Council for Voluntary Organisations).

Beresford, P. (1992) Researching Citizen Involvement: A Collaborative or Colonising Enterprise?, in Barnes, M. and Wistow, G. (eds) *Researching User Involvement* (Leeds: Nuffield Institute for Health Services Studies).

Beresford, P. (2012) What service users want from social workers, *Community Care*, 27(April), available at: www.communitycare.co.uk/Articles/27/04/2012/118171/ What-service-users-want-from-social-workers.htm accessed 13 February 2013.

Beresford, P. and Branfield, F. (2012) Building solidarity, ensuring diversity lessons from service users and disabled people's movements, in Barnes, M. and Cotterell, P. (eds) *Critical Perspectives on User Involvement* (Bristol: The Policy Press), pp.33–47.

Berridge, D., Biehal, N. and Henry, L. (2012) *Living in Children's Residential Homes,* Research Report DFE-RR201 (London: Department for Education).

Beveridge, W. (1942) *Report of the Inter-Departmental Committee on Social Insurance and Allied Services* (London: HMSO).

Blair, T. (1997) *The Will to Win,* speech at the Aylesbury Estate, Southwark, 8 May.

Blunkett. D. (2003a) *Civil Renewal: A New Agenda* (London: Home Office).

Blunkett. D. (2003b) *Active Citizens, Strong Communities: Progressing Civil Renewal* (London: Home Office).

Boffey, D. (2012) Serco Set to Take Charge of 'Big Society' Initiative, *The Observer,* 5 August.

Botes, L. and van Rensburg, D. (2000) Community Participation in Development: Nine Plagues and Twelve Commandments, *Community Development Journal,* 35(1): 41–58.

Boylan, J. and Dalrymple, J. (2009) *Understanding Advocacy for Children and Young People* (Maidenhead: McGraw-Hill).

Bradford, S. (2005) Modernising Youth Work: From the Universal to the Particular and Back Again, in Harrison, R. and Wise, C. (eds) (2005) *Working With Young People* (London: Sage), pp.57–70.

Braye, S. (2000) Participation and Involvement in Social Care, in Kemshall, H. and Littlechild, R. (eds) *User Involvement and Participation in Social Care* (London: Jessica Kingsley Publishers), pp.9–29.

Brent, J. (2009) *Searching for Community: Representation, Power and Action on an Urban Estate* (Bristol: Policy Press).

Brewer, P. (1993) 'The Future of Community Education', in *Adults Learning,* 4(6): 165–166

Brodie, E., Hughes, T., Jochum, V., Miller, S., Ockenden, N. and Warburton, D. (2011) *Pathways through participation: What creates and sustains active citizenship?* (London: NCVO/ Institute for Volunteering Research/Involve).

Bryant, A. (2006) *Report of Results from HAI Evaluation of Bibi Bulak Community Drama* (Seattle: Health Alliance International).

Budapest Declaration (2004) http://www.iacdglobal.org/publications-and-resources/conference-reports/budapest-declaration

Burgess, C. (1998) Saplings in the Forest: A Community Development Project with Young Survivors of Torture and Trauma, *Community Development Journal,* 33(2): 145–149.

Burke, T. (2010) *Listen and Change: A Guide to Children and Young People's Participation Rights,* 2nd edn (London: Participation Rights).

Burns, D., Hambleton, R. and Hoggett, P. (1994) *The Politics of Decentralisation* (Basingstoke: Hampshire).

Cabinet Office (1999) *Modernising Government* (London: The Stationery Office).

Cabinet Office (2010) *Building a Stronger Civil Society: A Strategy for Voluntary and Community Groups, Charities and Social Enterprises* (London: Office for Civil Society). Available at: www.cpa.org.uk/cpa_documents/building_stronger_civil_society.pdf accessed 12 February 2013.

Cabinet Office (2012) *Government Supports Decade of Social Action Opportunities for Young Britons,* CAB 046-12. Available at: http://www.cabinetoffice.gov.uk/news/government-supports-decade-social-action-opportunities-young-britons accessed 13 February 2013.

Cameron, C., Petrie, P., Wigfall, V., Kleipoedszus, S. and Jasper, A. (2011) *Final Report of the Social Pedagogy Pilot Programme: Development and Implementation* (London: Thomas Corum Research Unit).

Cameron. D. (2009) *Putting Britain Back on Her Feet*, speech at Conservative Party Conference, 8 October.

Cameron, D. (2010) *The Big Society*, speech at Liverpool Hope University, 19 July.

Cameron, D. (2011) *The Big Society*, speech at Milton Keynes, 23 May.

Carr, S. (2010) *Personalisation, Productivity and Efficiency* (London: Social Care Institute for Excellence).

CDX (n.d) *What is Community Development?* Available at: http://www.cdx.org.uk/community-development/what-community-development accessed 11 February 2013.

Chanan, G. (2003) *Searching for Solid Foundations: Community Involvement and Urban Policy* (London: Office of the Deputy Prime Minister).

Channel 4 News (2008) *FactCheck: Glasgow worse than Gaza?* Available at: www.channel4.com/news/articles/society/health/factcheck+glasgow+worse+than+gaza/2320267.html accessed 13 February 2013.

Chelimsky, E. (1997) The Coming Transformations in Evaluation, in Chelimsky, E. and Shadish, W. (eds) *Evaluation for the 21st Century: A Handbook* (London: Sage).

Citizenship Foundation (2007) *The Citizens' Day Framework: Building Cohesive, Active and Engaged Communities* (London: Citizenship Foundation).

Coats, M. (1994) *Women's Education* (Buckingham: Open University Press).

Cohen, S. (1972) *Folk Devils and Moral Panics* (London: MacGibbon and Kee).

Colley, H. (2003) *Mentoring For Social Inclusion* (London: Routledge).

Commission on Social Justice (1994) *Social Justice: Strategy for National Renewal* (London: Vintage/IPPR).

Commission on the Future Delivery of Public Services (2011) *Commission on the Future Delivery of Public Services* (Edinburgh: APS Group Scotland).

Community at Heart (2010) *New Deal for Communities: Final Report* (Bristol: Community at Heart). Available at: www.eastonandlawrencehill.org.uk/wp-content/uploads/2010/07/2000-2010-ndc-final-report.pdf accessed 13 February 2013.

Cooper, F. (2012) *Professional Boundaries in Social Work and Social Care* (London: Jessica Kingsley).

Cooper, S. (2011) Reconnecting with Evaluation: The Benefits of Using a Participatory Approach to Assess Impact. *Youth & Policy* 107, 55–70.

Cornwall, A. (2008) Unpacking Participation: Models, Meanings and Practices. *Community Development Journal*, 43(3): 269–283.

Cortis, N. (2007) What do Service Users Think of Evaluation? Evidence from Family Support. *Child and Family Social Work*, 12: 399–408.

Cotterell, P. and Morris, C. (2012) The Capacity, Impact and Challenge of Service User's Experiential Knowledge, in Barnes, M. and Cotterell, P. (eds) (2012) *Critical Perspectives on User Involvement* (Bristol: Policy Press), pp.57–69.

Coulter, A. (2011) *Engaging Patients in Health Care* (Maidenhead: Open University Press).

Cowden, S. and Singh, G. (2007) The User: Friend, Foe or Fetish? A Critical Exploration of User Involvement in Health and Social Care. *Critical Social Policy*, 27: 5–23.

Craig, G. (2007) Community Capacity Building: Something Old, Something New ...? *Critical Social Policy*, 27(3): 335–359.

Crick, B. (1998) *Education for Citizenship and the Teaching of Democracy in Schools: Final Report of the Advisory Group on Citizenship* (London: QCA).

Crick, B. (2002) *A Note on What is and What is Not Active Citizenship?* Available at: www.excellencegateway.org.uk/media/post16/files/033_BernardCrick_WHAT_IS_CITIZENSHIP.pdf accessed 13 February 2013.

Crowther, J. and Martin, I. (2010) Adult Education and Civil Society, in Rubensen, K. (ed) *Adult Learning and Education* (Oxford: Elsevier).

Cunningham, J. and Cunningham, S. (2008) *Sociology and Social Work* (Exeter: Learning Matters).

Davies, R. and Dart, J. (2005) *The 'Most Significant Change' (MSC) Technique: A Guide to Its Use*. Available at: www.mande.co.uk/docs/MSCGuide.pdf accessed 13 February 2013.

Davis, M. (1999) *Sylvia Pankhurst: A Life in Radical Politics* (London: Pluto Press).

DCLG (Department for Communities and Local Government) (2006) *The Community Development Challenge* (London: DCLG).

DCLG (Department for Communities and Local Government) (2007) *An Action Plan for Community Empowerment: Building on Success* (London: DCLG).

DCLG (Department for Communities and Local Government) (2008) *Communities in Control: Real People, Real Power* Cm 7427. Available at www.official-documents.gov.uk/document/cm74/7427/7427.pdf accessed 20 February 2013.

DCLG (Department for Communities and Local Government) (2011a) *A Plain English Guide to the Localism Act* (London: DCLG).

DCLG (2011b) *Best Value: New Draft Statutory Guidance*. Available at: www.gov.uk/government/uploads/system/uploads/attachment_data/file/8488/1885419.pdf accessed 20 February 2013.

DCLG (2011c) *Best Value Statutory Guidance*. Available at: www.gov.uk/government/uploads/system/uploads/attachment_data/file/5945/1976926.pdf accessed 20 February 2013.

De Silva, M.J., McKenzie, K., Harpham, T. and Huttly, S.R. (2005) Social Capital and Mental Illness: A Systematic Review. *Journal of Epidemiology and Community Health*, 59(8): 619–627.

de St. Croix, T. (2011) Struggles and Silences: Policy, Youth Work and the National Citizen Service. *Youth & Policy*, 106: 43–59.

Delanty, G. (2000) *Citizenship in a Global Age: Society, Culture, Politics* (Buckingham: Open University Press).

DETR (Department for the Environment, Transport and the Regions) (2000) *National Strategy for Neighbourhood Renewal: Joining it up Locally* Report of Policy Action Team 17 (London: DETR).

DH (Department of Health) (2001) *Valuing People: A New Strategy for Learning Disability for the 21st Century – A White Paper* Cm 5036 (London: HMSO).

DH (Department of Health) (2002) *National Standards for the Provision of Children's Advocacy Services* (London: Department of Health).

DH (Department of Health) (2006) *Our Health, our care, our say; a new direction for community services* (London: Department of Health).

DH (Department of Health) (2008) *An Introduction to Personalisation*. Available at: http://webarchive.nationalarchives.gov.uk/+/www.dh.gov.uk/en/SocialCare/Socialcarereform/Personalisation/index.htm accessed 13 February 2013.

Dickinson, H. and Glasby, J. (2010) *The Personalisation Agenda: Implications for the Third Sector*, Working Paper 30 Third Sector Research Centre.

Dinham, A. (2007) Raising Expectations or Dashing Hopes? Well-being and Participation in Disadvantaged Areas, *Community Development Journal*, 42(2): 181–193.

Dinham, A. (2011) 'What is a faith community?'*Community Development Journal*, 46(4): 526–541.

Dixon, J. (1996) Community Stories and Indicators for Evaluating Community Development. *Community Development Journal* 30(4): 327–336.

Doel, M., Allmark, P., Conway, P., Cowburn, M., Flynn, M., Nelson, P. and Tod, A. (2010) Professional Boundaries: Crossing a Line or Entering the Shadows? *British Journal of Social Work*, 40: 1866–1889

DuBois, D.L., Holloway, B.E., Valentine, J.C. and Cooper, H. (2002) Effectiveness of Mentoring Programs for Youth: A Meta-Analytic Review. *American Journal of Community Psychology*, 30(2): 157–197.

Duffy, S. and Etherington, K. (2012) *A Fair Budget*, Centre for Welfare Reform. Available at: http://www.centreforwelfarereform.org/library/by-az/a-fair-budget.html accessed 13 February 2013.

Duncan Smith, I. (2009) *Broken Britain Can Be Fixed by Its Army of Social Entrepreneurs*. Available at: www.centreforsocialjustice.org.uk/default.asp?pageRef =361, accessed 1 June 2012.

Dunning, A. (2005) *Information, Advice and Advocacy for Older People: Defining and Developing Services* (York: Joseph Rowntree Foundation).

Dunning, J. (2011) Expert Guide to Personalisation, in *Community Care*, 19 August.

Dwyer, P. (2010) *Understanding Social Citizenship*, 2nd edn (Bristol: Policy Press).

Eden District Council (n.d.) Available at: www.eden.gov.uk/your-community/big-society/ accessed 12 February 2013.

Education Scotland (2012) *Education for Citizenship*. Available at: www. educationscotland.gov.uk/learningteachingandassessment/learningacrossthe curriculum/themesacrosslearning/globalcitizenship/educationforcitizenship/index. asp accessed 13 February 2013.

Education Scotland (n.d.) *Community Capacity Building*. Available at: www. educationscotland.gov.uk/communitylearninganddevelopment/communitycapacity building accessed 11 February 2013.

Edwards, M. (2009) *Civil Society*, 2nd edn (Cambridge: Polity Press).

Engeström, Y. (ed.) (1999) *Perspectives on Activity Theory* (New York: Cambridge University Press).

Eraut, M. (2002) Conceptual Analysis and Research Questions: Do the concepts of 'Learning Community' and 'Community of Practice' provide added value?' Paper presented at the Annual Conference of the American Educational Research Association, New Orleans, April.

Eriksson, L. (2011) Community Development and Social Pedagogy: Traditions for Understanding Mobilization for Collective Self-development. *Community Development Journal*, 46(4): 403–420.

Etzioni, A. (1995) *Spirit of Community: Rights, Responsibilities and the Communitarian Agenda* (London: Fontana Press).

EU (European Union) (1997) *Treaty of Amsterdam: Consolidated Version of the Treaty on European Union, Part Two: Citizenship of the Union*. Available at: http://eur-lex.europa.eu/en/treaties/dat/11997D/htm/11997D.html#0145010077 accessed 13 February 2013.

Evans, S., Hill, S. and Orme, J. (2012) Doing More for Less? Developing Sustainable Systems of Social Care in the Context of Climate Change and Public Spending Cuts. *British Journal of Social Work*, 42(4): 744–764.

Everitt, A. and Hardiker, P. (1996) *Evaluating for Good Practice* (Basingstoke: Macmillan).

Eversole, R. (2012) Remaking Participation: Challenges for Community Development Practice. *Community Development Journal*, 47(1): 29–41.

FactCheck blog (n.d.) Available at: http://blogs.channel4.com/factcheck/ accessed 13 February 2013.

Faulkner, A. (2012) Participation and Service User Involvement in Research, in Harper, D. and Thompson, A. (eds) *Qualitative Research Methods in Mental Health and Psychotherapy* (Chichester: Wiley-Blackwell), pp.39–54.

Faulks, K. (2000) *Citizenship* (Edinburgh: Edinburgh University Press).

Fetterman, D. (1996) Empowerment Evaluation: An Introduction to Theory and Practice, in Fetterman, D., Kaftarian, S. and Wandersman, A. (eds) *Empowerment Evaluation: Knowledge and Tools for Self-Assessment & Accountability* (London: Sage), pp.3–48.

Fielding, M. (1996) Empowerment: Emancipation or Enervation?', *Journal of Education Policy*, 11(3): 399–417.

Fielding, M. (2004) Transformative Approaches to Student Voice: Theoretical Underpinnings, Recalcitrant Realities. *British Educational Research Journal*, 30(2): 295–311.

Foucault, M. (1980) *Power/Knowledge: Selected Interviews and Other Writings 1972–1977* (London: Harvester Wheatsheaf), pp.78–108.

Fox, J. and Sandler, S. (2004) *Bringing Religion in to International Relations* (Basingstoke: Palgrave Macmillan).

Fox, M. (1988) Plain Talk: On Empowerment Talk. *The Ladder*, 27(2) (Washington DC: PUSH Literacy Action Now).

Freire, P. (1972) *Pedagogy of the Oppressed* (Harmondsworth: Penguin)

Fulton, K. and Winfield, C. (2011a) *Community Engagement* (Sheffield: Centre for Welfare Reform).

Fulton, K. and Winfield, C. (2011b) *Peer Support* (Sheffield: Centre for Welfare Reform).

Gaffney, M. (2005) *Civic Pioneers: Local People, Local Government, Working Together to Make Life Better* (London: Home Office).

Gibb, S. (1994) Evaluating Mentoring, in *Education and Training*, 36(5): 32–39.

Gilchrist, A. (2004) Developing the Well-connected Community, in Miller, P., Skidmore, P. and McCarthy, H. (eds) *Network Logic – Who Governs in an Interconnected World?* (London: Demos), pp.143–154.

Gilchrist A. (2009) The *Well-Connected Community*, 2nd edn (Bristol: Policy Press).

Gilligan, R. (2000) Adversity, Resilience and Young People: the Protective Value of Positive School and Spare Time Experiences, *Children & Society*, 14: 37–47.

Glasgow City Council (2010) *Council Moves towards Personalisation for Social Work Service Users*, News RSS Feed, 14 October. Available at: www.inclusionscotland. org/news/story.asp?id=2635 accessed 20 February 2013.

Goodson, L. and Phillimore, J. (eds) (2012) *Community Research for Participation: From Theory to Method* (Bristol: Policy Press).

Grayling, A.C. (2008) *Social Evils and Social Good* (York: Joseph Rowntree Foundation).

Great Britain (1989) *Children Act 1989* (London: HMSO), ch. 41.

Great Britain (1990) *NHS and Community Care Act 1990* (London: HMSO), ch. 19.

Great Britain (1996) *Community Care (Direct Payments) Act 1990* (London: HMSO), ch. 30.

Great Britain (1999) *Local Government Act.* (London: The Stationery Office), ch. 27.

Great Britain (2000) *Local Government Act* (London: The Stationery Office), ch. 22.

Great Britain (2002) *Adoption and Children Act 2002* (London: The Stationery Office), ch. 38.

Great Britain (2005) *Mental Capacity Act 2005* (London: The Stationery Office), ch. 9.

Great Britain (2006) *Immigration Asylum and Nationality Act 2006* (London: The Stationery Office), ch. 13.

Great Britain (2007) *Local Government and Public Involvement in Health Act 2007* (London: The Stationery Office), ch. 28.

Great Britain (2009) *Borders, Citizenship and Immigration Asylum Act 2009* (London: The Stationery Office), ch. 11.

Great Britain (2011) *Localism Act* (London: The Stationery Office), ch. 20.

Greenop, D. (2011) Mentoring: A Qualitative Evaluation of What Works and What Does Not. *Youth & Policy*, 107: 34–54.

GSCC (General Social Care Council) (2010) *Code of Practice for Social Care Workers* Available at: www.skillsforcare.org.uk/developing_skills/GSCCcodesofpractice/GSCC_codes_of_practice.aspx accessed 13 February 2013.

GSCC (General Social Care Council) (2011) *Professional Boundaries: Guidance for social workers.* Available at: http://www.scie-socialcareonline.org.uk/repository/fulltext/122181.pdf accessed 13 February 2013.

Hall, I. and Hall, D. (2004) *Evaluation and Social Research: Introducing Small-Scale Practice* (Basingstoke: Palgrave Macmillan).

Hall, P.A. (1997) Social Capital: A Fragile Asset. *DEMOS Collection*, 12: 35–37.

Hambleton, R. and Howard, J. (2012) *Public Sector Innovation and Local Leadership in the UK and The Netherlands* (York: Joseph Rowntree Foundation).

Hancock, L., Mooney, G. and Neal, S. (2012) Crisis Social Policy and the Resilience of the Concept of Community. *Critical Social Policy*, 32(3): 343–364.

Hargreaves, J. and Twine, R. (2006) Community Development, in Macdowall, W., Bonell, C. and Davies, M. (eds) *Health Promotion Practice* (Maidenhead; Open University Press), pp.152–163.

Haslam, A., Jetten, J., and Waghorn, C. (2009) Social Identification, Stress and Citizenship in Teams: A Five-phase Longitudinal Study. *Stress Health*, 25(1): 21–30.

Hawkins R.L., and Maurer K. (2012) Unravelling Social Capital: Disentangling a Concept for Social Work. *British Journal of Social Work*, 42(2): 353–370.

Hayes, D. (2008) Do Practitioners Know the Limits of Inappropriate Behaviour? *Community Care Magazine*, 3 September.

HCPC (Health and Care Professions Council) (2012) *Standards of Conduct, Performance and Ethics* (London: Health and Care Professions Council).

Heater, D. (2004) *Citizenship: The Civic Ideal in World History, Politics and Education*, 3rd edn (Manchester: Manchester University Press).

Henderson, R. (2006) Defining Non-instructed Advocacy. *Planet Advocacy*, 18: 5–7.

Hodgson, L. (2004) Manufactured Civil Society: Counting the Cost. *Critical Social Policy*, 24(2): 139–164.

Hoggett, P. (1997) *Contested Communities: Experience, Struggle and Policies* (Bristol: Policy Press).

Hoggett, P., Mayo, M. and Miller, C. (2009) *The Dilemmas of Development Work: Ethical Challenges in Regeneration* (Bristol: Policy Press).

Home Office (2001) *Building Cohesive Communities* (London: Home Office).

Home Office (2004) *Firm Foundations: The Government's Framework for Community Capacity Building* (London: Civil Renewal Unit).

IBSEN (Individual Budgets Evaluation Network) (2008) *Evaluation of the Individual Budgets Pilot Programme: Summary Report* (York: Social Policy Research Unit/University of York).

In Control (2011) *An Introduction to Self-Directed Support* fact sheet 01, updated 4 February 2011. Available at: www.in-control.org.uk/media/16696/01.%20introduction%20to%20self-directed%20support%202011%20v1b.pdf accessed 13 February 2013.

Jeffs, T. and Smith, M. (2005) *Informal Education: Conversation, Democracy and Learning*, 3rd edn (Nottingham: Education Heretics Press).

Jochum, V., Pratten, B. and Wilding, K. (2005) *Civil Renewal and Active Citizenship, A Guide to the Debate* (London: NCVO).

John, M. (1996) Voicing: Research and Practice with the 'Silenced', in John, M. (ed) *Children in Charge: The Child's Right to a Fair Hearing* (London: Macmillan), pp.3–24.

Jones, M., Kimberlee, R., Evans, S. and Deave, T. (2011) *South West Well-Being Programme: Final Evaluation Report* (Bristol: University of the West of England). Available at: www.southwestwellbeing.co.uk accessed 13 February 2013.

Keay, D. (1987) Aids, Education and the Year 2000! *Woman's Own* 31 October, 8–10.

Keller, J.E. and Pryce, J.M. (2010) 'Mutual but Unequal: Mentoring as a Hybrid of Familiar Relationship Roles', *New Directions for Youth Development*, 126: 33–50.

Kemshall, H. and Littlechild, R. (eds) (2000) *User Involvement and Participation in Social Care* (London: Jessica Kingsley).

Kendrick. M (2006) The Inevitable Loneliness of Personal Advocacy. *Planet Advocacy*, 18: 8–9.

key2europe (n.d.) *Acquire EU Citizenship and Permanent Residency via Property Investment*. Available at: www.key2europe.com/en/Acquire-EU-citizenship-and-permanent-residency accessed 11 February 2013.

King, A. (2011) Service User Involvement in Methadone Maintenance Programmes: The 'Philosophy, the Ideal and the Reality'. *Drugs: Education, Prevention and Policy*, 18(4): 276–284.

Knight, A. and Oliver, C. (2007) Advocacy for Disabled Children and Young People: Benefits and Dilemmas. *Child and Family Social Work*, 12: 417–425.

Koubel, G. and Bungay, H. (eds) (2012) *Rights, Risks and Responsibilities: Interprofessional Working in Health and Social Care* (Basingstoke: Palgrave Macmillan).

Kruger, D. (2011) Death by a Thousand Cuts for Big Society, *Financial Times*, 6 February.

Kvarnström, S., Willumsen, E., Andersson-Gäre, B. and Hedberg, B. (2012) How Service Users Perceive the Concept of Participation, Specifically in Interprofessional Practice, *British Journal of Social Work*, 42, 129–146.

Lansdown, G. (2010) The Realisation of Children's Participation Rights, in Percy-Smith, B. and Thomas, N. (eds) *A Handbook of Children and Young People's Participation: Perspectives from Theory and Practice* (Abingdon: Routledge).

Lather, P. (1991) *Getting Smart. Feminist Research and Pedagogy with/in the Postmodern* (London: Routledge).

Ledwith, M. (1997) *Participating in Transformation: Towards a Working Model of Community Empowerment* (Birmingham: Venture Press).

Ledwith, M. and Springett, J. (2010) *Participatory Practice: Community-based Action for Transformative Change* (Bristol: Policy Press).

Lee, S. (2007) *The Independent Mental Capacity Advocate (IMCA): Helping People who are Unable to Make Some Decisions Themselves* (London: The Mental Capacity Implementation Programme).

Lepper, J. (2010) 'Old Step In To Stop Youth Offending', *Children & Young People Now* 15 June. Available at: www.cypnow.co.uk/Archive/1009778/News-Insight-Old-step-stop-youth-offending/.

Lindsay, G. (1995) Values, Ethics & Psychology, *The Psychologist*, 8: 493–498.

Lipsky, M. (1979) *Street Level Bureaucracy* (New York: Russell Sage).

Lister, R. (2003) *Citizenship: Feminist Perspectives*, 2nd edn (Basingstoke: Palgrave Macmillan).

Lockyer, A. (2003) Introduction and Review, in Lockyer, A., Crick, B. and Annette, J. (eds) *Education for Democratic Citizenship: Issues of Theory and Practice* (Aldershot: Ashgate).

Lombard, D. (2010) How to End a Working Relationship with a Service User. *Community Care Magazine* 21 October. Available at: www.communitycare. co.uk/Articles/21/10/2010/115642/how-to-end-a-working-relationship-with-a-service-user.htm accessed 13 February 2013.

Lymbery, M. (2012) Social Work and Personalisation: Fracturing the Bureau-Professional Compact? *British Journal of Social Work*, 1: 1–17.

Mackenzie, M. (1975) *Shoulder to Shoulder* (Harmondsworth: Penguin).

Mair, V. (2012) Serco Wins Big in National Citizen Service Contracts. *Civil Society*, 13 September. Available at: www.civilsociety.co.uk/governance/news/content/13373/serco_wins_biggest_bulk_of_national_citizen_service_contracts accessed 13 February 2013

Marshall, T. (1950) Citizenship and Social Class, in Marshall, T. and Bottomore, T. (1992) *Citizenship and Social Class* (London: Pluto Press), pp.3–51.

Mathiesen, R. (1999) An Examination of the Theoretical Foundation of Social Pedagogy. *Journal of the European Association of Training Centres for Social Educational Care Work*, 3: 3–28.

May, T. (2010) Immigration speech to Policy Exchange, London, 5 November. Available at: www.jcwi.org.uk/2010/11/05/theresa-mays-speech accessed 5 January 2013

Mayo, M. (1975) Community Development: A Radical Alternative, in Bailey, R. and Brake, M. (eds) *Radical Social Work* (New York: Pantheon Books), pp.129–143.

Mayo, M. and Rooke, A. (2006) *Active Learning for Active Citizenship: An Evaluation Report*. Available at: www.gold.ac.uk/media/active-learning-report-A41.pdf accessed 20 February 2013.

Melville-Wiseman, J. (2012) 'Taking Relationships into Account in Mental Health Services', in Koubel, G. and Bungay, H. (eds) (2012) *Rights, Risks and Responsibilities: Interprofessional Working in Health and Social Care* (Basingstoke: Palgrave Macmillan), pp.123–142.

McCall, A. (2012) *The Sunday Times Giving List*, 29 April. Available at: https://www.cafonline.org/media-office/press-releases/2012/giving-list-2012.aspx accessed 13 February 2013.

McGonigal, K. (2005) Teaching for Transformation: From Learning Theory to Teaching Strategies. *Stanford University Speaking of Teaching Newsletter*, 14: 2.

McLauglin, H. (2009) 'What's in a Name: Client, Patient, Customer, Consumer, Expert by Experience, Service User – What's Next? *British Journal of Social Work*, 39: 1101–1117.

Mickel, A. (2008) 'Do I Know You From Somewhere?' *Community Care Magazine*, 13 August.

Milewa, T., Dowswell, G. and Harrison, S. (2002) Partnerships, Power and the 'New' Politics of Community Participation in British Health Care, *Social Policy and Administration*, 36(7): 796–809.

Mohan, J. and Bulloch, S. (2012) *The Idea of a 'Civic Core'; What are the Overlaps between Charitable Giving, Volunteering, and Civic Participation in England and Wales?* Working Paper 73 Third Sector Research Centre.

Nairn, A. (2011) *Children's Well-being in UK, Sweden and Spain: The Role of Inequality and Materialism. A Qualitative Study* (London: UNICEF).

Natorp, P. (1904) *Sozialpadagogik* (Stuttgart: Framanns).

Nelson, L.G., Summers, J.A. and Turnbull, A.P. (2004) Boundaries in Family-Professional Relationships: Implications for Special Education, *Remedial and Special Education*, 25(3): 153–165.

New Economics Foundation (NEF) (2004) *A Well-Being Manifesto for a Flourishing Society* (London: NEF).

Newbigging, K. (2012) *The Right To Be Heard: Review of the Quality of Independent Mental Health Advocate (IMHA) Services in England* (Preston: UCLAN).

NSPCC (National Society for the Prevention of Cruelty to Children) (2012) *Gillick Competency and Fraser Guidelines* NSPCC factsheet July 2012. Available at: www.nspcc.org.uk/inform/research/questions/gillick_wda61289.html accessed 13 February 2013.

NYA (National Youth Agency) (2004) *Ethical Conduct in Youth Work*. Available at: http://nya.org.uk/dynamic_files/workforce/Ethical%20Conduct%20in%20Youth%20Work%20(Reprint%202004).pdf accessed 13 February 2013.

Ofsted (2011) *Choosing to Volunteer*. Available at: www.ofsted.gov.uk/resources/110119 accessed 13 February 2013.

Oliver, B. (1994) *Tutor Support in Community Education* (Bristol: WEA).

Oliver, B., Percy-Smith, B. and Young, P. (2011) *Report of the Knowledge Cafe Evaluation Event* (Bristol: University of the West of England).

Oliver, B. and Pitt, B. (2005) Youth Work, in Barrett, G., Sellman, D., and Thomas, J. (eds) *Interprofessional Working in Health and Social Care: Professional Perspectives* (Basingstoke: Palgrave), pp.170–183.

OPG (Office of the Public Guardian) (2007) *Making Decisions: The Independent Mental Capacity Advocate (IMCA) Service* No. 606 Ministry of Justice Available at: www.justice.gov.uk/downloads/protecting-the-vulnerable/mca/making-decisions-opg606-1207.pdf accessed 13 February 2013.

Packham, C. (2008) *Active Citizenship and Community Learning* (Exeter: Learning Matters).

Pankhurst, E. (1914) *My Own Story* (London: Eveleigh Nash).

Pankhurst, E.S. (1931) *The Suffragette Movement: An Intimate Account of Persons and Ideals* (London: Chatto and Windus).

Parsloe, E. and Leedham, M. (2009) *Coaching and Mentoring*, 2nd edn (London: Kogan Page).

Payne, M. (2005) *Modern Social Work Theory*, 3rd edn (Basingstoke: Palgrave).

Petrie, P. (2011) Interpersonal Communication, in Cameron, C. and Moss, P. (eds) (2011) *Social Pedagogy and Working with Children and Young People: Where Care and Education Meet* (London: Jessica Kingsley), pp.69–83.

Petrie, P., Boddy, J., Cameron, C., Wigfall, V. and Simon, A. (2006) *Working with Children in Care* (Maidenhead: Open University Press).

Philip, K. (2000) Mentoring and Young People. Available at www.infed.org/learningmentors/mentoring.htm accessed 13 February 2013.

Philip K. and Hendry, L.B. (2000) Making Sense of Mentoring or Mentoring Making Sense? Reflections on the Mentoring Process by Adult Mentors with Young People. *Journal of Community and Applied Social Psychology*, 10: 211–223.

Phinney, A., Chaudhury, H. and O'Connor, D. (2007) Doing as much as I can do: The meaning of activity for people with dementia. *Ageing and Mental Health*, 11, 4: 384–393.

Portas, M. (2011) *Portas Review: An Independent Review into the Future of our High Streets* (London: Department for Business, Innovation and Skills).

Prior, D., Stewart, J. and Walsh, K. (1995) *Citizenship: Rights, Community and Participation* (London: Pitman Publishing).

Pugh, R. (2007) Dual Relationships: Personal and Professional Boundaries in Rural Social Work. *British Journal of Social Work*, 37: 1405–1423.

Purvis, J. (2002) *Emmeline Pankhurst: A Biography* (London: Routledge).

Putnam, R. (2001) *Bowling Alone: The Collapse and Revival of American Community* (London: Simon and Schuster).

Rhodes, J.E. (2001) Youth Mentoring in Perspective, The Center Summer. Republished in *The Encyclopedia of Informal Education*. Available at: www.infed.org/learningmentors/youth_mentoring_in_perspective.htm accessed 13 February 2013.

Rimmer, A. (2005) What is Professional Social Work? Social Work and Social Justice, in Nelson, P. and Shardlow, S. (eds) *Introducing Social Work* (Lyme Regis: Russell House Publishing), pp.1–20.

Robertson, S. (2005) *Youth Clubs: Association, Participation, Friendship and Fun!* (Lyme Regis: Russell House Publishing).

Robson, C. (2011) *Real World Research*, 3rd edn (Chichester: Wiley).

Rose, J. (2010) Monitoring and Evaluating Youth Work, in Jeffs, T. and Smith, M. (eds) *Youth Work Practice* (Basingstoke: Palgrave Macmillan), pp.156–170.

Sage, D (2012) A Challenge to Liberalism? The Communitarianism of The Big Society and Blue Labour. *Critical Social Policy*, 32(3): 365–382.

SCDC (Scottish Community Development Centre) (2012) What is Community Engagement? Available at: www.scdc.org.uk/what/national-standards/what-is-community-engagement/ accessed 13 February 2013

Schön, D. A. (1983) *The Reflective Practitioner: How Professionals Think in Action* (New York: Basic Books).

Scott, M. (2011) Reflections on 'The Big Society'. *Community Development Journal*, 46(1): 132–137.

Scottish Executive (2001) *Independent Advocacy: A Guide for Commissioners* (Norwich: The Stationery Office).

SEU (Social Exclusion Unit) (2001) *A New Commitment to Neighbourhood Renewal* (London: Cabinet Office).

Shaping Our Lives (n.d.) Definitions. Available at: www.shapingourlives.org.uk/definitions.html accessed 13 February 2013.

Shaw, M. (2011) Stuck in the Middle? Community Development, Community Engagement and the Dangerous Business of Learning for Democracy. *Community Development Journal*, 46(2): 128–146.

Sheppard, M., MacDonald, P. and Welbourne, P. (2008) Service Users as Gatekeepers in Children's Centres. *Child and Family Social Work*, 13(1): 61–71.

Shier, H. (2001) Pathways to Participation: Openings, Opportunities and Obligations. A New Model for Enhancing Children's Participation in Decision Making. *Children & Society*, 15: 107–117.

Shier, H. (2006) Pathways to Participation Revisited, *Middle Schooling Review*, 2: 14–19.

Shier, H., Hernández Méndez, M., Centeno, M., Arróliga, I. and González, M. (2012) How Children and Young People Influence Policy-makers: Lessons from Nicaragua. *Children & Society*.

Shiner, M., Young, T., Newburn, T. and Groben, S. (2004) *Mentoring Disaffected Young People: An Evaluation of Mentoring Plus* (York: Joseph Rowntree Foundation).

Simons, K. (1993) *Citizen Advocacy: The Insider View* (Bristol: Norah Fry Research Centre).

Sinclair, R. (2004) Participation in Practice: Making it Meaningful, Effective and Sustainable. *Children & Society*, 18: 106–118.

Skills for Care (2011) *Capable Confident Skilled: A Workforce Development Strategy for People Working, Supporting and Caring in Adult Social Care* (Leeds: Skills for Care).

Skinner, S. (1997) *Building Community Strengths: A Resource Book on Capacity Building* (London: Community Development Foundation).

Slocock, C. (2012) *The Big Society Audit 2012* (Civil Exchange).

Sloman, A. (2012) Participatory Theatre in Community Development. *Community Development Journal*, 47(1): 42–57.

Smith, M.K. (1999) Learning Mentors and Informal Education. *Encyclopedia of Informal Education*. Available at: http://www.infed.org/learning mentors/lrn-ment.htm accessed 20 February 2013.

Smith, M.K. (2001) Community. *Encyclopedia of Informal Education*. Available at: www.infed.org/community/community.htm accessed 13 February 2013.

Smith, M.K. (2002) Youth Work: An Introduction. *Encyclopedia of Informal Education*. Available at: http://www.infed.org/youthwork/b-yw.htm 2002, updated January 2005 accessed 20 February 2013.

Smith, M.K. (2005) Introducing Informal Education. *Encyclopedia of Informal Education*. Available at: www.infed.org/i-intro.htm accessed 13 February 2013.

Smith, M.K. (2011) Young People and the 2011 Riots in England – Experiences, Explanations and Implications for Youth Work. *Encyclopedia of Informal Education*. Available at: www.infed.org/archives/jeffs_and_smith/young_people_youth_work_and_the_2011_riots_in_england.html accessed 13 February 2013.

Smith, R. (2012) Why Do Children Talk to Social Workers in Cars? *Community Care*, 27 June. Available at: www.communitycare.co.uk/blogs/childrens-services-blog/2012/06/why-do-children-talk-to-social-workers-in-cars.html accessed 13 February 2013.

Somerville D. and Keeling, J. (2004) A Practical Approach to Promote Reflective Practice within Nursing. *Nursing Times*, 100(12): 42.

Spence, J., Smith, M. K., Frost, S. and Hodgson, T. (2011) *MySpace Evaluation – Final Report* (London: Department for Education).

Stephens, P. (2009) The Nature of Social Pedagogy: An Excursion in Norwegian Territory. *Child and Family Social Work*, 14: 343–351.

Tam, H. (2010) The Importance of Being a Citizen, in Mayo, M. and Annette, J. (eds) *Taking Part? Active Learning for Active Citizenship; and Beyond* (Leicester: NIACE), pp.7–15.

Tam, H. (2011) The Big Con: Reframing the state/society debate. *Public Policy Research* March–May: 30–40.

Tambini, D. (2001) Post-national Citizenship. *Ethnic and Racial Studies*, 24(2): 195–217.

Taylor, M. (1992) *Signposts to Community Development* (London: Community Development Foundation).

Taylor, M. (2011) *Public Policy in the Community*, 2nd edn (Basingstoke: Palgrave).

Taylor, P. (2007) The Lay Contribution to Public Health, in Orme, J., Powell, J. Taylor, P. Harrison, P. and Grey, M. (eds) *Public Health for the 21st Century: New Perspectives on Policy Participation and Practice*, 2nd edn (Maidenhead: Open University Press), pp.99–117.

Taylor, P. (2008) Where Crocodiles Find Their Power: Learning and Teaching Participation for Community Development, in *Community Development Journal*, 43(3): 358–370.

Taylor, P. and Upward, J. (1995) *Bridge Building for Effective User Involvement in Primary Care* (Birmingham: FHSA).

Teasdale, K. (1998) *Advocacy in Health Care* (Oxford: Blackwell Science).

Tedmanson, D. (2003) *Whose Capacity Needs Building? Open Hearts and Empty Hands: Reflections on Capacity Building in Remote Communities*, paper presented at the 4th International Critical Management Studies Conference, University of South Australia.

Tew, J. (2008) Researching in Partnership: Reflecting on a Collaborative Study with Mental Health Service Users into the Impact of Compulsion. *Qualitative Social Work*, 7(3): 271–287.

The Guardian (2007) Ask not what your country can do for you. Speech delivered by John F Kennedy during his inauguration 20 January 1961. Available at: www.guardian.co.uk/theguardian/2007/apr/22/greatspeeches accessed 11 February 2013.

Thomas, D. (2012) Well Being and Community Action, in Walker, P. and John, M. (eds) *From Public Health to Well Being* (Basingstoke: Palgrave), pp.128–143.

Thompson, N. (2007) *Power and Empowerment* (Lyme Regis: Russell House Publishing).

Tierney, J.P., Grossman, J.B. and Resch, N.L. (1995) *Making a Difference: An Impact Study of Big Brothers Big Sisters* (Philadelphia: Public/Private Ventures).

Toynbee, P. (2011) Big Society isn't New, but the Tories are Purging the Past, *The Guardian* 21 May.

Treseder, P. (1997) *Empowering Children and Young People: Promoting Involvement in Decision Making* (London: Save the Children).

Turner, A. (2009) Bottom-up Community Development: Reality or Rhetoric? The Example of the Kingsmead Kabin in East London. *Community Development Journal*, 44(2): 230–247.

Turner, R. (2012) Mentoring Programmes. *Children & Young People Now*, 15 May.

United Nations (1989) *Convention on the Rights of the Child (1989)* (New York: United Nations).

Van der Veen, R. (2003) Community Development as Citizen Education. *International Journal of Lifelong Education*, 22(6): 580–596.

WAG (Welsh Assembly Government) (2006) *Education for Sustainable Development and Global Citizenship – A Strategy for Action* (Cardiff: Welsh Assembly Government).

Watts, A.G. (2001) Career Guidance and Social Exclusion: A Cautionary Tale. *British Journal of Guidance and Counselling*, 29(2): 157–178.

West, A. (1997) Citizenship, Children and Young People. *Youth and Policy*, 55: 69.

White, S. and Pettit, J. (2004) *Participatory Approaches and Measurement of Human Well-Being* (New York: World Institute for Development Economics Research).

Wilkinson, H. (2012) Knitting the Community, private conversation: Bristol.

Williams, F. (1992) Somewhere over the Rainbow: Universality and Diversity in Social Policy, in Manning, N. and Page, R. (eds) *Social Policy Review 4* (Canterbury: Social Policy Association), pp.200–219.

Williams, R. (1958) *Culture and Society* (Harmondsworth: Penguin).

Woodward, V. (2004) *Active Learning for Active Citizenship*. Civil Renewal Unit, Home Office.

Woolcock, M. M. (2001) The Place of Social Capital in Understanding Social and Economic Outcomes. *Canadian Journal of Policy Research*, 2(1): 11–17.

Yerbury, H. (2012) Vocabularies of Community. *Community Development Journal*, 47(2): 184–198.

Young, K. (1999) *The Art of Youth Work* (Lyme Regis: Russell House Publishing).

Index

Printed in China